JUN 3 '08

53517 9.65 BT

I1039400

History of Ethics
Volume II

History of Ethics

Volume II

Modern and Contemporary Ethics

Vernon J. Bourke

Axios Press

P.O. Box 118

Mount Jackson, VA 22842

888.542.9467 info@axiospress.com

History of Ethics, Vol. 2: Modern and Contemporary Ethics © 1968 by Vernon J. Bourke. Published by arrangement with Doubleday, a division of Random House, Inc. All rights reserved. Printed in the United States of America. No part of this book may be used or reproduced in any manner whatsoever without written permission except in the case of brief quotations used in critical articles and reviews.

Distributed by NATIONAL BOOK NETWORK.

Library of Congress Cataloging-in-Publication Data

Bourke, Vernon J. (Vernon Joseph), 1907–1998.
History of ethics / Vernon J. Bourke.
p. cm.
Includes bibliographical references and index.
ISBN 978-0-9753662-3-3 (v. 1 : pbk. : alk. paper) —
ISBN 978-0-9753662-5-7 (v. 2 : pbk. : alk. paper)

1. Ethics—History. I. Title.

BJ71.B66 2008
170.9–dc22

2007051386

Contents

Part Four

Modern Theories

X: Utilitarian and Subjectivist Ethics in Britain . . 3
XI: German Idealistic Ethics 33
XII: Franco-Latin Spiritistic Ethics 59
XIII: Societal Ethics in Europe 89

Part Five

Contemporary Ethics

XIV: Axiological Ethics. 125
XV: Self-Realization and Utilitarian Ethics 149
XVI: Naturalistic Ethics 175
XVII: Analytic Ethics 207
XVIII: Existential and Phenomenological Ethics 237

Notes 265
Bibliography 299
Index 371

Part Four

Modern Theories

Chapter X

Utilitarian and Subjectivist Ethics in Britain

IT WAS IN the eighteenth and nineteenth centuries that the contrast between the utilitarian and the intuitionist approaches to ethics came to the fore. This division is not restricted to British thinkers but it is most evident in their attempts to do practical philosophy. The utilitarian thinks that judgments about human actions to the effect that they are good, right, and ought to be done (or contrariwise, that they are bad wrong and ought to be omitted) are justified by considering the knowable consequences of such actions to the agent or to other persons, or to both.

These consequences or results may be viewed either in terms of the advantage of the individual agent (egoistic utilitarianism), or in the light of the advantage of a plurality of persons other than the agent (universal utilitarianism). Sometimes the first type is called hedonism and the second simply "utilitarianism."[1] In its broadest sense utilitarianism maintains "that the right or wrong of an action is to be judged by its utility in the production of happiness."[2] J. S. Mill thought that he had picked up the term "utilitarianism" from John Galt's novel *Annals of the Parish* (1821), but it had been used as early as 1781 by Jeremy Bentham.[3]

Ethical intuitionism, on the other hand, is the view that a person directly knows or feels the good (or "oughtness") of an action or moral judgment, without any need to consider other items, such as consequences, in justification. As Henry Sidgwick understood the term: "Writers who maintain that we have 'intuitive knowledge' of the rightness of actions usually mean that this rightness is ascertained by simply 'looking at' the actions themselves, without considering their ulterior consequences."[4] Broadly understood, intuitional ethics would include some right reason theories, some types of deontology, moral sensism, and psychological approbative types of ethics. For the present chapter, we will simply understand intuitionism as the ethics that concentrates on the subjective attitude of the moral agent, rather than on the results of his action, in discussing what is morally good or bad. In the eighteenth century, what is under discussion is not always the individual action but may be the premises of moral reasoning. This is why the term "subjectivist" is used in the title of this chapter: it simply means an ethical approach that starts from something experienced within the moral person or subject. We shall see that many ethicians manage to combine intuitionism with utilitarianism; it is only as pure positions that they are mutually incompatible.

At the end of the seventeenth century, Richard Cumberland had introduced the theory, but not the name, of universal utilitarianism into English ethics. In his Latin *Treatise of the Laws of Nature* (1672), he had argued that it is not "possible to determine what is the best thing a man can do in each instance, unless the effects, remote as well as near, which may result in every variety of circumstances, be foreseen and compared among themselves."[5] This statement of the method of utilitarianism is followed by a remarkable enunciation of the principle of the greatest happiness to the greatest number. Cumberland calls this proposition the "fountain of all natural laws."

The greatest benevolence of every rational agent towards all, constitutes the happiest state of all in general and of each in particular, as far as is in their power to procure it; and it is necessarily requisite in order to attain the happiest state, to which they can aspire; and therefore the common good of all is the supreme law.[6]

This brand of utilitarianism (combined in Cumberland with a right reason view of moral law) was not acceptable to David Hume (1711–1776). He tended to distrust deductive reasoning in ethics and he could not see why the common good should take precedence over private interests. The complicated ethical position which Hume eventually reached is still a most important factor in the thinking of twentieth-century British ethicians. He rejected the notion that reason can command or move the human will and insisted that ethics should concentrate on certain impressions or feelings of approval or disapproval within the agent. In Hume's thinking, "an action, or sentiment, or character, is virtuous or vicious, because its view causes a pleasure or uneasiness of a particular kind."[7] He adopted, then, an ethical position which is subjectivist in the sense that we have just seen.

The problem of interpreting Hume's ethics is made more difficult by his own later dissatisfaction with the doctrine of his famous *Treatise on Human Nature* (1739–1740). Its third book is frequently made the basis for expositions of Hume's ethical position but Henry Sidgwick[8] claims that the *Treatise* was "expressly repudiated" (apparently referring to Hume's admitted disappointment with the reception of the *Treatise,* as noted in the *Autobiography),* and Sidgwick confines his analysis to the *Inquiry concerning the Principles of Morals* (1751). We will take a look at the doctrine of both works. There is also some material of ethical significance in the popularly written *Essays, Moral and Political* (1741–1742).

To understand Hume's argument in his practical philosophy we should think briefly of his view of man. Both the *Treatise* and the *Enquiry concerning Human Understanding* (1748) give a phenomenalistic account of the human agent. Hume tried to use Newton's method of empirical science in the whole field of philosophy. What is given in initial human experience is a series of "perceptions." These are both cognitive and emotional presentations. They combine in various patterns of association and thus form more complicated events in experience. Psychology (not yet developed as a distinct discipline in Hume's day) would be the study of these atoms of experience and their various modes of association. There is no mind, in the sense of an immaterial substance or power that thinks or feels these data; there is no person, in the sense of an individual being endowed with intelligence and volitional freedom. Hume continues to speak of persons and selves but in a very special way. A mind or person is a series of separately existing and discrete perceptions, occurring in such a way that one perception seems to give rise to the next.[9] When perceptions occur forcefully they are called impressions; when they are weak they are termed ideas. Perceptions are related according to three modes of association: resemblance, contiguity in time or place, and cause-effect.

In Book III of the *Treatise* (sec. 1) we are told that "reason or science is nothing but the comparing of ideas, and the discovery of their relations." So viewed, reason is wholly inactive and cannot be a source of moral experience. As Hume now says:

> Those who affirm that virtue is nothing but a conformity to reason; that there are eternal fitnesses and unfitnesses of things which are the same to every rational being that considers them; that the immutable measures of right and wrong impose an obligation, not only on human creatures, but also on the Deity himself: All these systems concur in the opinion, that morality, like truth, is discerned merely by ideas, and by their juxtaposition and comparison. . . . Since morals, therefore, have an influence on the actions and affections, it follows, that they cannot be derived from reason; and that because reason alone, as we have already proved, can never have any such influence.[10]

This neatly disposes of Cudworth and all such rationalists, From this point onward, in British ethics, it will be generally agreed that Hume has shown the folly of speaking about natural laws, right reason, and all such nonsense.

In this same section of the *Treatise,* Hume introduces the approbative portion of his theory. To say that an act or character is vicious simply means that one has a feeling or sentiment of blame in viewing it. Vice and virtue are perceptions in the mind, just as sensible qualities (sounds, colors, heat) are perceptions and not present in objects. So, in the second section of Book III, he offers his version of a moral sense theory. This is the function of feeling pain at the perception of an action which is then called vicious, and of reeling pleasure in viewing another action which is virtuous. Some such moral feelings are original instincts and are "natural"; other virtuous feelings arise by means of artifice from the needs of mankind and are called "artificial." Justice is an example of such an artificially contrived virtue.[11]

Book II of the *Treatise* is devoted to the passions as moral principles. If reason cannot be a source of action, then feelings can. Some passions are primary and simple feelings and others are derivative and follow upon ideas. There are also self-regarding and other-regarding feelings. Of the latter, sympathy is important in Hume's ethics. As he sees it, sympathy arises when there occur ideas of the effects in others of something such as a painful surgical operation: these ideas may give rise to stronger impressions which, in turn, precede feelings of pain in the observer who is not under surgery.[12] As a vicarious emotion and other-directed, sympathy is an important principle for moral feelings and actions. Along with self-interest and custom, sympathy is used to explain the working of moral sense.[13]

One final contribution of the *Treatise* to the history of ethics may be noted. In a famous passage he states the "is-ought" problem very clearly:

> In every system of morality, which I have hitherto met with, I have always remarked, that the author proceeds for some time in the ordinary way of reasoning, and establishes the being of a God, or makes observations concerning human affairs; when of a sudden I am surprised to find, that instead of the usual copulations of propositions, is, and is not, I meet with no proposition that is not connected with an ought, or an ought not. . . . As this ought or ought not expresses some new relation or affirmation, it is necessary that it should be explained; and at the same time that a reason should be given for what seems altogether inconceivable, how this new relation can be a deduction from others which are entirely different from it.[14]

Many ethicians, particularly in the twentieth century, have attempted to solve this problem of the relation of *ought* to *is.* In alternative terminology it may be stated as the problem of how to get *values* from *facts.*

The *Enquiry concerning the Principles of Morals* is Hume's own revision of the third book of the *Treatise,* done after ten years in which few readers paid any attention to this new start in British ethics. There are important differences between the two works. Instead of "sympathy" the *Enquiry* dwells upon "humanity" as a sentiment which all men have in common and which gives a sort of open and public character to moral attitudes. The distinction between "natural" and "artificial" is excluded as a verbalism in the *Enquiry*. More important, the handling of justice shifts from a Hobbesian emphasis on self-interest modified by sympathy as a basis for the virtue of justice to the concept of utility to society.[15] Utility has the meaning of "tendency to *ulterior* good"; it is the basis for several moral virtues but it is not the sole source of virtue; other qualities—courtesy, modesty, cheerfulness—contribute to virtue.

The following summary passage shows how Hume tried to combine a sentimental approbative theory of ethics with a measure of public agreement that is closely related to utility.

> The notion of morals implies some sentiment common to all mankind, which recommends the same object to general approbation, and makes every man, or most men, agree in the same opinion or decision concerning it. It also implies some sentiment, so universal and comprehensive as to extend to all mankind, and render the actions and conduct, even of the persons the most remote, an object of applause or censure, according as they agree or disagree with that rule of right which is established.[16]

Hume's influence in ethics has been extensive and profound. His stress on social utility leads into British utilitarianism in its several varieties. His emphasis on feelings of approval or disapproval is eventually taken up by psychological approbative ethics and, especially, by the school of emotive ethicians. In the *Essays, Moral and Political* ("Of the Original Contract") these two aspects of his thought are clearly brought out. Of two kinds of moral duties, one proceeds from natural instinct and is quite independent of ideas of obligation or public utility: love of children, gratitude to benefactors, and pity for the unfortunate are given as examples. A second type of moral duty is performed solely from a sense of obligation, an awareness of the necessities of human society. This is Hume's ethics in brief.

An almost immediate reaction to Hume's ethics is found in the *Review of the Principal Questions in Morals* (1758) by a Unitarian minister named Richard Price (1723–1791). Price disagrees with the epistemology and psychology which he finds in Hobbes, Locke, and Hume. Bluntly, Price says that Hume's assertion that all our ideas are either impressions or copies of impressions is "destitute of all proof."[17] Combining in a surprisingly consistent way the views of Cudworth, Samuel Clarke, and Butler, Price proposes a theory of "eternal and immutable" morality. He tries to reinstate "understanding" as the human power to grasp the unchanging natures of actions and realities. What Price contributes to the discussion is something which may have been implicit in earlier writers but is only now made explicit. The "understanding" is not the same as the "power of reasoning." By the latter we investigate certain relations between objects—but that is not what understanding does. As he explains it, to understand is to see something:

> As bodily sight discovers to us visible objects; so does understanding (the eye of the mind, and infinitely more penetrating) discover to us intelligible objects; and thus, in a like sense with bodily vision, becomes the inlet of new ideas.[18]

In effect, Price teaches that men enjoy an intellectual intuition of certain principles of moral judgment. This, plus his insistence that "rectitude" must be the motive for virtuous activity, may be the reason why some historians treat Price as a precursor to Kant.[19]

More impressed by Hume's position was Adam Smith (1723–1790), who is well known as a pioneer political economist but not so well recognized as an ethician. Smith was professor of moral philosophy at Glasgow and wrote his *Theory of Moral Sentiments* (1759) long before his famous *Wealth of Nations* (1776). Taking the principle of "sympathy" from Hume's *Treatise,* Smith investigated this altruistic feeling at great length and made it the sole foundation of ethical judgment.[20] He did not accept a special "moral sense," as such, but spoke of a sense of propriety quite distinct from the perception of utility. In fact, Adam Smith disliked the idea that usefulness to society might be taken as a criterion of morality. We make certain judgments of approbation or disapprobation of the conduct of other persons and these other-directed views and feelings are fundamental to ethics. When we attempt to judge our own conduct, we reverse the process, as it were, and try to see ourselves as others see us. Here Smith made considerable use of the "impartial spectator"—a disinterested observer whose attitudes provide a foundation for the sense of obligation and for ethics.[21] David Hume had used the idea of the impartial spectator throughout the third book of the *Treatise.* Adam Smith was the last important exponent of the moral sense theory, even though he substituted other terms (such as the sense of propriety) for it.[22] Smith's "impartial spectator" was not far removed from an active Presbyterian conscience, and that is close to a sense of morality.

Much of the activity in British ethics at this time centered in Scotland. Adam Smith's successor as professor of moral philosophy at Glasgow was Thomas Reid (1710–1796), founder of the school of "common-sense" philosophy. (Actually, a French Jesuit named Claude Buffier had first proposed the appeal to common sense against Cartesianism. Buffier's ideas are found in the *Traité des premières vérités* published in 1717. Both Reid and Dugald Stewart read Buffier.) The platform of this "common-sense" philosophy was very much like one part of the teaching of Boethius. In reaction to what seemed the excessive subtlety and complication of British epistemology from Locke to Hume, Reid asserted (in his *Inquiry into the Human Mind on the Principles of Common Sense,* 1764) that it is wrong to make "ideas" the objects of human knowledge. As far as Reid was concerned, when I see a tree I know an existing thing and not an idea.[28] In the moral area, there are certain universally accepted principles which need no philosophic proof. An example is: "No man ought to be blamed for what it was not in his power to hinder."[24] Man's moral faculty is his conscience which, on the basis of the common principles of right and wrong, dictates man's duty. Moral instruction and guidance are needed to develop good ability in moral reasoning but the whole business is not as tricky and sophisticated as Hume would suggest.[25]

At Edinburgh, Adam Ferguson (1723–1816) taught moral philosophy from 1764 to 1785 and was much influenced by his friend David Hume. Dugald Stewart (1753–1828) became professor in 1785 and introduced a modified version of Reid's common-sense ethics. His *Philosophy of the Active and Moral Powers of Man* (1828) was one of the first English textbooks in ethics used in the United States. Stewart taught that ethical propositions are just as true as mathematical ones: "In both cases we have a perception of *truth,* and are impressed with an irresistible conviction that the truth is immutable and independent of the will of any being whatever."[26] Stewart's pupil Thomas Brown (1778–1820) carried on the common-sense tradition at Edinburgh and exerted some influence on French ethicians of the nineteenth century, such as Victor

Cousin. At Aberdeen, James Beattie (1735–1803) was a critic of Hume and taught ethics in the common-sense tradition.

In 1768 John Witherspoon (1723–1794) came to America from Scotland to serve as president (and *ex officio* to teach philosophy) at the College of New Jersey, later to be known as Princeton University. A century later, James McCosh (1811–1894) brought the common-sensism of the Scottish school to the same American institution.[27] In this manner, the realistic, Biblically oriented, middle-of-the-road ethics from Scotland became a pioneer influence on higher education in the United States.

The great conservative thinker in British politics, Edmund Burke (1729–1797), was not a great ethician but he deserves to be mentioned here. He was not—contrary to what one recent study has tried to show—an exponent of the ethics of Thomas Aquinas.[28] There are superficial resemblances among all supporters of tradition and of natural law—but the differences can be more remarkable. Burke's *Philosophical Inquiry into the Origin of Our Ideas on the Sublime and Beautiful* (1756) and his *Appeal from the New to the Old Whigs* (1790) reveal a man who is eager to reinstate the classical function of "understanding" into English practical philosophy.[29] The idea that "utility" is the criterion of moral judgment is clearly under widespread discussion at this time, for Burke takes a whole section to reject it. He shares, however, his era's general distrust of any attempt to found ethics on metaphysical abstractions, as this text from the *Appeal* indicates:

> Nothing universal can be rationally affirmed on any moral, or any political subject. Pure metaphysical abstraction does not belong to these matters. The lines of morality are not like the ideal lines of mathematics. They are broad and deep as well as long. They admit of exceptions; they demand modifications. These exceptions are not made by the process of logic, but by the rules of prudence.[30]

Much more confident of his knowledge of ethics was the Anglican cleric and Cambridge tutor William Paley (1743–1805). He is usually remembered for his version of the argument for the existence of God from mechanical design in the universe; however, Paley's *Principles of Moral and Political Philosophy* (1785) was used as a textbook at Cambridge for more than fifty years.[31] Rejecting the notion of a moral sense, Paley made "utility" (in regard to both the particular and the general consequences of actions) the test of moral goodness.[32] The will of God determines the difference between moral right and wrong. It is conveyed to men in two ways: as revealed in Scripture and as known through the "light of nature." Virtue consists in "doing good to mankind, in obedience to the will of God, and for the sake of everlasting happiness." The ethics of William Paley is a neat combination of Christian morality with the principle of social utility.

A major figure in the history of British ethics, even though he did not pretend to be an ethician, was Jeremy Bentham (1748–1832). His primary interest was in the philosophy of law and politics but this required him to develop certain notions as to the relationship between moralitv and social organization. Estimates of the value of his suggestions in ethics vary widely. John Stuart Mill has called Bentham "the great subversive," yet Mill learned a great deal from Bentham.33 It has been asserted that Bentham deliberately reduced all moral problems to technical ones.[34] In any case, the treatise that is ethically significant is Bentham's *Introduction to the Principles of Morals and Legislation* (1789). John Bowring's compilation, entitled *Deontology* (1834), is of doubtful value as a source.

In an anonymous publication in the year 1776 *(Fragment on Government),* Bentham revealed his early distrust of "natural law" thinking. The *Fragment* is an open attack on Sir William Blackstone (1723–1780) for his advocacy of natural law in his famous *Commentaries on the Laws of England* (1765–1769). Blackstone had maintained that

> the law of nature being coeval with mankind, and dictated by God himself, is of course superior in obligation to any other. It is binding over all the globe, in all countries, and at all times: no human laws are of any valid-

> ity if contrary to this; and such of them as are valid derive all their force and all their authority, mediately or immediately, from this original.[35]

At one point in the *Fragment* Bentham characterized a view such as Blackstone's as "a sink that with equal facility will swallow any garbage that is thrown into it."[36]

Bentham helped to introduce the teaching that all laws governing human conduct are commands of a sovereign, backed by sanctions, and retained by a habit of obedience. The test of a good law is its "utility," which means "that property in any object, whereby it tends to produce benefit, advantage, pleasure, good, or happiness . . . to the party whose interest is considered."[37] The interest involved may be that of the individual person or that of the community but Bentham is inclined to take the interest of the individual as more basic, since the community is nothing more than a collection of individuals. He admits that he took the notion of "utility" from the French thinker Claude Adrien Helvétius (1715–1771), who had defined probity as that which has some usefulness *(utilité)* for the individual or his country.[38] In his treatise *De l'Homme* (1772), Helvétius described virtue in terms of "the confused idea of some quality useful to society."[39] In point of fact, the notion of utility as an ethical principle was becoming a commonplace in the late eighteenth century.

Perhaps Bentham is best known in ethics for his description of pleasure and pain in terms of quantity, and for his consequent theory of a "calculus of pleasures." As Mill noted,[40] Bentham could see no qualitative distinctions in pleasures: "quantity of pleasure being equal, pushpin is as good as poetry." So Bentham developed a method of calculating the amount of pleasure to the individual by using the four determinants: (1) intensity, (2) duration, (3) certainty or uncertainty, and (4) propinquity or remoteness. In relation to the interest of a group of persons, Bentham added two more circumstances of pleasure to be included: (5) fecundity and (6) purity. To decide morally between two proposed actions, then, one has only to add up and compare their respective quantities of pleasure and select the greatest!

Motivation is not ignored by Bentham; the tenth chapter of his *Principles of Morals* is devoted to this subject. He thinks that "motive" has two senses: literally it means an incident that tends to arouse pleasure or pain, and so move the will; figuratively motive designates any fictitious entity within the mind (such as avarice, indolence, benevolence) considered as prompting the mind to take a certain course. Bentham makes an extended list of such motives at the end of his *Principles of Morals.*

Perhaps the most competent follower of Bentham was James Mill (1773–1836), the father of John Stuart.

The elder Mill published an *Analysis of the Phenomena of the Human Mind* (1829) which simplified associationistic psychology by concentrating on the relation of contiguity. Personal pleasure and pain clearly function as the internal motives of moral action. Education is the chief means for the development of a better awareness of how to employ the utilitarian principle.

Not all British practical thinkers at this time agreed with Bentham. William Godwin (1756–1836) was also a utilitarian in his ethics, and, like Bentham, he was not primarily interested in ethical theory. Godwin's *Inquiry concerning Political Justice and Its Influence on Morals and Happiness* first appeared in 1793. It was intended as a rebuttal to Burke's *Reflections on the Revolution in France* (1790). Godwin was an ardent advocate of political and social freedom. However, he disagreed with Bentham's espousal of individual pleasure and pain as the key factors in moral judgment. Godwin's utilitarianism used the principle of the greatest happiness for the greatest number of people, long before John Stuart Mill formulated it. Of course, it should be remembered that this formula occurs in Bentham. The first note (written by Bentham) to the *Principles of Morals* speaks of "the greatest happiness or greatest felicity principle" and explains it.[41] However, Bentham had put little stress on the social dimension of utility, whereas Godwin insisted that personal pleasure and pain are not morally good motives for action. The latter thought that "reason" was the best moral motivation and in this he approached the better-known position of Immanuel Kant.[42]

One of the first British scholars who really knew something about Kant's ethics was the poet Samuel Taylor Coleridge (1772–1834). As his *Philosophical Lectures* (1818) reveal, Coleridge was reading Kant as early as 1804. He was much taken by Kant's arguments and tried to make them known in England. However, it was not until late in the nineteenth century that Kant's ethics made much impression on the British universities. Professors of ethics (John Grote, 1813–1866, at Cambridge; and James Ferrier, 1808–1864, at St. Andrews) distrusted the apparent agnosticism in the sage of Königsberg. Another well-known philosopher, Sir William Hamilton (1788–1856), was somewhat influenced by Kant but chiefly in the area of epistemology and in the direction of phenomenalism. Hamilton's views were brought to a wider audience by means of J. S. Mill's *Examination of Sir William Hamilton's Philosophy* (1865). As far as ethics is concerned, Hamilton combined Kant's teaching on the absolute and necessary character of primary moral principles with the down-to-earth moderation of Reid.

The "positivistic" quality of Bentham's theory of law was found also in the writing of John Austin (1790–1859). His *Province of Jurisprudence Determined* (1832) is not only the initiation of analytic jurisprudence; it is a forthright essay in utilitarianism. More clearly than Bentham, Austin taught that whatever the sovereign commands and can enforce is the law. This is what "positivism" means in the philosophy of law: there can be no appeal to a law of nature, a "higher law," or to the will of God. Even in morals, what the state law enjoins is what is right. Austin obviously influenced John Stuart Mill. One commentator writes that "Mill learned more of moral philosophy [from John Austin] than he could have learned from Bentham."[43]

A British Catholic thinker who had some impact on the ethics of this period was John Henry Newman (1801–1890). At Oxford he had been a pupil of Richard Whately (1787–1863), who was an outstanding logician and an authority on the ethics of Paley.[44] So, the ethics that Newman originally learned was doubtless a Christian approbative theory. However, in his *Grammar of Assent* (1870) Newman showed a highly personal approach to some of the problems of ethics. First of all, he distinguished notional from real assent: the former is abstract and unrelated to life, the latter is directed toward things and is concrete and unconditional.[45] There is a certain impatience with conceptual knowledge and system building, in Newman, that resembles the attitude of the twentieth-century existentialist. Reason is able to create a world of ideas for itself; it is also able "to investigate its reasonings."[46] It is the second function that interests Newman. He thinks that informal inference is more important (especially in practical matters) than the syllogistic of Aristotle. So, we are offered the theory of the "illative sense"—

the mind's power of concluding to a concrete and certain judgment. As Newman sees the matter:

> An ethical system may supply laws, general rules, guiding principles, a number of examples, suggestions, landmarks, limitations, cautions, distinctions, solutions of critical or anxious difficulties; but who is to apply them to a particular case? Whither can we go, except to the living intellect, our own, or another's? . . . It is a capacity sufficient for the occasion, deciding what ought to be done here and now, by this given person, under these given circumstances.[47]

Newman adds that this illative sense (which is a function of reason) is very much like Aristotle's *phronēsis,* the habit of reasoning well about practical matters. It is not really ethical theory, then, but the problem of applying any theory to life, that concerns Newman. In this he much resembles St. Augustine. His influence on the moral thinking of recent Catholic philosophers, such as Maurice Blondel (1861–1949) and Erich Przywara (1889–1972), is widely recognized.

Another British ethician, James Martineau (1805–1900), produced a much read survey of the subject in his *Types of Ethical Theory* (1885). Besides its obvious historical value, his work brings the whole problem of psychological motivation to the forefront in British ethics. To Martineau, morality is not an affair of the consequences, or even of the human action in itself. "That in which we discern the moral quality is, we have found, the *inner spring of action. . . .*"[48] The motive is known as good or evil by an immediate intuition. In addition to this view, Martineau is also recognized for his advocacy of indeterminism in the perennial problem of free will.[49]

The outstanding personality in nineteenth-century British ethics, however, was John Stuart Mill (1806–1873). A precocious child educated under the direction or his father, James, but without any training in revealed religion, John Stuart Mill made ethics the focal point of his personal interests. His contributions to theory of knowledge, psychology, and logic are well known. Against the realism of Hamilton, he argued that what we know consists of mental states, and his notion of man and his mind is basically that of David Hume. In logic Mill's theory of induction is a landmark.

We will confine our examination of Mill's ethical theory to the two key works. *On the Logic of the Moral Sciences* is actually the last part of his *System of Logic,* first published in 1843. At this time he was in close touch with the French social positivist Auguste Comte, and Mill's treatment of the methods of social science shows this influence. The other work is from twenty years later: it is the essay entitled *Utilitarianism* (1863).

The *Logic of the Moral Sciences* is prefaced by a lengthy quotation in French from Antoine Nicholas de Condorcet (1743–1794), who, in his *Historical Sketch of the*

Progress of the Human Mind (1794), had insisted that the philosopher should form his opinions on the basis of experience. With this empirical note established, Mill argues that a general science of human nature is possible, and that within this science the subject of psychology would be "the uniformities of succession, the laws, whether ultimate or derivative, according to which one mental state succeeds another—is caused by, or at least is caused to follow, another."[50] Next, Mill proposes a new science, "Ethology," which is to study the formation of character, national and collective, as well as individual character. This ethology is to be deductive in its method, contrasting with psychology, which is inductive, as Mill sees it.[51] Character study, however, is not ethics. Mill proceeds to discuss the methodology of the various social sciences: economics, sociology, political science, and also history. He does not think that they should, or can, use purely experimental methods; nor need these social sciences pretend to the sort of accuracy that is characteristic of chemistry.

The twelfth chapter brings Mill to moral knowledge and he immediately makes it clear that he regards ethics as an "art" and not a science. Ethics employs the imperative mood and this is typical of an art. Where there is an established law or rule (e.g. in a court of law) the process of reaching a judgment is ratiocination or syllogism. This contrasts with the procedure of the legislator whose function of establishing laws employs the opposite method. The legislator must look for the reasons or grounds for his rule. Matters of fact (expressed in terms of "is") are quite different from ought-propositions. Even in injunctions and recommendations (where "ought" is employed) some matter of fact is asserted, of course, namely "that the conduct recommended excites in the speaker's mind the feeling of approbation."[52] This is not enough; ethics must find general premises and deduce certain principal conclusions from them, in order to form a body of doctrine which will be the "Art of Life." It will have three divisions: morality, policy, and aesthetics—corresponding to the Right, the Expedient, and the Beautiful. This ethics as the art of life remains to be developed. Intuition of moral principles, if possible, would only take care of the start of the division of morality. Practical policy (prudential judgment) and aesthetics would require a different sort of principle. So, John Stuart Mill admits:

> I merely declare my conviction, that the general principle to which all rules of practice ought to conform, and the test by which they should be tried, is that of conduciveness to the happiness of mankind, or rather, of all sentient beings: in other words, that the promotion of happiness is the ultimate principle of Teleology.[53]

This is as far as the principle of universal utilitarianism is developed in Mill's *Logic.*

We have noticed how John Austin influenced John Stuart Mill. In Bentham there was always some ambiguity as to whether resultant utility was a test of the morality of a proposed individual action, or of a general type of activity. Speaking of human action, Austin said:

> Trying to collect its tendency . . . we must not consider the action as if it were *single* and *insulated,* but must look at the *class* of actions to which it belongs. The probable *specific* consequences of doing that single act, or forbearing from that single act, or of omitting that single act, are not the objects of the inquiry. The question to be solved is this:—If acts of the *class* were *generally* done, or *generally* forborne or omitted, what would be the probable effect on the general happiness or good?[54]

This helps us to understand the approach to the subject which Mill used in his *Utilitarianism* (1863).

First, Mill rejects the moral-sense theory: the existence of such a sense is not proved and even if we take it to be a function of our reason the deliverances of such a moral faculty would only be "the general principles of moral judgments."[55] The question of the morality of an individual action is not to be solved by direct perception but by applying a law to this case. Mill thinks that both ethical intuitionists and inductivists agree on this point. So he puts forth the utilitarian "creed" as his solution to the problem, after warning that it has nothing to do with the popular notion of "utility" as opposed to pleasure. Here is Mill's best statement of what it does mean:

> The creed which accepts as the foundation of morals, Utility, or the Greatest Happiness Principle, holds that actions are right in proportion as they tend to promote happiness, wrong as they tend to produce the reverse of happiness. By happiness is intended pleasure, and the absence of pain; by unhappiness, pain, and the privation of pleasure.[56]

To this Mill adds two clarificatory points. What is involved is not the greatest happiness of the individual agent but "the greatest amount of happiness altogether." Moreover, there are different kinds of pleasure; variations in quality must be noted, as well as in quantity. On this point Mill is departing from Bentham.

The main way of justifying the principle of utility seems to Mill to consist in an examination of its ultimate sanction. He frankly asks: "What is the source of its obligation?"[57] The only answer that he can give is that his test is "the same as of all other moral standards—the conscientious feelings of mankind." Mill is convinced that it is generally agreed that men do desire happiness—and he concludes that virtue is what is truly conducive to happiness.

The fifth chapter of *Utilitarianism* associates utility

with the notion of justice. Mill is well aware that many people have thought that men have a natural instinct or feeling for the just. He offers a very thoughtful account of the historical origin of men's acceptance of justice. Stressed in this is the idea that intelligent beings tend to grasp a "community of interest" and to develop the capacity to sympathize with human beings generally.[58] He even suggests that Kant's formula "So act, that thy rule of conduct might be adopted as a law by all rational beings" is an acknowledgement of the interest of mankind collectively. At the end, Mill decides that the duties of justice are simply the highest kind of social utilities; there are other things to do that are of utility, besides the obligations of justice. Justice has more definite commands and its sanctions are sterner.

Probably the outstanding British follower of John Stuart Mill was Alexander Bain (1818–1903). His *Mental and Moral Science* (1868) combined two works that developed the psychological and ethical implications of Mill's thought. Bain's *John Stuart Mill,* A *Criticism: With Personal Recollections* (1882) is a still-useful introduction to utilitarianism. It was Bain who introduced this way of thinking into the universities of Glasgow and Aberdeen.

Some people think that Henry Sidgwick (1838–1900) was the greatest of British ethicians. Certainly he was one of the best informed historically and the most learned. His *Methods of Ethics* (1874) and *Outlines of the History of Ethics* (1886) are evidences of the scholarship that he brought to his teaching at Cambridge. Sidgwick felt that, in the long run, there were really only three distinct approaches to the central problem of ethics, which is the justification of ethical or moral judgment. These are egoistic hedonism, universalistic hedonism (or utilitarianism), and intuitionism.[59] Of these, Sidgwick bluntly rejected Hobbes's egoism. This seemed to Sidgwick to be no ethics at all. Like a good academician, he tried to combine the best features of the other two theories, intuitional and utilitarian ethics. Yet he differed from John Stuart Mill on the matter of the ground of the greatest happiness principle. Mill, he thought, had confused the issue by attempting to show what men *ought* to desire from what they *do* desire. In other words, Sidgwick was concerned about something like the naturalistic fallacy well before G. E. Moore invented that striking name.

It was to avoid what seemed a circle in Mill's argument (happiness is desirable because we all desire it) that Sidgwick claimed an intuition of the principle of utility.[60] Of course, there are places in Mill's *Utilitarianism* where some recognition is given to the suggestion that we instinctively intuit the ground of moral obligation. But of all his predecessors, Samuel Clarke was the moral philosopher who seemed to Sidgwick to have had the most to offer. In this judgment, Sidgwick was also passing sentence on British ethics of the nineteenth century.

In his poem entitled *The Latest Decalogue,* Arthur

Hugh Clough (1819–1861) expressed his cynical verdict on the utilitarian ethics of his century:

> Thou shalt have one God only; who
> Would be at the expense of two?
> No graven images may be
> Worshipped, except the currency:
> Swear not at all; for, for thy curse
> Thine enemy is none the worse:
> At Church on Sunday to attend
> Will serve to keep the world thy friend:
> Honour thy parents; that is, all
> From whom advancement may befall:
> Thou shalt not kill; but need'st not strive
> Officiously to keep alive:
> Do not adultery commit,
> Advantage rarely comes of it:
> Thou shalt not steal; an empty feat,
> When it's so lucrative to cheat:
> Bear not false witness; let the lie
> Have time on its own wings to fly:
> Thou shalt not covet, but tradition
> Approves all forms of competition.

Chapter XI

German Idealistic Ethics

IN THE NINETEENTH-CENTURY German tradition ethics remained very much under the influence of Kant. The theoretical philosophy is generally idealistic, i.e. most thinkers in this period take it as granted that the objects of understanding and reasoning are ideas of some sort. Philosophy was considered to begin with an investigation of the inner presentations of human consciousness. These "ideas" were not merely cognitive, of course; they revealed feelings, volitions, human attitudes, laws, and obligations. A good deal of the German philosophy of this century was subjectivistic but there were attempts to reach an objective ground for both speculative and practical knowledge. Much of it was also dialectical, in the sense that some sort of step-by-step pattern of development was attributed to the ongoing process of reality. Finally, German ethics in this century becomes more and more divorced from the religious commitments of the Judaeo-Christian tradition. This is not universal but the general trend is toward a secular ethics.

Hundreds of German scholars were occupied with ethics at this time; it had become a popular subject in the university curriculum. We shall concentrate on four key figures: Fichte, Hegel, Schelling, and Schopenhauer. Less influential ethicians will be noted in passing.

Johann Gottlieb Fichte (1762–1814) initiates and personifies the main tendencies of idealistic ethics. All his writings are of ethical significance but three of them will be sufficient for a brief treatment of his ethics. Almost from the start of his writing career he showed his conviction that the domain of practical reason is most important. We see this in the *Basis of Natural Right* (1796) and the *System of Ethics (Das System der Sittenlehre,* 1798). Written in more popular style is the *Vocation of Man* (1800) which, however, presents most of the basic themes of Fichtean ethics. There is, finally, the *Addresses to the German Nation* (1807–1808), in which Fichte tried to rally his fellow countrymen by telling them that the Germans have as their destiny the duty of becoming "culture bearers" to the rest of humanity.

The aim of Fichte's methodology was to develop philosophy into a general theory of scientific knowledge (*Wissenschaftslehre).* This requires one organizing principle to explain all the presentations *(Vorstellungen)* of consciousness. Such data might be explained dogmatically and deterministically by attributing their origin to the "natural" world of matter. Such a move is repugnant to Fichte. The events of consciousness may also be explained mentally and freely by relating them to the mental character of the self or ego. This is what Fichte decides to do. From the very beginning, he takes the self as free, active, and moral.

One may think of the ego as contrasted with the nonego (or of the subject positing itself as object) within consciousness. One may experience the ego as a mental energy (will) which in acting meets with opposition—which is eventually revealed as but another aspect of will. As object or obstacle the nonego remains a function of the "Ich," the ever-present ego. So, Fichte's philosophy becomes an ethics as soon as it leaves the level of methodology. What is real for him is not some nonmental world of physical matter: the real is the resultant of the expression of volitional energy. He thinks that this is immediately evident within individual consciousness. "My will is mine, and it is the only thing that is wholly mine and entirely dependent on myself; and through it I have already become a citizen of the realm of freedom and of pure spiritual activity."[1]

Ethics deals with the realization of the ideal activity, both in the individual consciousness and in the moral order of the universe, which is a field for the development of infinite will. The ego first "posits" itself and thereby exists (thesis). It next sets up the nonego in opposition to itself, thereby becoming conscious of an otherness within itself (antithesis). Third, there comes an awareness that the ego without limitation (as absolute) must posit a certain limitation (or finitude) in both the ego and the nonego (synthesis). These are the stages of Fichte's dialectic: progress in knowledge and in morality will follow this triadic pattern.

There is an ordinary knowledge of morality common to all men because the "voice of conscience" speaks clearly and unequivocally within each of us.[2] In the second place, there is a philosophical science of what is right (ethics) that entails the understanding of the ground of morality in terms of Fichte's theory of knowledge. The main purpose of ethics is to show the development and realization of will, or moral consciousness, toward independence *(Selbständigkeit).* The resolve to become independent and free, in this sense, is called "Faith."[3] Thus, Fichte's ethical imperative is: "Act according to thine own conviction of duty." To act from motives arising from nature or authority is to abandon what is distinctively moral.

Fichte's moral conception of the state is in direct continuity with the foregoing. Will is not simply your mental energy or mine: there is the greater "will" (obviously reminiscent of Rousseau's general will), which posits itself in the life of the national state. Politics is but an extension of ethics. In the social community, the individual will must learn to limit itself in relation to the interests of other individual wills. Society, then, is "the relation of reasonable beings to each other . . . a free reciprocal activity founded on ideas."[4]

This ethics of Fichte is an important example of the self-realization theory. The process takes place in the ego, viewed both individually and cosmically. It is also a voluntarism but not an irrationalism, for Fichte's "will" remains within the limits of practical reason. In its social and political implications the doctrine of Fichte influenced some of the theoreticians of Hitler's national socialism. Fichte took a high-minded approach to the idea of a "national will"; it is easy enough to prostitute it. We shall see how the more personal facets of Fichte's voluntaristic ethics appear again in some existentialists of the twentieth century.

If Fichte neglected the Kantian realm of "things-in-themselves" and stressed the basic character of practical reason, one of his contemporaries, Friedrich Schleiermacher (1768–1834), took the contrary path. His main treatise in ethics is entitled: *Outlines of a Critique of the Doctrine of Morals up to the Present* (1803). Schleiermacher felt that we do know Kant's noumena, and so he was very much opposed to what he saw as Fichte's extreme subjectivism. That philosophy is concerned with a dialectic and that God is the transcendent identity of thought and being, Schleiermacher agreed. It is not through practical reason that we reach God but by way of religious feeling and intuition. Schleiermacher's natural theology has been called a "fusion of Spinozism and idealism."[5] Although human egos are parts of the universal substance, for Schleiermacher, they remain free, self-determining, and quite individual. Reason is present in a lower sense in nature, and on a higher level in man. All reality is rational; hence, the laws of nature and moral law are entirely compatible. The fundamental imperative in Schleiermacher's ethics is: "Be a unique person and act in accord with your own distinctive nature."[6]

The place of G. W. F. Hegel (1770–1831) in the history of ethics is not easy to determine. Some histories of the subject simply omit him. It could be argued that he has a philosophy of law, of history, of society, and so on, but no ethics as such. However, he has influenced, positively and negatively, so many later writers in ethics that it is necessary to pay some attention to his views. We cannot attempt a complete exposition but will try to single out some of the more important teachings.

A group of early writings by Hegel dates from the last decade of the eighteenth century and contrasts Christian morality with Kant's philosophical ethics. These are the works translated as the *Early Theological Writings.* One of these studies *(Life of Jesus,* 1795) treats Christ as a teacher of ethics. The *Phenomenology of Mind* (1807) marks the beginning of Hegel's personal approach to philosophy. This work has a good deal to say about the relation of ethics to the rest of philosophy. In 1821 Hegel published his *Outlines of the Philosophy of Right;* it is a major source for the study of his ethics. Various other volumes have been edited from Hegel's courses of lectures. The *Philosophy of History* is of this type. The posthumously published *System of Ethics* was outlined in 1802 by Hegel but it is a very imperfect formulation of Hegelian ethics and is only mentioned here for the sake of completeness.[7]

In the early works Hegel seems to have thought of ethics in terms of Kant's system. *The Spirit of Christianity,* for instance, teaches that Jesus advanced from the legalism (a morality of externally imposed commands) of the Judaic tradition to a new morality concerned with the satisfaction of human needs. This new morality of Jesus is grounded in the autonomy of the human will. In spite of the Kantian cast of this interpretation, Hegel accuses Kant himself of mistakenly speaking of a "command requiring respect for a law which commands love." It is wrong, Hegel thinks, to base love on an imperative: "In love all thought of duties vanishes."[8]

During the first decade of the nineteenth century, Hegel worked out his own general notion of what philosophy is and does. His views now represent a reaction to those of Kant, Fichte, and Schelling (who, though a contemporary, published several works that were read by Hegel). Hegel remained an idealist but pushed the theory beyond the original meaning of "idea" as a presentation of individual consciousness toward a doctrine in which all things and events occur in Mind objectified. Reality is completely rational:

there is an intelligible explanation for everything and the method of philosophical explanation is dialectical. Hegel's dialectic is a three-step process moving from an original positive affirmation of some event or thing (thesis), through a second stage of negation or denial of the first (antithesis), to a final stage which cancels and transmutes the two preceding stages into a higher combination (synthesis). What is canceled but then rises to a higher meaning is said to be *aufgehoben.* The blooming of a rose is used as an example of the dialectic. First, there must be a rosebud (thesis); then the bud must stop being a bud (antithesis); and third, the canceled bud must give rise to a new item, the flower, which comes from the first two steps (this culmination is the synthesis). This is the patterned triadic process of all developments in mind and reality: all philosophical interpretation should make use of this new logic. The dialectical theory is described at great length in the *Phenomenology of Mind.*[9] Nature, consciousness, history, culture, art, and religion develop dialectically. So also does ethics, for it is but a distinctive way of tracing the evolution of Mind.[10]

God is the Idea, the universe considered potentially; Mind or Spirit *(Geist)* is the realization of the Idea in concrete evolution. Mind expresses itself in many lines of development. The *Phenomenology of Mind* traces the dialectical process through methodology, various phases of consciousness and self-consciousness, reason in itself, in nature and in self-consciousness, through objectified spirit, morality, religion, art, to the ultimate stage of general philosophical science. Considering the phenomena of morality, Hegel says this:

> When we look at the moral view of the world. . . . The first stage, which forms the starting-point, is the actual moral self-consciousness. . . . And, since what is moral only is at all so far as it is complete,—for duty is the pure unadulterated ultimate element (*Ansich*), and morality consists merely in conforming to this pure principle—the second proposition runs: "there is no actual existence which is moral." Since, however, in the third place, it is a self, it is inherently the unity of duty and actual reality. . . . In this final goal or aim of the synthetic unity of the two first propositions, the self-conscious actuality, as well as duty, is only affirmed as a transcended or superseded moment.[11]

In other words, ethics advances from some low-grade common concept of morality, through a stage which recognizes that this sort of morality is unrealistic, to a synthesis in which a philosophy of morality is proposed.

Hegel's *Philosophie des Rechts* offers such a higher ethics, expressed in terms of right and wrong. As objectified, Mind gives rise to "abstract right." The term *Recht* (like *jus* in Latin) has no precise English equivalent. In a broad way, it names the moral, the lawful, the approvable good. Concretely, for Hegel, the institution of property (one's actuated right to possess a thing) provides a thesis from which to begin the development of ethics.[12] A property right is one sort of objectification of the universal or rational will.[13] Will is that aspect of consciousness in which freedom becomes actual: there is both individual and universal will. Voluntary actions running contrary to rational will are wrong and antithetic to the original rightness.[14] For such wrongs there is a logical demand for punishment and retribution. Morality itself is the abstract harmony between the individual volition and the rational will or notion of what ought to be.

At one point in the *Phenomenology of Mind*[15] Hegel speaks of the ethical life as substantially realized in a set of customs *(Sittlichkeit)* as something lower than morality *(Moralität)*. However, the *Philosophy of Right* (some fifteen years later) sees morality as an abstract concept that is concretely objectified in the substance of the ethical life *(Sittlichkeit)*. The latter is social, objective, and more profound than morality.[16] In the ethical dialectic a key series moves from (1) *purpose,* as the subjective inclination of the individual person, through (2) *intention* and *well-being,* as the essential character of the act that is proposed, to (3) the final synthesis of *goodness* or *wickedness.* Fundamental to this is the concept of the "ethical system." This is described as follows:

> The ethical system is the idea of freedom. It is the living good, which has in self-consciousness its knowing and willing, and through the action of self-consciousness its actuality. Self-consciousness, on the other hand, finds in the ethical system its absolute basis and motive. The ethical system is thus the conception of freedom developed into a present world, and also into the nature of self-consciousness.[17]

Duty, for Hegel, is the moral law issuing from the rational nature of will; while moral conscience is simply duty made effective.[18] The notion of "subjectivity" is important here to Hegel. Whether recent phenomenology is in lineal descent from the thought of Hegel is a matter of dispute today.[19] However, the phenomenological term "subjectivity" is used in a distinctively ethical manner by Hegel. This is evident in lines such as these:

> Substantive ethical reality attains its right, and this right receives its due, when the individual in his private will and conscience drops his self-assertion and antagonism to the ethical. . . . Subjectivity is the absolute form and the existing actuality of the substance. The difference between the subject and substance, as the object, end, and power of the subject, forthwith vanishes, like the difference between form and matter.[20]

Hegel goes on to say that subjectivity is the foundation for the real existence of the conception of freedom, and in ethics subjectivity is the existence of personal self-determination and moral freedom.

Another very important Hegelian approach to the notion of "ethical system" lies in the development of social life. This may be one of Hegel's greatest contributions to ethics; it implies a special theory of history and of politics. As morality concretizes and becomes "substantial" in the family, civil society, and eventually the state, there is an evolution of the ethical life *(Sittlichkeit).* The family is the union of at least two persons in love.[21] Civil society is a condition in which there is a mutual dependence of all persons on all, yet as a collection of independent individuals. It is founded on a system of wants. The state is a concrete institution that unifies and gives a higher reality to the ethical lives of its individual members. At times, there is a sort of mystique about Hegel's state. In his *Philosophy of History* we are told that the state is "the embodiment of rational freedom," and that it is the "Idea of Spirit in the external manifestation of human Will and its Freedom."[22] Since God is also the Idea of the Spirit *(Geist),* this amounts to a rather extravagant divinization of the national state. It is but one step away from totalitarianism or *étatisme.*[23]

The later influence of Hegel's ethical writings has been extensive. At times (see the Preface to the *Philosophy of Right)* Hegel presented himself as the philosopher of Protestantism and the successor to Luther in the reformation of the religious life of Europe. A group of German theologians (including Karl Daub, 1763–1836, at Heidelberg; and P. K. Marheineke, 1780–1846, at Berlin) applied his dialectic and ethical system to the study of Christian religion. They became known as right-wing Hegelians. Another school picked up Hegel's notion that religion is but a stage in the movement toward the synthesis which is his ethical philosophy and decided that Christianity had outlived its usefulness. These left-wing Hegelians (David F. Strauss, 1808–1874; and Ludwig Feuerbach, 1804–1872) stressed the materialistic and atheistic implications of Hegel's thought and influenced the thinking of Karl Marx. Practically all recent historians of philosophy have come under the influence of Hegel's methodology. One of the first histories of ethics was written by a pupil of Hegel, Leopold von Henning (1791–1866), under the title *Principien der Ethik im historischer Entwicklung* (Berlin, 1824). Finally, we might note that existentialists from Kierkegaard to the present agree on little other than a shared suspicion and dislike for the conceptualizing system-building of Hegel.

A follower of Kant who turned Kantian ethics into a spiritualistic eclecticism was Jakob Friedrich Fries (1773–1843). Fries's main writings in ethics were his *Doctrine of Right* (1804) and his *Ethics* (1818). The role of ethics in these works is to analyze and verify the moral deliverances of common experience. In his psychology Fries made much use of the method of introspection and his ethics also stresses inner experience. There is in Fries's understanding of Kant's practical reason a notion of moral faith viewed as an expression of religious feeling. Leonard Nelson (1882–1927) brought Fries's teachings to the United States, where the "Nelson Foundation" is still devoted to this school of thought.

Reaction to the prevailing idealism of nineteenth-century Germany is represented by Johann Friedrich Herbart (1776–1841). His pluralistic metaphysics is reminiscent of the philosophy of Leibniz but Herbart's work in psychology helped to bring attention to the importance of empirical data in ethics. Apart from his *Textbook in Psychology* (1816), the *Practical Philosophy* (1808) is Herbart's chief contribution to the literature of ethics. His theory of knowledge is realistic: we know the material world as an aggregate of simple essences, in which real events occur.[24] On the other hand, the human soul is not known in itself, as this text indicates:

> The soul has no innate natural talents nor faculties whatever, either for the purpose of receiving or for the purpose of producing. . . . It has originally neither concepts, nor feelings, nor desires. It knows nothing of itself, and nothing of other things; also in it lie no

> forms of perception and thought, no laws of willing and action, and not even a remote predisposition to any of these.[25]

This vigorous rejection of the a priori leads to Herbart's claim that feelings and desires include acts of preference and rejection, plus "something objective." He is a pioneer in attempting an experiential approach to a science of objective and real values.

Herbart investigates the functions of feeling and willing from the point of view of aesthetics, of which one branch for him is ethics. Five kinds of will relations give rise to ethical judgments. We approve of (1) the relation of a person's will that is in keeping with his basic convictions (the idea of freedom); (2) the relation of an act of will in one person that is in accord with other efforts of the same will (idea of harmony); (3) the relation of one person's will to the satisfaction of the will of another person (idea of benevolence). We disapprove of (4) the relation in which several wills impede each other (idea of justice); and (5) the relation in which the intended good or evil is not compensated (idea of retribution). This is an interesting attempt to discover certain basic ethical notions in immediate experience.[26]

A somewhat similar use of psychology to establish a value theory and an ethics is found in the work of Friedrich E. Beneke (1798–1854). His *Outlines of a Natural System of Practical Philosophy* (1837) rejects the ethics of Kant and suggests a detailed theory of the process of valuing in terms of good and evil. He is more inclined than others to attribute to human nature a certain predisposition toward some types of valuation. Beneke describes five relations or bases for grading perceptions of good and evil: (1) the nature of the elementary faculties; (2) the development of the elementary faculties through impressions; (3) the degree of complexity in the products of these faculties; (4) the duration of these products; and (5) the purity of these products.[27] This is obviously an effort to provide an empirical scale for rating ethical values.

Another direction taken by German idealistic ethics is illustrated by the views of Friedrich W. J. von Schelling (1775–1854). Historians usually treat him before Hegel because he influenced Hegelianism, especially in the area of methodology and the notion of the Absolute in the development of nature. Like Fichte and Hegel, Schelling also uses the logic of dialectic (action, reaction, synthesis) to interpret various processes. However, we are interested here in the later ethical position of Schelling, when he turned away from rationalistic logic to the romanticism of religious feeling. The beginning of this romantic period can be set at the publication of his treatise *On University Studies* (1803), in which his whole early philosophy is summarized for popular reading. Key works in the later period are the *Philosophical Investigations on the Essence of Human Freedom* (1809) and *The Ages of the World* (1811).

Lecture XIV is the end of the series *On University Studies* and already in it we find the suggestion that the philosophy of art may be a source of religious and ethical information. As Schelling grew older and came under the influence of the two Schlegel families at Jena, and of the Catholic fideist Franz von Baader (1765–1841), he put more and more emphasis on the irrational, dark, obscure depths of human and divine consciousness. God and the world are one, in a sense, but Schelling defended himself against the charge of pantheism by explaining that God is the antecedent and the world the consequent. This comes out in the treatise *On Human Freedom.* He is sure that man is free, because he has the power of good and evil.[28] In the dark depths of man's spirit Schelling finds urges and impulses toward unreasonable and evil feelings and actions. As a person matures, these lower instincts are brought to light and somewhat controlled by increasing rationality. They remain something of the basis for human freedom, however. Perhaps this is the main point in his later ethical thought (which is much neglected in secondary studies of Schelling): there is a dimension of feeling and imagination in the ethical life that exceeds the limits of reason. If most German ethicians up to Schelling thought of ethics as a reasoned account of voluntary activities, he now insisted that there is more to ethical personality than that. Doubtless he influenced, directly or indirectly, the growing interest in the unconscious (Eduard von Hartmann,

1842–1906) and in the subconscious drives, which were stressed by Sigmund Freud (1856–1939).

The last major figure in the German ethics of the nineteenth century was Arthur Schopenhauer (1788–1860). Yet he was never fully accepted as a serious philosopher by the academic thinkers of the day. Schopenhauer's first great work was *The World as Will and Idea* (1819), in which a portion (secs. 55–71) of the fourth book is devoted to ethical topics. Years later, in 1839–1840, Schopenhauer wrote two lengthy *Prize Essays,* one on the freedom of the will, the other on the basis of morality. These were published (1841) together as *The Two Basic Problems of Ethics.* Finally, he has a miscellaneous collection of essays and notes, gathered under the title *Parerga und Paralipomena* (1851). It is from cheap editions and translations of selections from these popular essays that Schopenhauer has come to be known as the "philosopher of nursemaids."

The World as Will and Idea is a huge metaphysical treatise that explains that the fundamental energy which evolves in all things and produces all events is "will."[29] As Schopenhauer expresses this metaphysics: "The world as idea is the complete mirror of the will, in which it knows itself in ascending grades of distinctness and completeness, the highest of which is man."[30] What we have here is another version of German idealism: instead of all things being variations of mind, they are now bubbles in an infinite will.

As individuals, men are part of the world of appearances, *phenomena;* as things-in-themselves (Kant's *noumena),* human beings are united in the eternal will. Freedom belongs to noumenal will but not to the order of individual phenomena; hence, individual men are not free.[31] Will is an ongoing process, ever striving, but with no ultimate objective. The whole series of volitional events which makes up the universe is non-purposive. Here, Schopenhauer is running against the Hegelian, and generally idealistic, tradition that there is a reason why for everything. He thinks not. Satisfaction or happiness is quite negative. It consists in release from pain.[32]

Good and bad are the basic ethical conceptions for Schopenhauer but they are essentially relative. Good mean "the conformity of an object to any definite effort of the will." What is good for one man may be bad for the next person. There can be no highest or absolute good (*summum bonum*); for that would be a final satisfaction of willing and, by the initial assumption of Schopenhauer, the will never ceases to desire and to strive. Intensity of volition is a source of inevitable suffering: the bad man must endure the sting of moral conscience and the good man must face the frustration of unending desire. To be just or right means to avoid denying the will that appears in another person. There is no moral imperative, or "ought," to prescribe to the eternally free will.[33]

53517

A "principle of asceticism" (to see that individual differences and strivings are merely phenomenal, and thus to renounce the effort of individual volition), which amounts to a denial of the will to live, is offered in this passage:

> After our investigation has brought us to the point at which we have before our eyes perfect holiness, the denial and surrender of all volition, and thus the deliverance from a world whose whole existence we have found to be suffering, this appears to us as a passing away into empty nothingness. Before us there is certainly only nothingness.[34]

This is a blunt statement of Schopenhauer's ethics of pessimism: not even suicide will remove one from the pointless flow of will power; the suicide is merely another negative event in an eternal process.

The essay on *Freedom of the Will* won the prize offered by the Norwegian Scientific Society in 1839. It was regarded as a brilliant *tour de force.* In it Schopenhauer argues for about ninety pages that there can be no freedom in human willing. "The result of our preceding exposition was to recognize the complete annulment of all freedom of human action and its thoroughgoing subjection to the strictest necessity."[35] However, Schopenhauer suddenly suggests at the end that, if we advert to the feeling of responsibility for our actions, we may take a new approach from this moral fact and conclude that human actions are "transcendentally" free, not as individual events but in the whole being and essence of man.[36] During the course of this essay, a very thorough and learned history of various theories of free will is provided by Schopenhauer.

In a second prize essay, *On the Basis of Morality* (which failed to win the prize offered by the Royal Danish Academy of Sciences in 1840), Schopenhauer offers a very severe and lengthy criticism of Kant's ethics.[37] He is briefer in subsequently rejecting Fichte's moral philosophy. Many of his remarks are unfair and intemperate and this is one reason why the Danes did not give him their prize. Yet in the latter part of this second essay Schopenhauer describes an ethical theory that is of some importance. His criterion, now, of an action of moral worth is that such action must be motivated by *compassion* for others.[38] This is Schopenhauer's famous ethics of pity or sympathy. "Only insofar as an action has sprung from compassion does it have moral value; and every action resulting from any other motives has none." His two great moral virtues, then, are altruistic. They are justice and loving-kindness; both have their roots in natural compassion. This feeling is the criterion of morality in ordinary knowledge. Metaphysically, Schopenhauer rests his ethics on the claim that the virtuous man "makes less of a distinction than do the rest between himself and others."[39] In other words, the real cause of evil is located in the phenomenal differences which separate people. To realize that we are all one will is ethically desirable. Schopenhauer was influenced by his reading in the religious writings of India to adopt a position which is similar to the Nirvana teaching.

Parerga and Paralipomena, the popular essays, include a wide variety of observations on life and people. Their style is terse and popular. In one he will explain why "there is a worm in every apple," and in another, why a beautiful woman always picks an ugly one as a companion. They illustrate his general pessimism in the moral order but are not of primary importance for the serious study of Schopenhauer's theoretical ethics. With important changes, Nietzsche carried on this voluntaristic movement in German ethics. We shall follow this line of influence in Chapter XVIII.

A very unusual development in German idealistic ethics is connected with the name of Max Stirner (1806–1856). He was a teacher in a Berlin school for girls and his real name was Johann Kaspar Schmidt. His book *The Individual and His Unique Quality* (1845) is a protest against the moral rules of society. Stirner seems to have been a nineteenth-century "beatnik" in his thinking but he is usually classified as an ethical anarchist. A left-wing Hegelian in his general philosophy, he felt that the individual person should be free to express himself without any social restraints. His ethical imperatives urged his contemporaries: "Be egoistic! Scorn the illusions of social morality! Don't be the slave of an idea!"[40] It is probable that Stirner pushed ethics as far as it would go in the direction of extreme egoism.

The medical doctor Rudolf Hermann Lotze (1817–1881) is noted in the history of philosophy for his revival of psychophysical parallelism in his large work entitled *Microcosmus* (1856–1864). His projected third volume on ethics, in his *System der Philosophie,* was never written but his *Metaphysics* (1841) shows something of what his approach would have been to moral philosophy. Student notes of his lectures (including those on ethics) were printed under the title *Kleine Schriften* (3 vols., 1885–1891). Lotze taught that the human will is powerless to cause anything to happen in the human body. If I have the impression that I can move my hand at will, this is due to the fact that "Nature" moves the body on the occasion of certain acts of will.[41] Ethically, this somewhat reduces the importance of the bodily aspects of moral activities.

In spite of an almost mechanistic view of human physiology and psychology, Lotze was much interested in Leibniz's metaphysics and in Fichte's ethical idealism. Rejecting the notion of a moral a priori predisposition in man, Lotze felt that there was some importance in Fichte's theory that a general moral consciousness expresses itselfin the lives or individual persons. Thus, Lotze thought, our moral consciousness testifies to the purposiveness of the world and human life. The end to which man's moral efforts should be directed is the supreme value, God.[42] His efforts to deal empirically with valuation are important in the history of axiology.

The famous pioneer in empirical psychology, Wilhelm Wundt (1834–1920), also did considerable work in ethics. His textbook on *Ethics* (1886) was widely used in late nineteenth-century classes in ethics and had quite a success in English. Besides the introduction of much empirical material from social psychology about the moral notions of various peoples, Wundt's use of the general will as the source of objective moral standards was reminiscent of Rousseau and, of course, Kant. The end of the century saw an increase in interest in Kant's ethics, not only in Germany but also in France, England, and the United States. The noted interpreter of Kantian ethics was Friedrich Paulsen (1846–1908). At Marburg, Hermann Cohen (1842–1918) went back to the original ethics of Kant.

A series of books that developed the theory of an ethics of spiritual life were written at Jena by Rudolf Eucken (1846–1926). As the teacher of Max Scheler, Eucken influenced the early directions of German phenomenological ethics. His *The Value and Meaning of Life* (1907) and *The Life of the Spirit* (1908) were translated into English. A theory of "types of life" (the naturalist, the aesthete, the spiritual man) was developed by Eucken to demonstrate the superiority of the life of spiritual freedom.

This brings us to the end of our account of nineteenth-century German ethics. Its contributions to the subject are not always fully appreciated today, particularly in English-speaking countries. But there was a period, early in the twentieth century, when American and even many British ethicians looked to graduate work at the great German universities as the crowning feature in their preparationas teachers of the subject. Even today, as we shall see in subsequent chapters, the idealism of German ethics remains significant in the axiological, existential, and spiritistic types of moral philosophy.

Chapter XII

Franco-Latin Spiritistic Ethics

THE KIND OF ethics to be examined in this chapter is not well known to English readers. It is a moral philosophy that has grown out of the movement which is called "*la philosophie de l'esprit*" in France but it is also very important in Italy and Spain and is the dominant ethical view in most parts of Latin America. The notion of *esprit* is not conveyed by one English term. It means spirit and mind, of course, but it also suggests that reality which is discovered in the higher functions of human consciousness and which is quite immaterial. This "spiritism" sometimes stresses the intuitional and cognitive aspects of mind; in other cases it emphasizes the volitional or affective functions. In all cases it rejects materialism.

Many of the thinkers to be considered here are known as "Christian personalists." This term is much favored in Italy and the Spanish-speaking countries. There is a certain amount of idealism implied: what is real is best investigated through personal consciousness. The existence of a physical universe is not usually denied but bodies are regarded as less important and less real than minds. Most people who hold this kind of personalistic or spiritistic ethics have strong Christian religious commitments; many are Catholics. This does not mean that they are Thomists. Few of them have more than a nodding acquaintance with the thought of Aquinas. It is St. Augustine who is the important early source of inspiration. Descartes's emphasis on the *cogito* is also an influence, as are some of the teachings of the German idealists and romantics. On the whole, British and North American ethicians have had little interest in this sort of thing. Personalism means something rather different in the context of philosophy in the United States. The closest approach in this country would be the "Christian philosophy" of Orestes Brownson (1803–1876) who, in fact, was indebted to the philosophy of two of our spiritistic ethicians, Victor Cousin and Gioberti.[1]

The first spiritistic ethician was Father Nicolas Malebranche (1638–1715), something of a Cartesian but also a great student of Augustine. Histories usually treat his striking theory of knowledge and reality and neglect his ethics. Malebranche speculated that all things exist in their Ideas in God's creative mind and we know them (bodies and finite spirits) by seeing the "ideas" which God (as universal Reason) furnishes to our thought. It would not be necessary for trees and the ocean, and so on, to exist physically: God could provide us with these objective ideas, even if these created things did not exist. However, we believe on the basis of divine revelation that the world of finite creatures is in existence—but we do not know it, except through the divinely implanted ideas. This is what we are told in Malebranche's *Search for Truth* (1674) and *Dialogues on Metaphysics* (1688). It is a theory that adapts the Augustinian doctrine of divine illumination to the problems of Cartesian metaphysics and psychology.

However, Malebranche wrote extensively in the field of moral philosophy. An early treatise is the *Christian Discussions in which One Justifies the Truth of Religion and Morality* (1675). His *Treatise on Morality* was first published in 1683. In a revised edition of the *Treatise* (Lyons, 1697), he printed his *Treatise on the Love of God.* In these works, as in the speculative writings, we are continually told that my individual mind *(esprit)* is not universal but it is impressed or enlightened by divine Reason in such a manner that the objects of my understanding are common to all minds *(esprits).* Knowledge is "objective" in the sense of having a "validity for spirits everywhere and at all times."[2] This is the beginning of French spiritism, as neatly summarized by Malebranche:

> The reason of man is the *word,* or the wisdom of God himself; for every creature is a particular being, but the reason of man is universal. If my own particular mind were my reason and my light, my mind would also be the reason of all intelligent beings. . . . The pain which I feel is a modification of my own proper substance, but truth is a possession common to all spiritual beings. . . . Thus, by means of reason, I have or may have some society with God, and all other intelligent beings; because they all possess something in common with me, to wit, reason.[3]

Any suggestion that pleasure could be the criterion of virtuous activity is strongly opposed by Malebranche. As he explains it: "Pleasure is the reward of merit, and therefore cannot be the foundation of it."[4] Nor can the order of nature (in the Stoic sense) be the ground for moral law. The only basis that Malebranche can see for moral or ethical judgment is the "love of order," the will to live in harmony with God's general will. Two dispositions are required for the virtuous acceptance of God's law in the love of order: "force of spirit" and "liberty of spirit." The habit of looking to universal Truth (another name for God) in order to acquire adequate ideas as to human behavior is the force of the spirit. On the other hand, the habit of rejecting all confused ideas, all notions which seem to come from the body (such as movements of concupiscence) is the liberty of the spirit. It is not easy to cultivate these two major virtues: the special assistance of divine grace is needed to advance in that love of God which culminates in eternal happiness.[5]

The ethics of Malebranche is a theological approbative theory: human actions are good because God immediately makes them so. Unlike William of Ockham, Malebranche does not suggest that God might, on occasion, "change His mind or will." The universality and objectivity of universal Reason are the bases for his confidence in the immutability of ethical principles. Implicit in this view of "spirit"—as transcending all individual limitations yet retaining the distinctive volitional and intellectual characteristics of personality—is the whole of later Christian personalism.

Another very unusual French Catholic thinker who belongs in this tradition is Maine de Biran (1766–1824). He was not a teacher or writer but a government official and the works that he has left are fragmentary and posthumously published. His essay on *The Relations between the Physical and the Moral in Man* was written in 1820 but only printed about ten years after his death. Also significant are the *Essay on the Foundations of Psychology* (1812) and the *New Essays in Anthropology* (1823). Henri Gouhier's selected texts (in French) is the most convenient for reference.

It is difficult to discover what Maine de Biran read; obviously Descartes and Malebranche lie in his background. He knew something of Kant and was influenced by him. The eighteenth-century philosophes were, of course, well known to him, in particular, Condillac. It is the soul, or spirit, that is of primary interest to Maine de Biran but, unlike Malebranche, he traces its basic energy to will. He looked not so much to God (although he was a pious man) for the explanation of the life of the spirit, as he did to the initial presentations of consciousness. "We feel our phenomenal individuality, or existence, but we do not feel the very substance of our soul."[6] What is important is to find the source, or primitive origin, of the activity that is the distinctive feature of the self. Maine de Biran introduces the "inner sense" *(sens intime)* as a function in which one intuits, or feels, his soul as a dynamic force. We have "an immediate feeling of force and that feeling is no other than that of our very existence, from which that of activity is inseparable."[7] This basic force, life, and existence in every person is what he calls will *(volonté);* it is efficient and free energy.[8] The starting point for his ethics is this psychological voluntarism, as he explains:

> I will, I act *(cogito),* therefore I am *(ergo sum).*
> I am not in some indeterminate way a think-

> ing being, but very precisely a willing force which passes from the virtual to the actual by its own energy, by determining itself or bringing itself to action.[9]

The good path for man's moral development is the way of self-determination, the improvement of the soul by the exercise of volitional freedom.

At one time, Maine de Biran tried to locate the original awareness of willing in the consciousness of muscular effort; this was offered as an alternative to Condillac's primitive fact of sensing. Maine de Biran always retained the notion that "effort" *(effort voulu)* is a most important feature of conscious moral life. Like Augustine, he thought that man's soul lives on an intermediate level between the life of the body, below, and the life of God, above. But he felt that it was best for man's spirit to stay on its own level.

> This is the proper and natural condition of man, that in which he exercizes all the faculties of his nature, develops all his moral power in fighting the unruly appetites of his animal nature, . . . Above and beneath that state, there remains no struggle, no effort, no resistance, consequently no ***I***; the soul is in that state of alienation, sometimes in deifying, sometimes in animalizing itself.[10]

What Maine de Biran has to offer, then, is not a theory of the basis of ethical judgment or obligation (he would simply point to God, if asked about that sort of thing) but rather an expansion of the meaning of the "spirit" of man. It is dynamic force, free activity, self-determining energy. It is a special mode of existence. This is important to later philosophers of the spirit and also to existentialists.

Not all French philosophers of the spirit are religiously inspired. In some, German idealism or Scotch common sense may substitute for the love of God. Victor Cousin (1792–1867) called his own brand of thought eclecticism. He was an able historian of philosophy and felt that the way to build a teachable and useful philosophy is to use the bricks gathered from the great philosophers of the past. He was one of the first French scholars to make a serious study of the thinking of men who lived in the Middle Ages. (His editions of the Latin works of Peter Abelard are still used.) After teaching for a few years (1815–1818) Cousin went into administration, eventually becoming the director of public education in France. His lecture notes were edited in several series. *The True, the Beautiful, and the Good* (published in 1837) and *History of Moral Philosophy in the Eighteenth Century* (published 1839–1840) are outstanding in the field of eclectic ethics. The latter contains much information on Scottish ethics and on moral sensism. He was well aware of developments in German idealistic ethics, also.

Apart from the methodological suggestion that the study of the history of philosophy, done in a scientific manner, may be essential to a professional approach to working in modern ethics, Cousin has little to say that is novel or startling. One should try to derive his notions of the "good" from a prior study of the "true." Obligation, in ethics, is the will to achieve what is true and reasonable. Moral duties depend on societal existence; they are concerned with man's relations to his fellows. He is somewhat indebted to the German idealists for the important moral function that he assigns to the state and to public education.[11]

Not a formal Christian, Cousin saw much value in the cultural tradition of Christendom. As to the philosophy of the spirit, in the mind of Cousin, it meant the cultivation of one's intellect and will, by study, and by efforts at self-improvement particularly in the area of the fine arts. For the French, at this point, "un homme d'esprit" was a person with some natural gifts, trained to think and write logically, educated to the appreciation of music and painting. His follower Théodore Jouffroy (1796–1842) shared and propagated this aesthetic ideal. As the translator of Thomas Reid, Jouffroy helped to popularize the common-sense philosophy in France. His *Nouveaux mélanges philosophiques* (1842) contains an essay on moral eclecticism that simply extends the views of Cousin.

In Switzerland, the philosophy of the spirit was given a religious setting by the Protestant thinker Charles Sécrétan (1815–1895). He published an exposition of the philosophy of Victor Cousin (1868) but his personal thought is found in the *Philosophy of Freedom* (1849) and *The Principle of Morality* (1884). Like Maine de Biran, Sécrétan was a metaphysical voluntarist: will is the fundamental reality. God is the Christian divinity and is the source of all ethical distinctions. However, God is essentially freedom and is not bound by the logic of nineteenth-century rationalism. His Christian personalism is fundamentally a Protestant moral theology.

Two Italian thinkers of this period are part of the Christian spiritist movement: Rosmini and Gioberti. Although both were Catholics, their views were not typical of their religious tradition. Antonio Rosmini-Serbati (1797–1855) was a priest who tried to adapt Hegelianism to the Italian intellectual scene. Every man, according to Rosmini, has an inborn intuition of the idea of being which grounds and illuminates all other ideas, and which establishes the soul of man as a "spiritual" reality.[12] This is not merely an effort to account for the origin of human thoughts; it is a metaphysics of the human person. In a sense, the idea of being is also divine. This teaching brought Rosmini under official censure from Catholic authorities. There is much debate as to what Rosmini actually meant by the intuition of an immutable object which is independent of all finite minds.

The fundamental ethical imperative for Rosmini is: "Follow the light of reason." There is a special science, *eudaemonology,* which treats of the human good, or happiness. Limited to the natural goods which may satisfy man's bodily and intellectual needs and aspirations, it is from the point of view of the *subjective* good (man's attainment of happiness) that eudaemonology is developed. Ethics, on the other hand is, the science of the *objective* good. Moral good is defined as objective good (identical with the idea of being) known by the intellect and willed by the will. As in Malebranche, the notion of "order" is a key one to Rosmini. Order is the relation between various grades of perfection and being. The good will loves the order of being. His position has been described as "an ethics in which 'obligation' and 'duty' find their foundation in the apprehension of ordered being by the light of natural reason . . . the free love of good acknowledged by intelligence and determined by reason."[13] There are many followers of Rosmini among the Christian spiritists of present-day Italy; the outstanding figure is M. F. Sciacca, whom we shall consider later in this chapter.

Contemporary with Rosmini was Vincenzo Gioberti (1801–1852), who also was a priest. He left Italy for political reasons and taught in Brussels for almost ten years. On his return to Italy, he became prime minister of Sardinia (1849) and then served as Italian ambassador to France. Eventually Gioberti died in poverty. At Brussels he had published a treatise *On the Good* (1848) and his *Primary Science (Protologia)* appeared in 1857. The *Course in Philosophy* (Brussels, 1841–1842) was published in 1947. Although he and

Rosmini criticized each other severely, there is much resemblance between their teachings.

Gioberti reacted against Cousin's effort to base metaphysics on psychological evidence. For the same reason, he always opposed Rosmini for providing a theory of knowledge rather than an ontology. Gioberti tried hard to show the difference between starting with an intuition of an idea of being and a seeing of being. What is ontologically first *(primum ontologicum)* is different from what is psychologically first *(primum psychologicum)*. He called his own position "ontologismo" and was criticized for practically teaching pantheism. But he tried to distinguish God in himself from God in us. The mature work *Della protologia* still maintains, however, that nature, providence, and revelation express variant views of the same reality.[14] Creation is simply the passage from being to concretely existing things.

The ethical theory offered in the treatise *Del buono* offers as a primary axiom "being creates existences," and insists that no thought or judgment is possible without this rule.[15] God is the prime cause of good, as He is of being. He not only puts forth existents by the first moment of creation, God also recalls these existents to being by a second phase of creation. Thus the notion of moral good as a return to God (which we saw as early as Plotinus) makes a new appearance in the history of ethics. Being creates the good through the mediation of human choice. In turn, choice produces virtue by submitting feelings to law, and virtue gives rise to beatitude by reconciling affections with law. Ethics is necessarily purposive and teleological, because the good is the ultimate end of human actions. Like Fichte and Hegel, Gioberti thinks that man achieves a special moral perfection in society. In his case, of course, Italy is the state that has a special religious and ethical role in the eventual redemption of the nations.[16]

This is another version of the ethics of the spirit. Gioberti is still read in Italy and the Spanish language areas, as witness the recent printing of his philosophy course. There is something pious but amorphous in this personalistic ethics. Much of it is rhetoric. However, it is seriously regarded by many people in the Latin tradition as a high-minded moral philosophy. It would appear to resemble an idealistic version of self-realization ethics.

France continued in the nineteenth and early twentieth centuries as the main center of the *philosophie de l'esprit.* Charles Renouvier (1815–1903) called his theory personalism and used Leibniz's theory of monads as a model for his doctrine of plural realities, each of which is living and personal. His *Moral Science* (1869) retains God as guarantor of good moral order but regards Him as a finite divinity, since evil is not always prevented by Providence. Ernest Renan (1823–1892) was a notorious critic of institutional religion but strongly supported the transcending importance of the spirit. "Everything appertaining to the soul is sacred," he claimed.[17] Renan was very critical of Auguste Comte (whom we shall consider in Chapter XIII) because positivism has no place for "morality, poetry, religion or mythology."[18] To free the spirits of men from obedience to law is the higher morality.

Not a philosopher of the spirit but a critic of the whole movement was the French thinker Hippolyte Taine (1828–1893). His works *On Intelligence* contrasted the literary explanations of psychic events in terms of spiritual "forces" with his own scientific analysis of the mind into its basic facts.[19] A novel by Paul Bourget *(The Disciple)* accused Taine of debasing the spirit of man. Yet Taine developed an important theory of aesthetics and was obviously under the impression that the human mind is capable of high-minded endeavors in the field of art.

In the case of Marie Jean Guyau (1854–1888) we have a nineteenth-century French ethics that is completely divorced from the Judaeo-Christian religious morality. His doctoral thesis was on *The Moral Teaching of Epicurus and Its Relations to Contemporary Teachings* (1886). Later he wrote a survey of British ethics, stressing utilitarianism. Two books present his personal thinking in the field of ethics (he also made noteworthy contributions to art theory): *Sketch of Morality Independent of Obligation or Sanction* (1885) and *The Non-Religion of the Future* (1887). His writings were translated into most modern languages and widely read.

The purpose of philosophy, as Guyau saw it, is to lead people to a better life. Scientific information should be used to find solutions to man's practical problems. He was particularly impressed with the possibilities of sociology but saw no reason to divorce it from metaphysics, as in the work of Auguste Comte. The older notions of moral "obligation" and "sanctions" seemed to Guyau to depend on outmoded religious teachings. In their place he offered an awareness of life and its potentialities for development.

Moral sensibility *(le sentiment moral)* is blended, as we see it, with the most intensive and extensive life that is possible, in the condition of awareness of its *practical fecundity.* The main form of this fecundity consists in action for others and sociability with other men.[20]

Life, so conceived, requires society for its full development. Morality is easier to treat in the social context, as a living part of a living whole. Life derives its "obligation" not from some mystical imperative but from the feeling of its own ability to act. Guyau's substitute for the famous Cartesian formula is: "I can, therefore I should" *(Je puis, donc je dois).*

In the *Sketch of Morality Independent of Obligation* we are presented with an "*anomie morale,*" which is a condition of human existence without any fixed or categorical commands. This does not mean that Guyau would leave mankind without moral guidance. He felt that the virtues of pity and charity live on after the disappearance of religious dogmas. There is a sort of moral enthusiasm that he would require for the propagation of ethical idealism, but without myths and without threats of punishment or promises of rewards.[21] He even agreed with the basic eclecticism of Cousin:

> We think, on the contrary, that from all the varied theories on the principles of morality we can now draw a certain common fund of ideas, and make of it an object of instruction and of popular dissemination.[22]

This point of view is typical of the ethics that was taught in France in the last half of the nineteenth century. It is likely that Guyau influenced the thinking of Nietzsche more than most historians realize.

One more feature in the background of the twentieth-century *philosophie de l'esprit* was added by Émile Boutroux (1845–1921). Since he always doubted the deterministic rigidity of the physical laws of nature, Boutroux came to think that there are many levels of reality, each distinguished from that immediately below it by a greater degree of freedom.[23] At the top is the most free being, which is God. On the level of human spirits, all men are bound together in a union of ideal love, described in the following quotation:

This teaching of an original community of souls, of a principle of life, one, infinite and perfect, in which we are able to come back together with our fellows, each of us recovering and attaining our most complete development, not at the expense of others but by virtue of their own fulfillment, of a principle which humanity calls God—this teaching seems to us the end and the climax of all the experiences and reflections of the mystics.[24]

Thus does Émile Boutroux set the stage for a return to a more religious meaning of "spirit" in contemporary French ethics.

Oddly, it was a thinker who started out as a biologist that restored French spiritistic ethics to the realm of theistic morality. Little in the early writings of Henri Bergson (1859–1941) pointed to the ethical position that he eventually took in his now famous *Two Sources of Morality and Religion* (1932). At first Bergson showed a great distrust of the work of conceptualizing reason and of the determinism of physical science. In good part he shared with many of his contemporaries an antipathy to the system-building of Hegel. In the vital force *(élan vital)*, which his early works pictured as progressively evolving into higher and higher levels of life and spirit, the basic characteristics were creativity and freedom. As he said in *Creative Evolution:* "God, thus defined, has nothing of the already made; He is unceasing life, action, liberty. Creation, thus conceived, is not a mystery: we experience it within us as soon as we act freely."[25] All of this is reminiscent of both Guyau and Boutroux.

After many years Bergson wrote the treatise that contains his mature ethics, the *Two Sources.* Its opening chapter treats moral obligation by contrasting two kinds of societies, the closed and the open ones. A society where almost every kind of activity is rigidly regulated by social and moral laws and by strict religious codes of conduct must be static or closed. For the majority of men, according to Bergson, "physical law, social or moral law, all law is in their eyes a commandment."[26] This legalism is a source of morality but Bergson leaves no doubt that it is second-rate, in his estimation. The man who lives well under such regulation is possessed of the closed soul *(l'âme close)* and he is not the human spirit at its best. On the other hand, there is a society which is dynamic, which gives full vent to the free development of the individual person. In a sense, this open society is humanity in its entirety.[27] It is the home of the open soul *(l'âme ouverte),* which is the spirit concerned with all mankind, whose love extends even to animals, plants, and all of nature.

To these two societies and types of men, Bergson applies their respective moralities. For the closed soul there is the ethics of law, strict codes of conduct, rigid moral obligation. For the open soul there is the ethics of freedom, of self-directed activity, of love rather than intelligence. It is not that obligation disappears in the life of the open soul: rather it is transformed. Of such obligation, Bergson writes:

> A constant vector force which is to the soul what weight is to the body assures the coherence of the group [in the open society] by

> inclining individual wills in the same direction. Such is moral obligation. We have shown that it may take on a new dimension in the society that is opened but obligation was made for a closed society.[28]

That there are two kinds of religion paralleling the two kinds of societies and souls, Bergson felt sure.

The third chapter of the *Two Sources* illustrates this theory of the two moralities by a discussion of certain human heroes. These are the people whom Bergson considers great souls, outstanding examples of the human spirit at its best. In turn, he reviews the characteristics of the Greek and Oriental mystics and the prophets of Israel. Though his own background was Jewish, he concludes that the finest examples of moral "heroes" are to be found among the Christian mystics. He names various saints-Paul, Teresa, Catherine of Sienna, Francis, and Joan of Arc.[29] Bergson is quite aware that his ethics culminates in mystical union with God. Indeed, he is convinced that this sort of experience is an experimental demonstration of the existence of God. As one of his most able pupils has written: "the doctrine is the last word of the school of thought initiated by Maine de Biran."[30]

Another clear example of a philosopher of the spirit who developed an ethical position not only independent of, but opposed to, institutionalized religion was Léon Brunschbicg (1869–1944). His is a thoroughly rationalized version of the *philosophie de l'esprit.* Brunschvicg was, during the late twenties and early thirties, the chief opponent of the "Christian philosophy" movement led by Jacques Maritain and Étienne Gilson (both pupils of Bergson). Descartes's theory of mind merges with Kant's critique of reason (pure and practical) to form the background for Brunschvicg's ethical thought. *On the Knowledge of Self* (1931) is not primarily a psychology but a study of the past of the person with the intent to discover rules of development and growth in the realm of spirit. His *philosophie de l'esprit* (1949) suggests that personal consciousness creates the values of truth and justice but not in an egocentric manner.[31] As men grow in rationality they find more ground for communion with each other; they are thus enabled to transcend selfish interests. This evolution of reasonable minds is the core theme of Brunschvicg's ethics.

Such moral thinking culminates in a religious teaching which is a sort of un-Christian Science. Brunschvicg's divinity is an impersonal but transcendent principle of value and goodness. As he explains it in *Reason and Religion* (1939), his God is not a being who reciprocates the love of men.

He is not that higher Power to whom a being turns who lives in duration yet prays to be removed from the laws of his duration. He is the eternal truth in whom a thinking soul gains the sense and intimate experience of the eternity of thought.[32]

Both Catholic and Protestant philosophers in France have objected to this theory of a rationalized God as the object of higher human love.[83] It has been said with complete accuracy that Brunschvicg's thought combines "almost all the purely rationalist elements in the thought of our century."[34]

Vladimir Jankélévitch (1903–) continues in the footsteps of Bergson but uses phenomenological technique to study the human spirit and its duties. He attempts to describe human consciousness in terms of fleeting moments of irony, boredom, remorse, and inner struggle. Two ways are available to explain the world and the spirit: the way of "quiddity" and that of "quoddity." The quidditive approach stresses *what* reality and events are, and expresses itself in terms of rational concepts, laws, and causes. The quodditive view adverts to the fact that events are radically contingent, irrational, and sometimes open only to feeling experience. To attempt to conceptualize such experience is banal. It is from the quodditive approach that Jankélévitch does his ethics.

Although the book entitled *Bad Conscience* (1933) already shows the character of his ethics, Jankélévitch's *Treatise on the Virtues* (1949) is generally regarded as his main contribution in this field. Certain virtues are more basic expressions of the quodditive impulse within the spirit: this is the contentless feeling that "one must do something." It is a sort of formal categorical imperative that cannot be justified by reasoning. Courage, love, and humility are high in the scale of moral values, because they are dispositions to act in accord with this initial impulsion. On the other hand, friendship, justice, and modesty are more sophisticated and rationalized virtues; they are quidditive and fall lower on the scale of values. It is not easy to see where the quidditive ends and the quodditive begins for Valdimir Jankélévitch. He is a man with religious commitments, a Christian personalist who takes us into the related school of existential ethics. We shall look at this type of ethics in Chapter XVIII.

Two Catholic philosophers of the spirit in twentieth-century France have shown that Thomism is not the only type of philosophy cultivated by adherents of this traditional religion. (Of course, Gabriel Marcel is still another example, but he will be treated with existentialist ethics.) René Le Senne (1882–1954) was a distinguished professor of moral philosophy at the Sorbonne. His contributions to metaphysics are at least as important as his work in ethics. We have made use, in this and earlier chapters, of his *Treatise on General Morality* (1942), which is a textbook with much material on the history of ethics. His other important books in the field of ethics are: *Duty* (1930) and *Obstacle and Value* (1934). Le Senne is an example of a first-rate French philosopher who is practically unknown to English readers.[35]

Like Bergson, Le Senne is opposed to "scientific" ethics. Science offers an account of what is and what cannot be; morality deals with what must be or cannot be. The moral is contingently subject to human decision. "Science is about the realized, morality about the realizable," is Le Senne's way of stating it.[36] He sees duty as something concrete and personal, as we may gather from this explanation:

> At the same time as it is the same for everybody, in the sense that no concrete duty can be a duty without applying the imperative universally, it is true, because of the inexhaustible fecundity of duty, that this duty, which imposes itself upon me, at such and such an instant, is a historical duty, that no other person is called upon to face, and which is incumbent upon me only by reason of what I am and what I want.[37]

The ethics of the *Traité de morale générale* is Bergsonian with overtones of Christian personalism and value theory. Le Senne makes a very thorough survey of various theories of moral conscience. After this, he asks whether, in the light of the history of ethics, one may still claim that metaphysics provides a basis from which morality may be deduced.[38] Le Senne is as much opposed to deductive rationalism as Bergson was. However, he is convinced that values do provide a ground for moral judgment and decision. Value is a deliverance of the human spirit. Le Senne describes it as whatever is worthy of being sought. The unity and infinity of value are manifested within our mental experience by a multitude of presentations of humanized values. Items like truth, good, beauty, and love are cardinal values. The Absolute Value is God. Moral value is but one among many kinds of value: it is the value of the "I" *(le moi)* insofar as it is will.

Moral value, then, may be defined as the ought-to-be-done *(le devoir-faire)*, where "done" means the doing of something. It is the value of action; and since action, in the sense in which it goes on according to a determination which serves as its end-directed or ideal rule, proceeds from the "I" that is made definite in the act of willing, moral value should be conceived as *the value of the will,* as truth is that of knowledge, beauty that of imagination, and love that of the heart.[39]

Part of what Le Senne means by "willing" is explained in the book entitled *Obstacle et valeur.* Man's spiritual energy is surging onward all the time; however, it sometimes meets obstacles or impediments which may be met with a special effort. Thus does will put forth volition and give rise to moral value.[40]

The other leading figure in the recent spiritistic school is Louis Lavelle (1883–1951). He was also a Catholic who worked through value theory toward a moral philosophy. Many of his insights are similar to what we have seen in Le Senne. Of Lavelle's extensive writings, we should mention *The Consciousness of Self* (1933), *The Error of Narcissus* (1939), *Four Saints* (1951), and *Conduct in Regard to Others* (1957). His basic moral theme is the notion of "participation." Some actions are creations but our potentially ethical actions are participations in a whole; they are "contained in the totality of things so that they are instrumental rather than creative."[41] To Lavelle, personal consciousness consists in freedom to initiate action. The same action displays both subjective and objective facets. Man does not create *things* but by his action he may make *beings* out of things. By participation the person consents to be; he thereby asserts the self on the level of value. This fulfillment of the person is the entry into the realm of morality and value.

Of philosophers who write in Spanish and Italian on ethical subjects many are in the school of Christian personalism. The "spirit" is the focal point of their attention, also. Some such thinkers are more in the tradition of Kant and the German idealists than of Descartes and Maine de Biran. Alejandro Korn (1860–1936), one of the greatest personalities in South American philosophy, was a practicing psychiatrist who also taught ethics at the University in Buenos Aires from 1906 to 1930. This is typical of many Latin American philosophers: they are not primarily engaged in teaching the subject but are lawyers, physicians, or politicians who teach and write philosophy as an avocation. Korn's books *Creative Liberty* (1922) and *Axiology* (1930) show the influence of both Nietzsche and Bergson. He was critical of any attempt to apply the findings or methods of physical science to the study of the spirit. Freedom is primarily experienced within spiritual consciousness and from this experience there stems an act of evaluation. Like Bergson, Korn taught that ethics must rely on intuition rather than reason. Will is very important in the constitution of the person. Culture and moral ideals are the product of the will, which is always seeking creative liberty *(libertad creadora)*. This is the peak of personality, for Korn. Personality is the ideal terminus of man's historical and cultural growth. Moral values (good-bad) are but one among many types of worth that are projected in man's spiritual consciousness.[42] As successor to Korn at Buenos Aires, Francisco Romero (1891–1962) has carried on the tradition of personalistic ethics in his *Philosophy of the Person* (1938).

In Mexico, the outstanding exponent of personalist ethics has been José Vasconcelos (1882–1959). He has written extensively on the social culture of Mexico and published the first edition of his *Ethics* in 1932. It was against the importation of philosophies from other countries into Mexico that Vasconcelos reacted. In particular he resented the "Anglo-Saxon" theory of evolution.[43] His own personalism, he argued, was not intentionally nationalistic but it led him to a heightened sense of patriotism. Art is one of the highest manifestations of the human spirit. For this reason, he argues that aesthetic rhythm is a key to the higher values of human life.[44] In place of the famous three stages of the cultural development of mankind enunciated by Auguste Comte (whom we shall treat in Chapter XIII), Vasconcelos proposed a broader triad. His first stage is the material or warlike condition; the second is the intellectual or political; and the third is the spiritual or aesthetic phase. As he sees the process: "These three stages represent a process which will gradually free us from the empire of necessity and will, little by little, submit the whole of life to the higher norms of feeling *(del sentimiento)* and of fantasy."[45] Vasconcelos fuses psychology, ethics, and an idealistic approach to politics into a view of life which avoids the materialism and mechanism of foreign philosophy. His basic themes are "individuality, freedom, purposive creativity, cosmic reality in process, personality and God."

In contemporary Spain, the outstanding representative of Christian personalism is Xavier Zubiri (1898–). He has studied at several European universities and wrote his doctoral dissertation at Madrid on the phenomenological theory of judgment. Both Husserl and Heidegger taught him. He also worked under Juan Zaraguëta, a Spanish priest who taught a modified version of Suarezianism. *Nature, History and God* (1953) is Zubiri's outstanding book.[46] A man of insights rather than a systematic philosopher, Zubiri appears to some scholars to be an existentialist. However, he would seem to be rather close on many points to the philosophers of the spirit. Thus, he is fond of saying, "Personality is the very being of man."[47] Philosophy, he thinks, has already run through its three stages. With Descartes it concentrated on the subject; in the speculative philosophy of Kant the ego was the center of attention; and now, following the lead of Kant's practical philosophy, the focal point is the person.[48] The volume of essays written by several Spanish writers, *Homenaje a Xavier Zubiri* (1953), testifies to the esteem in which this unusual philosopher is held by his compatriots. His most recent book, *Sobre la esencia* (1962), develops a metaphysics of the individual person which is not far removed from the views of Suárez.[49]

An Italian philosopher whose ethics is similar to that of the tradition in this chapter is Michele Federico Sciacca (1908–). Undoubtedly he is the leading representative of Christian personalism in Italy. Sciacca has lectured in many countries and his books are widely translated. As editor of the *Giornale di Metafisica* (Turin), he has had a great influence on other Catholic philosophers. His study, *The Moral Philosophy of Antonio Rosmini* (1955), indicates his debt to this earlier Christian ethician. He has also made an intensive investigation of the thought of St. Augustine, but Sciacca has little interest in Thomas Aquinas. His book in Portuguese on *Ethics and Morality* (1952) and the Italian work *Ethical Reason and Moral Intelligence* (1953) are representative publications in our field.

In an address delivered in 1963, Sciacca summed up his personalist ethics and showed how close he is to several of the thinkers that we have considered above. His words exemplify both the high-minded idealism and the unfortunate vagueness of this kind of ethics:

> The unconditioned character of the norm is not an obstacle to liberty but rather a "guarantee" of its more valid exercise. It is liberty itself that takes on its own order and the absolute end that is constitutive of the will, which can refuse to choose or, having chosen, reject its choice. The determination of ends falls in the moral order, not the physical . . . there is no liberty without law and no law without liberty. What is free in the normative order is the Idea. Morality consists in acting according to the essence of the ideal *(secondo l'idealità)* "without any necessity stemming from reality" (Rosmini), with a view to the actuation of its extent in all things. And to actuate the essence of existing is the absolute choice, coinciding with the initiative of Existence.[50]

There is a good deal of similarity between this spiritistic ethics and the ethics of existentialism, which we shall take up in our final chapter.

Chapter XIII

Societal Ethics in Europe

DURING THE PAST three centuries a good many people have thought that a basis for ethical judgment is to be found in human societies as they develop historically. Most of these people are convinced that there are stages in the evolution of groups of men and that there is some sort of meaningful pattern to the sequence of these various periods of history. Some think that mankind as a whole is an ongoing group that gives rise to moral values as it moves forward through time. Others feel that a certain class of people (say the nobility, or the proletariat) are the bearers of a special set of ideals that may give direction to the ethical considerations of all men, whether they belong to the favored class or not. Still others have the idea that a certain people or nation (their own, of course) has a sort of corporate "soul" that carries with it the seeds of all human perfections. Some have been quite sure that a certain "race" of men are born to lead mankind to higher and better things, because they have better bodies or purer blood. And finally, some men have thought that ethics must be grounded in history itself, in those special meanings that are to be found in a philosophy of history. This sort of theory of ethics should not be confused with any version of utilitarianism. Societal ethics does not attempt to explain moral good and evil in terms of the consequences of certain personal attitudes or actions to the social welfare. Rather, this kind of ethics springs from the conviction that *prior to* any given moral action or ethical finding there is in the human group a ground for the justification of "oughts." People who hold this societal ethics, in one of its many varieties, usually think that the common good of the group takes precedence over the private interest of individual members. Such an ethical attitude is important to understand, because extremists in this school of thought feel that they are ethically justified in sacrificing the individual person for the sake of the general welfare which they see so clearly.

Early in the eighteenth century a rhetoric teacher in Naples wrote the first version of a work that pioneered in this school of thought. The *New Science* of

Giambattista Vico (1668–1744) first appeared in 1725. His second and definitive edition was printed in 1744. What he tried to do was to find wisdom in the history of mankind. One of Vico's greatest admirers in the twentieth century, Benedetto Croce, has expressed the project in a way that helps us to understand it:

> For Vico, politics, force, the creative energy of States, becomes a phase of the human spirit and of the life of society, an eternal phase, the phase of certainty, which is followed eternally, through dialectic development, by the phase of truth, of reason fully explained, of justice and of morality, or ethics.[1]

The first book of the *New Science* attempts a chronological account of the early history of man and then proceeds to establish the axioms, principles, and method to be used in the interpretation of the historical evolution of humanity. The key to much of his theory is found in Axiom XII, where he explains that common sense *(senso commune)* is not the same for all men. Rather, every group of men, or nation, or people may have its own distinctive ideals and standards of right and wrong. However, there are some general notions about natural justice that are found in all peoples and these are the bases of the law of peoples *(diritto delle genti).* It is taught to all by divine Providence.[2] This natural law is concerned with the "human necessities or utilities of social life." Vico also shows a strong sense of the evolution of civilization *(evoluzione della civiltà).*[3] History itself has its own reality and its own laws of development. This theory is *historicism.* The temporal movement of the human spirit, in its collectivity, from finite to infinite, from the sensible to the idea, from passion to wisdom, is the object of Vico's philosophical interest.

Vico did not like Cartesianism but some of the things that he said about wisdom in Book II of the *New Science* are reminiscent of Descartes's ideas on practical wisdom. In general, wisdom is the power that commands the acquisition of all the arts and sciences constituting the humanities. The highest wisdom would be that of metaphysics but Vico is sure that men have not yet reached the metaphysical stage of development. At this point in history one must settle for the "poetic" wisdom of the great theological poets. Homer is central here; in effect, he has provided the ideals of beauty, goodness, and virtue on which Western civilization is still living. From the trunk of poetic wisdom there is one great branch that produces logic, ethics, politics, and economics (the societal disciplines); from the other side springs the branch of physics and the other studies of nature. As far as Vico is concerned, it is time for men to concentrate at least as much of their efforts on the study of the branch concerned with society, as on the branch of nature. When we look at Croce's ethics (later in this chapter), it will become evident how important this emphasis on the reality of history and society can be.

France, in the same period, provides us with some good examples of both opposition to, and espousal of, societal ethics. A Benedictine monk, Dom Léger-Marie Deschamps (1716–1774), gave one of the most peculiar presentations of this kind of thought. His views are found in two works written in the 1770s: *The Voice of Reason* (1770) and *The True System, the Metaphysical and Moral Enigma* (published in 1939). Briefly, he thought that our present ethical standards are simply the product of human society; but, in order to get back to the true principles of morality, we will have to abolish society.[4] Deschamps was, then, a social anarchist. He was not precisely a societal ethician, for he did not think that society has provided us with an adequate morality. We are now in the stage of positive laws *(état des lois);* we look forward to that future state when laws will be replaced by morality *(état des moeurs).* This he saw as a dialectical process with the development of a true ethics as the final stage. In the period in which he was writing men had no moral consciences, no natural sense of right and wrong, of what is just or unjust. All the conceptions of human behavior were, to Deschamps, mere aspects of positive legality, of the law of the state.[5] An associate of thinkers like Rousseau and Diderot, Deschamps must have seemed somewhat extreme even to them.[6]

This is the place to mention the position of the Marquis de Sade (1740–1814). He was not a theoretical ethician but a man who wrote a number of books in which he expressed his violent rejection of the moral code imposed by the society of his day, particularly in the area of sexual behavior. If we recall that Rousseau's theory of the origin of moral distinctions in the general will was really a type of societal ethics, we can see that it was this sort of assumption that the Marquis de Sade professed to oppose. He makes this evident in the *Histoire de Juliette,* where he complained:

> Almost always, moreover, the laws of government are our compass for distinguishing just and unjust. We say, the law forbids such an action, therefore it is unjust. Nothing is more deceptive than this way of judging, for the law is directed towards the general interest; now nothing is in greater contradiction with the general interest than individual interest, and at the same time, nothing is more just than individual interest. Therefore, nothing is less just than law, which sacrifices all individual interests in the general interest.[7]

A contemporary of the Marquis de Sade, with equally impeccable family background, was the Marquis de Condorcet (1743–1794). The book which is of interest here is his *Sketch of a Historical Table on the Progress of the Human Mind* (1794). In the Introduction to this work, he tells us that metaphysics studies the development of the faculties of the human mind (this is from Condillac) and that his historical philosophy "studies this development as it manifests itself in the inhabitants of a certain area at a certain period of time." Obviously, Condorcet is not far removed from the historicism of Vico. He is studying the history of the evolution of various societies through time, with a view to the discovery of the general laws of such progress and the steps which mankind may take toward happiness. As a mathematician, Condorcet divides the history of civilization into ten neat stages. The ninth period runs from Descartes to the foundation of the French Republic and it has shown how the rights of man may all be deduced from the axiom "that man is a sentient being, capable of reasoning and of acquiring moral ideas."[8] Convinced that all errors in politics and morals are due to mistakes in philosophy and science, Condorcet looked forward to an ultimate period in history. The tenth stage of mankind will take place in that indefinite future of society in which all men will rise to the level of civilization that is characteristic of the French and Anglo-Americans! In it the moral code will be free of selfishness and superstition.[9]

Another member of the French nobility, Count Claude Henri de Saint-Simon (1760–1825), insisted that ethics is the science which aims at producing the greatest good for the greatest number of men. Of the continental thinkers in this period he most closely approaches the social altruism of British utilitarianism. There is but one kind of progress that is common to the whole of humanity: this is the development of the sciences.[10] The purpose of the New Christianity is to promote the social welfare of the human race. The science of ethics is far more important for the social community than all the physical and mathematical disciplines. In his *Dialogue between a Conservative and a Reformer,* Saint-Simon equated this ethics with the teachings of Christ:

> It is more than eighteen centuries since its fundamental principle has been produced, and since then none of the researches of the men of the greatest genius has been able to discover a principle superior in universality or precision to that formulated by the Founder of Christianity.[11]

The morality of "enlightened self-interest" is always negative and limited in character; true morality must be social in scope. A perfect ethics will make more use of feeling and love than of reason.

Another French social reformer who believed that all that is required for the improvement of human morality is the development of societal organizations in which life may be lived most fully was François Marie Charles Fourier (1772–1837). His ethical views are found in a large treatise entitled *The New World of Industry and Society* (1829–1830). He planned and helped to establish small social groups (about eighteen hundred persons) in which men would live simply and idealistically on a communal basis. Only one of these "phalansteries" was founded in France but many were started in the United States of America. A pupil and ardent follower named Victor Considérant (1808–1893) set up one such community in Texas (near Dallas). Another such establishment was the famous Brook Farm, in Massachusetts.[12] Albert Brisbane, Charles A. Dana, Nathaniel Hawthorne, Father Thomas Hecker, and Orestes Brownson were Americans who came under the influence of Fourier's societal ethics during the nineteenth century.

The man who erected this societal ethics into a religion was Auguste Comte (1798–1857). His early thought was expressed in the six volumes of his *Course of Positive Philosophy* (1830–1842). This was soon published in a condensed form, by Harriet Martineau, in English (1853). In 1848, Comte published his *Discourse on the General View of Positvism,* which was followed by the *Catechism of Positive Religion* (about 1852). These works of the later period (after 1848) show a thinker who has moved away from his original faith in "science" to a faith in a new religion of Humanity, of which Comte is the founder.[13]

That Comte was the father of sociology is well known. He adopted and developed the view that we have seen in the opening pages of this chapter: the way to understand man and the laws governing human behavior lies in the study of the development of society. As he says at the start of the *Cours de philosophic positive,* "No conception can be understood otherwise than through its history."[14] Like Condorcet and the other French societalists, Comte thought that there is a dialectical pattern of the evolution of civilization and culture. Knowledge starts with *theology* (where explanations are fictitious), moves through a *metaphysical* period (in which abstract concepts are used), and reaches its ultimate growth in the *scientific* stage (where the positive method is employed). This is the famous law of three stages.

A famous classification of the "sciences" in the order of their logical development is next developed by Comte: mathematics (the "source of positivity"), astronomy, physics, chemistry, physiology, and social physics.[15] Sociology becomes the peak science in the original course of positive philosophy. The second volume of this *Course* divides the work of sociology into two parts, corresponding to the "anatomical" study of the order of society (statical sociology), and the study of the progress of society (social dynamics). Morality is best understood, according to the writings of this early period, by considering how the notions of human duties have changed in passing from the indirect and contradictory sentiments of the theological period, through the stress on self-interest in the metaphysical period, to the altruism of the positive period. This is explained as follows:

> Human faculties, affective as well as intellectual, can be developed only by habitual exer-

> cise; and positive morality, which teaches the habitual practice of goodness without any other certain recompense than internal satisfaction, must be much more favorable to the growth of the benevolent affections than any doctrine which attaches devotedness itself to personal considerations.[16]

With the *General View of Positivism,* in 1848, Comte begins to give a special status to ethics. At this point he is moving away from Fourier's idea that the answer to all human problems lies in scientific knowledge toward the late Comtian view that makes a religion out of the cult of Humanity. Now the talk is about a new moral power that is rising in France which will lead to the complete reorganization of society. Its guiding idea is the service of Humanity.[17] Within a few years, Comte will have quite definitely differentiated between sociology and ethics, as the following lines suggest: "Sociology studies the structure and the evolution of the collective beings formed by man. Ethics, on the contrary, studies individual man as developed for and by the collective beings: Family, Fatherland, Humanity."[18]

Humanity is now deified and its cult and liturgy are formed into a complex religious institution, with Auguste Comte as high priest. Social feeling is proposed as the first principle of the new religion of humanitarian ethics. This Comtian ethics has "love for principle, order for basis, and progress for end."[19]

No theoretical or systematic exposition of the positive ethics can be given, for that would be to reduce it to a metaphysical abstraction.

Still another version of societal ethics has greater contemporary significance. In Europe as of mid-twentieth century an astute observer of the history of philosophy could identify three major schools: the Communist, the Catholic, and the existentialist.[20] This may occasion some surprise to people not directly acquainted with contemporary philosophy on the Continent. Few in the English-speaking countries of the world would select Communism as a major type of philosophy. Yet it is that for many people today: and that fact is our justification for including a brief survey of the ethical thinking of Marx and his followers in this history. We shall see that Marxist ethics is but a variant of the societal movement which is now under examination.

Karl Marx (1818–1883) was twenty years younger than Comte and read many of the same historical-minded and socially-oriented writers as the founder of positivism. Marx knew more about the German idealists, and one of his first important writings was a study of the Hegelian *Philosophy of Rights* (1843). From the beginning Marx was suspicious of the idealist metaphysics and the abstract system-building of Hegel. Yet he was impressed by the concept of a dialectical pattern in the development of human history. Such a dialectic is found not only in Hegel but in many other

German idealists; it is also characteristic of nearly all the societal ethicians treated in this chapter. The names and notions of the stages may vary somewhat but the triadic pattern remains throughout. Marx's noted writings *(The Communist Manifesto,* 1848; and *Capital,* 1867–1894) have a very simple message. Up to his time, social philosophers concentrated on ethics or politics to the neglect of economics. As Marx saw things in the middle of the nineteenth century, Europe had had its Reformation, and Enlightenment, and even the start of its industrial revolution, but the ordinary man was worse off than ever. Only a radical change in the economic condition of that vast class of workers who make up the "proletariat" could result in real progress for mankind. The development of a truly human ethics, according to Marx, must await the coming of that future condition of mankind in which it will be possible to live well.

It will be recalled that Hegel taught that all development and progress take place in the ideal order and follow the dialectical pattern of thesis, antithesis, and synthesis. When young Marx was a university student at Bonn, Berlin, and Jena, this notion of dialectical evolution in all things was very much in the air and Marx accepted it in part. He did not agree with Hegel that all reality is ideal but he did have a high regard for the triadic dialectic as a principle of change. Marx felt, however, that Hegel's claim that the dialectical movement is always from a lower and more simple *thesis* to a higher and more complicated *synthesis* was simply wrong. Hegel had put the dialectic "on its head," and Marx undertook to turn it "right side up again" by making it move from the complexity of a prior synthesis to the simplicity of an eventual thesis.[21] The most important application of this reversal of the Hegelian dialectic, for Marx, was in the economic order. Here he saw the bourgeois system of private ownership, which had reached its peak in the industrial revolution, as an over-organized and objectionable synthesis. It would have to break down and be negated in an inevitable moment of revolution—which is the antithesis. Then would come the new thesis in human life, the simpler condition which is Communism.

The ultimate reality in which Marx sees this dialectic taking place is man. Left-wing Hegelians in early nineteenth-century Germany had tried to turn the idealism of Hegel into a materialism. Ludwig Feuerbach (1804–1872) represented a less radical view within this school, for he maintained that what is real is the concrete man. This influenced Marx, although he could not agree to the supposition that man's environment is exclusively physical and that man is subject to complete determination by the forces of material nature. There is always in Marx's picture of man a certain emphasis on the importance of *society,* as the milieu in which human progress may be made and there is even a stress on the ability of mankind to achieve certain ends that are not dictated by the rigid laws of physical nature.

While Marx's view of man has been called "materialistic," it should be remembered that this label was originally applied by historians with idealistic prejudices, to whom any nonidealistic position concerning human nature would be a materialism.[22]

One of the most important notions in Marx's teaching, from the point of view of ethics, is that of "alienation." He is convinced that the proletariat, that vast class of productive workers being exploited by a smaller class of rich owners, is the class of people on whom the ultimate salvation of mankind depends. Now, in the present industrial and economic system the worker becomes more and more separated from the product of his labor: it has a distinct existence, it is not controlled by the worker, it is alienated from him. Moreover, the worker is even separated from his activity as a human being; his own work becomes a means whereby other men dominate and exploit him.[23] What is necessary for the good life, according to Marx, is that this economic system be overthrown so that the proletariat may become the only class (the "classless" society) and its members may be enabled to live full and perfect human lives.

The ethics of Karl Marx is not, and cannot be, a theoretical system of morality. Rather, Marxian ethics would be that future condition of concrete moral practices which would characterize the real life of the worker under Communism. Such Marxist ethics grows inevitably out of the dialectical progress of man in society. For Marx, as one astute biographer stated it, "the only sense in which it is possible to show that something is good or bad, right or wrong, is by demonstrating that it accords or disaccords with the historical process, assists it or thwarts it, will survive or inevitably perish."[24] This ethics is a "Naturalism"—both in the sense of describing the moral good in terms of a life of economic well-being, and also in the negative sense of being opposed to all supernatural notions of divine obligation or eternal rewards and punishments. Moreover, Marx's ethics is normative. At the same time that Marx would call the present standards of morality merely relative and without absolute imperatives, he would also claim that the (as yet undeveloped) morality of the classless society of the future will impose absolute standards of moral judgment and behavior.[25]

Friedrich Engels (1820–1895) was a businessman with socialist interests who helped Marx to write several of his key works. In the book called *Anti-Dühring* (1878), Engels added one important thing to the preceding sketch of Marxist ethics. This was the notion that no morality can have absolute validity. All the ethical systems of the past have been produced by the economic stage of the societies in which they appear.[26] The three classes of modern society (feudal aristocracy, bourgeoisie, and proletariat) have their own special and purely limited morality. Even proletarian ethics is not eternal. There are eternal truths in mathematics and physics but not in the sociohistorical area. A truly human morality must await the coming of the classless society. It will contain the "maximum of durable elements," Engels felt, but even the morality of the proletariat will not be eternal.[27]

Among the older followers of Karl Marx the man who made the greatest effort to write a formal ethics was Karl Kautsky (1854–1938). His *Ethics and the Materialist Conception of History* (1927) compared Marxist ethics with other types and stressed the claim that all morality grows out of societal impulses.[28] There is some argument as to whether the term "dialectical materialism" is typical of Marx's original position. In Kautsky, who regarded himself as a very orthodox Marxist, the theory of Communism and its ethics come very definitely under the head of dialectical materialism. He is violently opposed to "revisionists," those who would modify the original thinking of Marx by combining it with some other type of philosophy. Kautsky sees the growth of society in purely economic terms and regards ethics as the set of human ideals emerging from the laws of the process of production. It is on these techniques that the entire future of mankind depends.[29]

Most of Marx's teachings were taken over and adapted to the conditions of Russian life and society by Vladimir Ilyich Lenin (1870–1924). With Lenin, Marxism became not only an organized economic crusade but also a political program. The Communist party now became a factor in world history and politics. On many points with some bearing on ethics, Lenin takes a more definite and harder line than Marx. Religion must be rooted out of socialist society and atheism must be adopted.[30] Lenin stressed the claim that Marxist thinking in all areas is solidly founded on positive science. The crude materialism of people like Ernst Mach is but a perversion of the true meaning of physical science.[31] Beyond giving support to the general Marxist claim that the proletarian class produces its own moral values, neither Lenin nor Joseph Stalin (1879–1953) contributed anything more to the theory of ethics. Before 1950 there is little use of the term "ethics" in Soviet academic literature. Morality is discussed under the ideology of dialectical materialism.[32] In the period between 1950 and 1965, a few articles, mostly historical in character, have dealt with moral philosophy in the U.S.S.R.

A prominent exponent of Marxist thought in contemporary Germany is Ernst Bloch (1885–). He objects to the emphasis on economic and historical determinism of human life, as he finds it in Russian Marxism, and stresses the "principle of hope" as a freer and more human factor in the personal effort to live a good life. Bloch is, of course, regarded as a revisionist by Soviet Marxists.[33] Another non-Russian Marxist who is considered very influential is Georg Lukacs (1885–), a Hungarian who writes in German. As far as ethics is concerned, Lukacs has brought out the importance of the concept of alienation. It is undoubtedly true that certain types and conditions of work tend to dehumanize the people engaged in them. He has, however, vigorously criticized the idealist-existentialist version of Marxist ethics recently proposed by Leszek Kolakowski (1927–) of Warsaw. Lukacs rejects any charge that he himself is a revisionist.[34]

The recent literature of Marxism in Soviet Russia shows some growing interest in morality as a special field of study. The fundamental attitudes are very similar to what we have seen in Marx: a good morality grows out of a rightly ordered society; all ethical systems are relativistic; all classes have their own moralities but the proletariat has the only progressive type; the value of a given moral or ethical position is determined by its political and social results; the Communist party as the spearhead of proletarian ideals is the ultimate norm of moral judgment.[35]

Quite opposed to Marxism is another school of Russian thought, which takes its origins in the Orthodox Christianity of the Eastern Church. There is also a strong societal thrust in this kind of ethics. To be a Russian and a non-Latin Christian is to participate in the "soul" of Mother Russia. The ethical position of such a school is not systematized; it is much opposed to the "legalism" of Roman Catholicism; and it is emphatic in promoting values such as spirituality, freedom, and the development of the person. Much attention is paid to moral evil as an almost inevitable feature of all human life. The Russian novelists of the nineteenth century are primary examples of this point of view. However, there are philosophical and theological writers who have made this into a rather definite kind of ethics. Vladimir Soloviev (1853–1900) is one of the most influential of these. *The Justification of the Good* (1897) presents an ethics based on the spirit of the universal Church, the unity of Christendom, and the fundamental unity of mankind. As Soloviev sees it: "The moral significance of life in the last resort consists in the struggle with evil and in the triumph of good over evil."[36] Vladimir Soloviev is generally considered to be the source of most of the ethical views characteristic of the later school of Russian Christian ethics.

During his long residence in France, Leon Shestov or Chestov (1866–1938) was a most influential representative of this kind of ethics. His studies of the relation between the thinking of writers like Tolstoy and Dostoyevsky and contemporary existentialism are widely respected in Europe but little known elsewhere. Shestov knew Kierkegaard and the German idealists very well. Critical of the whole program of Christian philosophy, he avoided putting his moral insights into systematic form. In fact, he taught that human life is absurd and irrational—long before Camus and the French existentialists picked up this view. Impressed by the omnipotence of God, Shestov tended to think that nothing can limit the divine power, not even apparent contradictions and the facts of history.[37]

If Shestov is little known, except in France, Nikolai Berdyaev (1874–1948) was another Russian philosopher in exile who popularized the tenets of this school. Many of Berdyaev's books (originally in Russian, German, or French) have been put into English and they are well known. The work which best presents his ethical views is *The Destiny of Man* (1935), which insists that "abstract *a priori* systems of morality have little value."[38] Throughout this book Berdyaev insists that it is what happens to man after death that gives meaning and value to his life. This eschatological emphasis involves the important notion of the finality of man. His view is not that of ancient or medieval eudaimonism, however; Berdyaev does not agree with Thomas Aquinas that a morally good life is the way to achieve everlasting happiness. Instead, Berdyaev argues that the more highly developed persons may suffer the most.[39] Actually, he does not think that the focal point of ethics is the norm of the good. Evil is just as important as good, ethically. The moral philosopher is concerned with the continual struggle during the course of time between good and evil. Much of Berdyaev's later ethical writing stressed the supreme value of personal freedom. He is often classified as a personalist. Creativity is the key to moral freedom.[40]

However, Berdyaev was also a societal and historical thinker from the beginning of his career as a writer. One of his first publications *(Subyektivizm i individualizm v obshchestvennoi filsofi,* St. Petersburg,

1901) stressed the objective and social character of ethics, in the following passage:

> Morality, of course, cannot be class morality, any more than truth can be class truth, but historically it takes on a class form and is borne by the social class which is carrying the banner of universal human progress. Later we will try to show that historically the *avant garde* of society always works to elevate the value of man and leads him toward consciousness of absolute justice.[41]

Though opposed to Communist proletarian ethics, Berdyaev remained convinced that ethics cannot be derived from speculative philosophy. It is the product of social values and the spiritual progress of man through history toward eternity. For Berdyaev, spiritual progress is a religious concept; his whole teaching in ethics is Christological.[42] Although he was not a cleric, his ethics came closer to being a moral theology than that of the other Christian ethicians from Russia.

Distinctively French societal ethics took a new start with the work of Émile Durkheim (1858–1917). In 1897 he founded one of the pioneer journals in sociology *(L'Année Sociologique)* and helped to develop the methodology of the social sciences. Durkheim held that "every social group naturally produces, as a sort of secretion, collective representations, beliefs, and rules of behavior. . . ."[43] Each society has its own collective *conscience,* from which arise a religion, a morality, a political point of view, and so on. Sociology studies these cultural emergents. Ethics is not a part of theoretical or systematic philosophy; it is a useful moral code that should be taught to enable young people to adapt harmoniously to the *mores* of their group.

Long associated with Durkheim and a contributor to his journal was Lucien Lévy-Bruhl (1857–1939). His early book, *The Notion of Responsibility* (1885), is an essay in Kantian ethics. It is in *Ethics and Moral Science* (1903) that Lévy-Bruhl launches the *science des moeurs.* All questions of morality are now reduced to social facts: the "science of morals or customs" deals with what *is* and not with what *ought to be.* This sociological approach can go through various stages, as he describes them:

In a primary form . . . the morality of a society is purely and simply a function of the other series of social phenomena. It may be called spontaneous. The second stage is that in which reflection begins to be applied to moral reality to validate it in the eyes of reason. This is the society of systems of morality which are attached to the rich complexity of moral life as to a single principle. Finally, today we see the beginning of a third period, in which social reality will be objectively studied.[44]

Thus, a purely theoretical ethics is, for Lévy-Bruhl, impossible. What one must do is to study what is transmitted from the collective consciousness *(la con-*

science) of a given society. In relation to this group, the product of philosophical and scientific reflection on the standards of behavior approved therein is a relatively valid ethics.[45] In a sense, Edward Westermarck (1862–1939) simply extended this view in *The Origin and Development of the Moral Ideas* (1906) and *Ethical Relativity* (1932).

In the empirically based method of Frédéric Rauh (1861–1909) we find still another version of French societal ethics. He was interested in the methodology of both psychology and ethics. His book on *Moral Experience* (1903) uses the device of the impartial observer ("l'honnête homme") to provide a certain objectivity for ethical judgment. Moral opinion must be tested by contact with the milieu in which the agent lives. The ultimate criterion of moral certitude is the social conscience, according to Rauh: "Morality appears at the point when collective aspirations are narrowed down and refracted in the conscience of an individual person, in a conscience which by living these aspirations personally remakes and recreates them."[46] Rauh, then, attempts a combination of the societal origin of moral views with a more personal elaboration of these views within the spirit of the moralist. In this teaching, he was more disposed to effect a compromise between the factual morality of the sociologists and the rationalized ethics of the metaphysicians.

Equally important is the recent growth of societal ethics in Italy. Italian ethics in the twentieth century is very largely identified with the practical philosophies of Croce and Gentile, but unfortunately their thought is not well known to English readers. Both fall within the category of ethicians who take a historical and societal approach to their subject. Vico's ideas are still important but Hegel and his dialectic are even more influential. Both Croce and Gentile lived through that unfortunate period in Italy's history when Benito Mussolini attempted to restorethe glories of ancient Rome. Croce was more opposed to Fascism than was Gentile but both contributed to a certain exaltation of the civil society, without which the philosophy of the fascist state would have been lacking in academic support. In any event Croce and Gentile are prime examples of men who identified the source of moral values with the history and social culture of the Italian people.

It was through reading the *Scienza Nuova* of Vico that Benedetto Croce (1866–1952) became interested in philosophy. Croce's basic contribution to philosophy lies in the fields of aesthetics and the philosophy of history. Always antagonistic to metaphysics, Croce made this attitude very clear in his famous address to the Sixth International Congress of Philosophy (1926). In it he denounced the concept of metaphysics as the study of a reality above and beyond experience, and as the notion of a systematic or final philosophy.[47] Croce there defined philosophy as "the abstract moment of historiography." The work of the philosopher he saw set forth in Hegel's *Philosophy of History:* to understand the laws and development of reality one must go back in history and relive the process whereby the Idea has moved dialectically in any given era. This is historicism: the meaning and value of human life can only be discovered from a philosophic study of the passage of the spirit of mankind through time.

In 1909 Croce published his *Philosophy of the Practical,* and it is the chief statement of his ethical position. In the order of *praxis* what is important is willing *(volizione).* Willing the particular belongs to economics; willing the universal pertains to ethics. The act of willing is not distinct from the practical action, since intention is realized in action only. Action is free every time there is a real volition. Some actions are amoral, being merely economic or political.[48] What characterizes the moral action, and the good action, for Croce, is its liberty. In the early works, freedom is identified with the good.[49] The laterwritings even more definitely make "liberalism" more than a merely political factor: thus, freedom becomes the form of what is ethical.[50] Right in the general sense *(diritto)* is not basically ethical and law *(legge)* is simply a willing of certain classes of actions, an abstract and unreal volition.[51]

Students of the practical philosophy of Croce point out his opposition to racism, imperialism, and dictatorship. He was, indeed, a stout critic of the aberrations of Italian Fascism. Yet there was in Croce's ethical thinking a certain exaltation of the state which is hard to reconcile with his support of personal freedom. Chapter thirty-six of the work translated as *The Conduct of Life (Frammenti di Etica,* 1922) deals with "The State as an Ethical Institution." In it he is opposed to the idea that "the State knows no law except its own power."[52] Yet he insists that the state requires its own virtues, that these are different from the ideals of Christianity, and he points to Machiavelli as a man who saw this truth. This is the way that Croce expresses his view: "The State is an ethical institution," and it is "the true Church," for it has "souls and not only bodies in its keeping."[53] It is not difficult to turn such a view to the support of totalitarianism.

An idealism of the human spirit which was much more personal and individualistic than Croce's historical idealism was meanwhile developed by Giovanni Gentile (1875–1944). Much influenced by both Kant and Hegel in his general theory of reality, Gentile shows in his treatise *The Theory of the Mind as Pure Act* (1912) that he identified the real with the ego (*Io*) in process of becoming. Both the particular and the universal meet and are combined, for Gentile, in the concrete spirit that is the individual ego.[54] This is the *actual idealism* of Gentile. *Act* does not designate an event but the existence or development of something in thought.

One might expect that Gentile's ethics would be a simple theory of the self-perfecting of the individual mind but this is not the case. He was very much impressed by Hegel's reification, and deification, of the state (as was

Croce). In a posthumously published work on the *Genesis and Structure of Society,* Gentile describes a dialectic that shows the connection between his political and ethical position. His thesis in this dialectic is the immediate individuality of particular being, which involves a natural spontaneity. The antithesis is the force of universal being of law. This conflict is resolved, according to Gentile, in the process of the real formation of the ego *(processo dell'autocoscienza)*. As he expands on this dialectical theme, Gentile makes it clear that this development of the individual mind or spirit only reaches its completion in the "bosom of society." There is no ethics of the individual as such. "The State completes the morality of the individual."[55] Whether he was "the philosopher of Fascism" or not (and there is still much debate on this question), Gentile was an ethician who thought that the good of the individual person is a function of, and is subordinate to, the higher good of the state or political society. This, of course, is the conclusion of nearly all societal ethics.

Societal ethics has held little attraction for English writers on ethics. Nearly every British philosopher is, of course, a social utilitarian at heart and convinced of the practical superiority of the moral ideals of society in England. The point is that usually he does not erect this prejudice into a substitute for ethical theory. So the mystique of the ethical State is not found in English ethics. A philosopher like R. G. – (1889–1943) stressed the role of history as a starting point for both metaphysics and ethics, of course, and he stoutly criticized the tendency of most British philosophers, and ethical intuitionists in particular, to ignore the historical dimension of their work. Plato is read as if he lived but yesterday. Ethics should be understood, according to Collingwood, in relation to the historical development of men and societies. Thus, Collingwood's *Autobiography* (1939) is a brief but eloquent defense of historicism in philosophy. Similarly, Morris Ginsberg (1889–) is a British sociologist who has written extensively on the relation between his subject and morality of law. His *Essays in Sociology and Social Philosophy* (1957–1960) show how a reflective application of sociological methods to the history of philosophy may produce new results. Ginsberg argues, for instance, that the observable diversity of cultural and moral views in different places and times is not a basis for concluding to ethical relativity.[56] That variations in moral opinion, when carefully examined, show an underlying pattern, is Ginsberg's basic contention. He argues as follows: (1) There is universal agreement that conduct has to be guided by reference to principle. (2) Variations of moral opinion are far from arbitrary; there are discernible levels of insight and experience corresponding to diEerent valuations. (3) There is an observable growth of moral insight which is associated with an increase in the experience of human needs and social cooperation. These conclusions challenge the long-accepted inference by Edward Westermarck from cultural to ethical relativity. Ginsberg has not, however, made much impression on British writers on ethics.

Our final example of societal ethics in Europe is found in a group of writers who have claimed that all moral and cultural ideals are carried in the blood of a given race of men, and that certain races are superior and others inferior in this as in other respects. The writers whom we shall consider, very briefly, have suggested that the Aryan race is the bearer of the highest seeds of human culture. Their teachings were made the basis of the philosophy of German national socialism under Adolf Hitler but they are by no means exclusively German in origin. Racism is an attitude with ethical implications and it is found in many parts of the world.

A Frenchman, Count Arthur de Gobineau (1816–1882), wrote a long treatise on the *Inequality of Human Races,* in the middle of the nineteenth century. In it he claimed that there was much scientific evidence to support the finding that the white race is in all ways superior to the black and yellow races. In energetic intelligence, courage, perseverance, physical power, and love of liberty, white people are outstanding, according to Gobineau.[57] He stressed the observations of some forgotten German physiologist who studied the capacity of different people to strike a blow with their fist. The best at this sort of thing were the English and the worst were the Negro and Australasian peoples. From "scientific" evidence of this kind, Gobineau concluded that the white race is by bodily and mental endowment naturally intended to lead and control the others. "I have been able to distinguish on physiological grounds alone, three great and clearly marked types, the black, the yellow, and the white." The negroid race "stands at the foot of the ladder."[58] He also assumed that the offspring of interracial breeding are inferior to the original stock of both races. (It should be unnecessary to point out, here, the flimsy factual and pseudoscientific foundation of this whole argument.)

Meanwhile, in Germany, Paul Anton de Lagarde (1827–1891; his father's name was Bötticher) picked up these notions and combined them with a violent dislike of Jews. Originally a Scripture scholar, Lagarde thought that St. Paul was responsible for corrupting the Christian Church by the introduction of Old Testament teachings into the New Testament. He published a set of essays entitled *German Writings* (1878–1881) that was very popular in Germany in the early 1930's. As the theoretical father of Nazi anti-Semitism, Lagarde stressed the nobility and moral value of the "spirit" that is found in all people of pure German blood.[59]

Another German writer with better academic credentials but similar racist attitudes was the sociologist Ludwig Gumplowicz (1838–1909). His family was actually Jewish, from Poland. This man was an advocate of what is called "conflict sociology"—the theory that primitive races originally hated each other and fought for supremacy. Civilization was supposed to have emerged out of this struggle. Gumplowicz's most influential work was called *The Race-Struggle* (1883) and it, ironically, was reissued in Germany during the period of Hitler's rise to power. The implication of his teaching was that the superior race is the one that wins all the battles.

England made its contribution to this school of writing through Houston Stewart Chamberlain (1855–1927). Educated in Germany, he married Eva Wagner, the daughter of the composer, and settled at Bayreuth. Chamberlain idealized German culture and institutions. His *Foundations of the Nineteenth Century* was first published in German, in 1899, and it preached the doctrine of the purity of the German blood. Unlike Gobineau (whom he much admired), Chamberlain felt that the Jews were a threat not because of inferiority but because of their aggressive ability. Afraid that they were taking over Europe, Chamberlain concluded:

> Were this to go on in this way for a few centuries, there would not be a single racially pure nation in Europe, other than the Jews. All others would be a herd of pseudo-hebraic half-breeds; without the slightest doubt they would be a physically, spiritually and morally degenerated people.[60]

We should note how Chamberlain included morality as a special inheritance within a race. This provided a ground for a version of societal ethics, in which the "society" is any group of people related by blood.

Leaders of the national socialist movement adopted what they found useful from the foregoing pseudotheories. One man was given the job of official philosopher for the Nazi party and he was told to publicize the doctrine of the cultural supremacy of the Aryan race. This writer was Alfred Rosenberg (1893–1946), whose *Myth of the Twentieth Century* (1930) sold hundreds of thousands of copies.He fabricated a new national religion based on the Teutonic myths in combination with the racial views that we have examined. Exalting the communal soul of the German people, Rosenberg insisted that "nobility is blood" *(das Edelste ist das Blut).*[61] The German is a *Kulturträger,* the natural bearer of cultural and moral values, and it is his duty to lead other nations to higher levels of culture.

This peculiar variant of societal ethics was taught for a few years in some German schools. It never gained wide academic recognition but it is a reminder that racist ethics is one tangent which societal morality may take. In ending this chapter with this unfortunate school of morality, we have no intention of suggesting that the inevitable climax of societal thinking is illustrated by the experience of national socialism; yet there is something of a totalitarian quality in most versions of societal morality.

Part Five

Contemporary Ethics

Chapter XIV

Axiological Ethics

AXIOLOGY IS THE study of values. Wilbur M. Urban thought that he was the first to use the adjective "axiological," but it had been used earlier in Europe.[1] Perhaps the most helpful general meaning of "value" is the famous definition by R. B. Perry: "Value is any object of any interest."[2] To be interested, in this usage, means to be for or against something. In the past century value theories have run the gamut from very realistic and objective views (which maintain that values are extraconscious realities in themselves or in things) to quite subjective theories (which equate values with affective or cognitive states or acts of consciousness). Recent philosophers speak of many kinds of value, in different fields of experience: aesthetic, economic, religious, logical, and moral values. In fact, value language is used, at least occasionally, by most contemporary philosophers and the usage is so broad that the meaning has grown very thin.

What we propose to examine in this chapter is not, then, the whole field of value ethics. John Dewey would have to be treated under such a heading, for his *Theory of Valuation* (1939) is quite important. Nor will we discuss R. B. Perry in the present chapter. They will be found with other ethical naturalists in Chapter XVI. Here, axiological ethics designates the theories of a group of German-Austrian philosophers and other related thinkers who have come under their influence. These people tend to offer an idealistic and objectivist teaching on values. In the moral order, they often claim to have some sort of rather direct experience of a realm of ethical values that serve as norms or standards for practical judgment. There is some direct relation between this ideal value school of axiology and phenomenology. We will devote Chapter XVIII to phenomenological ethics, however.

The kind of axiological ethics that we are now to consider is closely related to two other approaches to the subject. Ideal value theorists are nearly always intuitionists. What they claim to "see" is not some concrete quality of good or bad in an action or attitude (as do the British intuitionists) but something like an essence of the good. Second, these axiological ethicians make use of the notion of self-realization: they tend to think (as do many other schools of ethics) that morally good activity fulfills or perfects the person in some distinctive way.

An Austrian priest, trained in Aristotelian and Scholastic philosophy, who left the Catholic Church after the First Vatican Council, initiated this movement. He was Franz Clemens Brentano (1838–1917), who taught philosophy and psychology at Vienna and had many distinguished pupils, including Sigmund Freud. His *Psychology from the Empirical Standpoint* (1874) and *On the Origin of Ethical Knowledge* (1884) provide the seeds from which Austrian axiological ethics developed. Brentano's theory of psychic activity stresses intentionality *(Intentionalität)*: this is the characteristic of all acts of knowing, feeling, or willing whereby they are directed toward objects. Such objects may consist in contents of consciousness, or, in other cases, they may stand for extramental realities. Brentano's explanation simply says:

> Every act of knowledge is characterized by what the Scholastics call the intentional (or mental) existence of an object; we call it the relation to an object, the direction toward an object; we could also call it immanent objectivity.[3]

The object *(Gegenstand)* for Brentano is not necessarily identical with an extramental reality. Rather, his object may owe its existence (and he argues that every object does exist, for consciousness) to some activity of the mind. Thus, while some objects may stand for physical realities (such as the Eiffel Tower), others may be imaginative items (such as a golden island), and still others may be meanings (such as the square root of three) that cannot be pictured. If ethical judgments are to be meaningful, they must refer to objective contents of psychic activity.[4]

One of Brentano's outstanding pupils, Alexius Meinong (1853–1920), organized the theory of objects *(Gegenstandstheorie)* into a definite type of philosophy and formally related it to value theory and ethics. In an essay on the *Theory of Objects,* Meinong suggested that, when we feel joy or pity, or other emotions, the objects are not "joy" or "pity" but some items to which these feelings are directed. He used the term "directedness" *(Gerichtetsein)* for this characteristic which Brentano had called intentionality.[5]

For Meinong, many objects do not exist in reality *(wirklich)* yet they subsist *(bestehen).* Such objects are neither merely subjective mental states or acts, nor are they actual existents in the world of realities. Hence, philosophy needs a third realm of being in which objects are given. A special and new part of philosophy is now to be devoted to the study of objects. "What can be known about an Object in virtue of its nature, hence *a priori,* belongs to the theory of Objects."[6] That some such objects are moral values, types of objective worth or oughtness, is brought out by Meinong in a study of *Emotional Presentation* (1917). Just as there is an objective content to what is presented in sense perception, so there are objects-with-properties that are given in emotional experience. These included items such as goals, desideratives, and dignitatives.[7] These are subsistent ethical values that are not just personal appearances *(phenomena)* but are valid over and above subjective experience *(metaphe-nomena)*. Whether this is to be called a realistic theory of values (Chisholm) or an idealistic theory (Hill) depends not so much on the theory as on how we use the terms "ideal" and "real." Another philosopher who came under Brentano's influence in Vienna during the early 1880s, was Edmund Husserl (1859–1938), who developed his "phenomenology" but stressing the realistic side of the theory of objects. Husserl influenced many of the phenomenological ethicians treated in our last chapter but had little to say about ethics for himself.

Still another follower of Brentano, Christian von Ehrenfels (1859–1932), took a more psychological approach to the study of values. His *System of Value Theory* (1897–1918) offers in its first volume a general account of the genesis of values and, in the second volume, an explanation of how ethics may be based on value theory. He understood value as an objective property arising from a person's act of desiring. Where Meinong regarded value as "given" in affective experience, Ehrenfels thought of value as projected from the subject's psychic inclination.

One of the greatest figures in the school of axiological ethics was Max Scheler (1874–1928). One of his earliest ethical works, after his dissertation *On Logical and Ethical Principles* (1899), was the study entitled *Ressentiment* (1912). He borrowed this word from the French to name the continued feeling of emotional reaction (or hostility) against a person or thing. This establishes Sender's interest in the domain of emotional experiences as a source of moral notions. His chief contribution to ethics is the book on *Formalism in Ethics and the Non-Formal Value Ethics* (1913–1916; printed in *Werke,* II, 1954). Of the later writings, *The Nature of Sympathy* (1921) is important. Much imprinted material left at the time of his death has since been edited.

Scheler was not an Austrian (he was born in Munich) but came under the influence of the phenomenology of values through Edmund Husserl. Of course, Scheler was also indebted to Augustine, Nietzsche, Bergson, and Eucken. Fundamental in his thought is the notion of the *Mitwelt* (literally, with-world), a realm of experience shared with other persons (I-Thou relation). Four such interpersonal feelings are described by Scheler: (1) community of feeling *(Miteinanderfühlen),* (2) fellow-feeling *(Mitfühlen),* (3) psychic contagion *(psychische Ansteckung),* and (4) emotional identification *(Einfühlung).* All are aspects of the basic feeling of sympathy.[8] The capacity to enter into such relations with others is part of what it means to be a person.

Such an interpersonal relation is viewed as a sort of entity: being-with-another subsists in the "ontic" realm of being, though it does not exist in the world of physical nature. This theory of real relations gives rise to Scheler's theory of "community" which is important in both his metaphysics and his ethics.[9] Ordinary feelings of bodily pain or hunger, and so on, are not thus shared; these are entirely within the individual. Primary physiological feeling *(Gefühl)* is nonintentional but the higher feeling-awareness of a feeling *(Fühlen)* is the value experience.[10] Since the higher, psychic feelings can be shared with others—emotions like joy and sorrow, remorse, despair, and happiness—it is on this level that ethical values are intuited. As interpersonal experiences, these feelings provide a certain objectivity, universality, and absolute character to their value-objects. Love is the most perfect feeling of community and it has a special status in moral experience. It is most important for ethics.[11]

Ethics studies the a priori content of what is given in such interpersonal feeling experience. Scheler's ethics is "material" (or nonformal) in the Kantian sense of having to do with the *content* ot moral lite. He thinks that Kant was generally right in his formal ethics but overlooked the whole area of objective moral values. Thus, there is no material a priori for Kant but there is for Scheler, who grants that there are many diverse "moralities" among different peoples, and at different times in history. The further question that Scheler asks is whether there is an underlying structure and unity in these various moralities which may be discovered in ethics. Ethics is a philosophical study of morality: the terms ethics and morality are not identical for Scheler.

One of the chief discoveries that Scheler makes as an ethician is a scale of nonformal values. Working from the lowest values to the highest, he finds four levels. His principle of ranking uses the following features: (1) duration (a lasting value is better than a fleeting one); (2) extension (the quality of a value that may be shared by many persons without disintegrating); (3) independence (the higher value is never the foundation for the lower value); (4) depth of satisfaction (the more profound the value experience the higher the value).[12] With these standards he proposes the following scale of values. First, there are sensible values *(sinnliche Werte),* which include objects of pleasure and pain, and various sorts of utility. Second, there are life values *(Lebenswerte)*: the noble and the mean, strength and weakness, good quality and bad quality. Third, there are cultural values *(geistige Werte)*, such as the beautiful and ugly, the legal and illegal, the knowledge of what is true. Final and highest are religious values *(Werte des Heiligen und Unheiligen):* beatitude and despair, feelings of holiness and the opposite.[13] This is a hierarchy of values which has had a great influence on recent European ethics.

For Scheler, oughtness *(Sollen)* is of two kinds (1) ought-to-be, and (2) ought-to-do. The second rests in the first and together they establish the ground of ethical duty. Moral values do not correspond to the four levels of general value that have just been described. Instead, moral value arises when a person acts in such a way as to realize, or prefer, a thing-value *(Sachwerte)* of a higher level to a similar value on a lower level. All moral values are thus personal *(Personwerte)*. Good as a value "rides on the back" of an act, as Scheler puts it.[14] In the long run, moral obligation consists in a special response in the person to the values that have been described.[15]

Much the same approach to value ethics is found in the work of Nicolai Hartmann (1882–1950). His three-volume *Ethics* (1926) is a more thoroughly organized version of Scheler's axiology. The first volume treats of moral phenomena; the second deals with moral values; and the third is devoted to moral freedom. His thought is better known to English readers than that of Scheler, because this large work of Hartmann's has been available for many years in translation. Born in Latvia of German parents, Hartmann did his university studies at Marburg. He came to know Aristotle quite well and was probably influenced by the Stagirite to take a slightly more realistic position on values than did Scheler. His historical study *Die Philosophie des deutschen Idealismns* (2 vols., 1923–1929) shows his extensive knowledge of earlier German idealism, particularly the thought of Hegel. Many people consider Nicolai Hartmann the greatest European ethician of the twentieth century.[16]

In Hartmann's view, values are essences in the ontic realm, essences somewhat like Plato's ideal forms. The world of subsisting values can be intuited through cognitive and affective acts of consciousness.[17] Value-objects are neither subjective phases of consciousness nor physically existing entities. They constitute a third realm of ideal reality.[18] Different persons are more or less open to the experience of values. All men perform some acts of approval, preference, and affective feeling of items which reveal an objective content of value. In this initial openness to value, feeling is most important.[19]

In the second volume of the *Ethics,* Hartmann makes a long investigation of the problem of ranking values and finding a value scale. Here he is indebted to Scheler but also critical of his simplicity. One must note that difference between the initial feeling of value and a secondary moment of ideal intuition of the value as object. Unlike Scheler, Hartmann thinks that the higher values are based on the lower ones; they depend, in some sense, on the inferior values.[20] Hartmann is very much aware of the history of philosophy, from Plato and Aristotle onward, and seems at times to get his gamut of lower to higher values from the great tradition of the ancient philosophers. On the other hand, he insists that higher values are not "stronger" but are generally "weaker" than the lower ones. What he means is that it is usually more serious to "sin" against a lower value than against a higher one. Yet to fulfill a higher value is better than to realize a lower one.[21] This means that Hartmann's table of values is not a unidimensional scale but a more complicated arrangement of objective standards of worth. The following value table attempts a summary of his teaching on this matter.

(I) Elementary values: modal oppositions of necessity and freedom, being and non-being, relational opposites of harmony and conflict, simplicity and complexity, qualitative and quantitative oppositions of universality and singularity, humanity and nation.

(II) Values conditioning contents within the subject: life, consciousness, activity, suffering, strength, freedom of will, foresight, purposive activ-ity;values in goods: existence, situation, power, happiness.

(III) Moral values:

- (A) fundamental moral values: the good, the noble, richness of experience (common to many types of behavior);
- (B) special moral values:
  - 1) values of the ancient moral system: justice, wisdom, courage, self-control, and other Aristotelian virtues;
  - 2) Christian values: brotherly love, truthfulness, trustworthiness and

fidelity, modesty, humility and aloofness, being true to one's own being, humor;

3) modern moral values (influenced by Nietzsche's transvaluation of values): love of the remote (humanity), radiant virtue, ethical ideals, personality, and personal love.[22]

It will be clear to the reader that an adequate account of this remarkable theory would require more space than can be given it here.

The study of the moral "ought" is much more fully developed in Hartmann than in Scheler. Both distinguish, of course, the "ought-to-be" from the "ought-to-do"—which latter brings us into the area of moral obligation and responsibility. All initial values have a teleological tendency toward being realized: "The *ought-to-be* is in its nature an *ought-to-be-real.*" Only some values are of moral significance and have an exigency for action: to them the *ought-to-do* corresponds. Since values are in themselves independent of moral consciousness, they confer or point to absolute obligations for the ethical person. Accountability and responsibility for one's free personal acts are the key features of the moral life.[23]

In his discussion of freedom, Hartmann is very critical of previous philosophic treatments of the subject. He is particularly opposed to indeterminism, for he feels that free acts are caused, both physically and psychically. Freedom is positive and entails the entry of new causal factors into an ongoing causal series. There is a freedom of the *ought-to-be* toward further realization—and there is a different freedom of action in the order of the *ought-to-do.* The nature of moral responsibility and obligation is restated in terms of personal freedom.[24] In brief, the fact that conflicts among values are quite possible leaves an opening for the person to intrude into the interobjective tension and play the role of a determiner of the manner in which "oughts" are fulfilled. Hartmann's ethics is, of course, a self-realization theory. What makes it distinctive is his claim that one can intuit a whole range of ideal possibilities that may, and in some cases should, be realized. The validity of the whole construction depends on his initial assumption that such a realm of objective values is reached in human experience.

Although there were British idealist ethicians at the end of the nineteenth and beginning of the twentieth century, and most of them used the language of value philosophy, the school of ethics under consideration in this chapter is not part of the English tradition. In the well-known anthology *Contemporary British Philosophy* (1925) neither Scheler nor Hartmann is mentioned. Hartmann's *Ethik* was published a year later, of course, but several of his studies in epistemology and ontology had appeared earlier.

The closest approach to an axiological ethics in England was made by William Ritchie Sorley (1855–1935).

Moral Life and Moral Worth (1911) and the Gifford Lectures, *Moral Values and the Idea of God* (1918), are Sorley's most significant books. Nearly all of Sorley's philosophy is ethically oriented. In his metaphysical thinking, he distrusted both materialism and naturalism. Persons, he viewed as the "bearers of value" but not the constructors of standards of worth. Hence, moral laws and values are just as objective as the "laws of nature."[25] However, Sorley repudiated any suggestion that such values are experienced and discovered philosophically through acts of feeling. If this means an irrational approach (he quotes, "The heart has its reasons which the reason knows not," from Pascal), then such a method leads to the bankruptcy of philosophy. Sorley is an *intellectual* idealist, not an emotional one, and this is where he differs radically from the Austro-German school of axiologists.

Objectivity of values means to Sorley that these standards are there, whether we know them and are guided by them or not. The point is that "they ought to be our guides."[26] These moral values are part of the total system of reality and they are simply revealed through the person. A second characteristic of moral values, for Sorley, is their purposiveness. They indicate a need of the human person for fulfillment. This is one of the rare instances of the recognition of finality or teleology in recent British ethics. The other context in which it appears is in some versions of evolutionary ethics.

In the United States, until comparatively recently, German-Austrian axiology has had few devotees. Howard O. Eaton's study, *The Austrian Philosophy of Values* (1930), introduced the thinking of Brentano, Ehrenfels, and Meinong to American readers but did not treat the work of Scheler or Hartmann. Almost the sole representative of axiological ethics on the American scene was Wilbur M. Urban (1873–1952). His major publications in this field are *Valuation. Its Nature and Laws* (1909) and *The Intelligible World—Metaphysics and Value* (1929). The textbook *Fundamentals of Ethics* (1930, reissued 1949) is also important. *Beyond Realism and Idealism* (1949) states his mature thought on values and reality. Urban studied in Germany from 1895 to 1897, hence his knowledge of continental value theory goes back to the first members of the school, Brentano and Meinong, and even more to pioneers in German axiology, such as Wilhelm Windelband (1848–1915) and Heinrich Rickert (1863–1936).

Urban's early thinking on values and their relation to moral obligation stressed a psychological study of all the discoverable kinds of value. *Valuation* (1909) sought to discover through cognitive and affective acts of consciousness the whole gamut of values and the underlying principles in this field. He then described the act of valuation as the feeling aspect of a conative process.[27] The object of the act of valuing is not the product of this act: the value is already there as an object. The realm of values is midway between being and nonbeing.

A more definitely ethical orientation is required in Urban's textbook. There value is very simply defined as "that which satisfies human desire," even though, in *The Intelligible World* he had suggested that value is indefinable.[28] Now, value becomes the "basal concept" of Urban's ethics. Since ethics tries to find a standard or norm of human conduct, it is a normative science. However, such a norm is simply a description of "the morally good or humanly valuable."[29] Moral responsibility is implied in the acceptance of moral freedom. Duty is grounded in the axiom that "the good ought to be chosen rather than the bad, the greater rather than the lesser good."[30]

In his last major work Urban returned to the whole problem of the ontological status of values. As the title, *Beyond Realism and Idealism,* implied, these are not ultimate philosophical classifications. A completely worked-out metaphysics will have to give first place to the realm of values, as Urban sees it:

> From our present standpoint the entire issue, it seems to me, is one of priority or primacy. This primacy belongs to value for the reason, as I have long maintained, that there is a synthetic relation between them, such that there is a judgment of an "ought-to-be" implicit in all acknowledgment of value . . . the "ought-

> to-do" of moral agents being secondary and derived from this acknowledgment.[31]

In his mature thought, then, Urban held that ethics depends on metaphysics and that it is a specialized section of the general philosophy of value. There are some affinities between this position and that of Ralph Barton Perry, but we shall consider Perry as a representative of naturalism (Chapter XVI). *Humanity and Duty* (1951) offers a very explicit version of self-realization ethics, as developed in Urban's last period. The moral good is the fulfillment of an "ought-to-be" that consists in a drive toward realization.[32]

Continental Europe, in the period between the two world wars, saw many changes in philosophical thinking. Austrian axiological ethics came full circle with the work of Moritz Schlick (1882–1936), for his *Problems of Ethics* (1930) rejected the whole notion that values are objective and that they constitute independent norms for ethical judgment. Ethics was treated by Schlick from the viewpoint of the scientific positivism of the Vienna Circle and he had no sympathy with the idealism, or phenomenological realism, of the Brentano to Hartmann school. Schlick firmly rejected the assumption that the purpose of ethics is to formulate a conception of the good.[33] For him, ethics is reduced to a psychological study of the various observable motives for human conduct. Nor is it a normative science, in the ordinary meaning of the term "normative," as Schlick bluntly explains:

For if ethics furnishes a justification it does so only in the sense just explained, namely, in a relative-hypothetical way, not absolutely. It "justifies" a certain judgment only to the extent that it shows that the judgment corresponds to a certain norm; that this norm itself is "right," or justified, it can neither show nor, by itself, determine.[34]

In his fifth chapter, Schlick gives a very accurate summary of the theory of absolute moral values. So conceived, value would have to be something wholly independent of man's feelings, identified with certain objects that are quite distinct from the ways in which we react emotionally to them. This absolutistic ethics would have as its moral imperative: "Act so that the events or things produced by your actions are as valuable as possible." In response to this, Schlick simply asks why he should obey this rule. His criticism of the theory of objective values uses the standard positivistic approach to verifiability. Value judgments are clearly not tautologies. If they are to be empirically verified, one may ask: Under what empirical conditions is the proposition, "this object is valuable," true? To say that moral values are any objects of pleasure is nonsense. One cannot find an objective fact in sense perception that would indicate objective value. It is necessary to conclude, according to Schlick, that values are not objective but are merely subjective feelings of pleasure.

Hartmann's claim that values are objective in the same sense that a mathematical proposition (2 plus 2 equals 4) is, being valid for all who think it, is not for Schlick a proper analogy. The hypothesis of absolute value is empty. What happens if I don't choose to realize a value? If values were in independent objective existence, "they would constitute an independent realm which would enter the world of our volition and action at no point."[35] Instead, Schlick suggests that moral values (and ethical judgments) are purely relative. Both pleasure and sorrow may be morally valuable feelings: "They owe their value to the joy they promise, which is the only measure of their value." Responsibility is simply the feeling that one is subject to punishment or reward for a given act.[36] It is generally agreed that Schlick's ethics amounts to ethical skepticism and that it is "axiological" only in the sense that this ethics continually uses the language of value.

If his positivism induced Moritz Schlick to create a far from idealistic type of value ethics, much the same diversity in theory now becomes apparent among his contemporaries. One group of philosophers in the United States represents a value theory of ethics that is not dependent on the Austrian school yet falls within the category of axiological ethics. C. I. Lewis (1883–1964), for instance, located value experience in the area of affective feelings. For Lewis, however, a value is not an object but a special and not easily described quality of the conscious experience of valuing. His book *An*

Analysis of Knowledge and Valuation (1946) is usually classified as a naturalistic study and it does resemble John Dewey's efforts to make "valuation" more primary than value. Some commentators even reduce his position to hedonism,[37] but his distinction between *intrinsic* value (valuable for its own sake) and *extrinsic* value (valuable for the sake of something else) is very much like the Thomistic distinction between the *bonum honestum* and *utile.* In fact, Lewis puts extrinsic value under the heading of utility.[38]

An outstanding American personalist who used value language in his approach to ethics, Edgar Sheffield Brightman (1884–1953) stoutly defended the normative character of ethics and maintained that the purpose of ethics is to enunciate a coherent system of moral laws. Eleven basic laws of ethics are grounded in the value of the person.[39] As a theist, Brightman regarded God as a necessary factor in any moral theory but he also insisted that moral law is more fundamental than religion.[40]

In his *Human Values: An Interpretation of Ethics Based on a Study of Values* (1931), DeWitt H. Parker (1885–1949) developed a teaching which depends on Perry's definition of value as "any object of any interest." Parker is more idealistic, or even subjectivistic, than Perry, since he places less stress on value as an object and more on the character of the "interest" involved. Ought-as-a-feeling has no meaning for Parker, unless it is related to some desire.[41] The highest good is a condition of harmony in which all desires are satisfied. Parker's ethics, in fact, fluctuates between the notion that the harmonious satisfaction of the individual is all-important and the view that universal satisfaction is the supreme goal.[42]

Among more recent teachers in the United States, William H. Werkmeister (1901–) has done a great deal to make the point of view of axiological ethics known in America. Born in Germany, Werkmeister finished his philosophical studies in the United States and has taught here for many years. His exposition of the ethics of Scheler and Hartmann has formed the starting point for most of the recent studies by American scholars in this field. Werkmeister's own view may be gathered from the tenth chapter of his *Theories of Ethics* (1961). One of the central problems of ethics, as he sees it, is to work out the relation between the axiological and the moral *ought,* for they are not identical.[43] Werkmeister finds a second pivotal problem in the many cases where one's obligations are in obvious conflict.

A surprising number of Catholic ethicians, with more or less background in Thomism, have gone into the field of axiological ethics. For example, Rudolf Allers (1883–1963) studied medicine in Vienna, psychology and philosophy at Milan, and then taught philosophy for many years at Catholic University and Georgetown University. One of Allers' most influential books was his study of the development of the ethical personality, entitled *The Psychology of Character* (1929) in the English version. Allers' work lies on the periphery of ethics but he taught and influenced many younger scholars who are doing promising work in the subject. It was in a paper entitled "Reflections on Cooperation and Communication" (1960) that Allers first supported the notion of a realm of "insistent being" which would seem to parallel the ontic realm of Hartmann. Participation in this ontological region (in which "meanings" and presumably values insist) enables human persons to communicate with each other.[44] In another paper, "Ethics and Anthropology," Allers suggested that the social sciences may make important factual contributions to ethics without forcing it into the camp of ethical relativism.

A German priest who started his scholarly career as a student of the thought of St. Augustine later became an ardent exponent of the personalistic ethics of Max Scheler. This is Johannes Hessen (1899–). Both his study of *Max Scheler* (1948) and his *Ethics: Foundations for a Personalist Ethics* (1954) remain untranslated but Hessen is regarded in Europe as an important figure in post-World War II German ethics. Similarly, Fritz von Rintelen (1898–) is another example of a Catholic ethician who has carried on the axiological approach to ethics in recent German scholarship.

Of course, Dietrich von Hildebrand (1889–), who taught for many years at Fordham University, is well known for his many books in the field of Christian ethics. Much of his thought is quite like the axiological personalism of Max Scheler. *Fundamental Moral Attitudes* (1950), *Christian Ethics* (1953), and *True Morality and Its Counterfeits* (1955) have made his views generally known in the United States. A symposium, *The Human Person and the World of Values* (1960), was issued as a tribute to von Hildebrand on his seventieth birthday. Its title was well chosen: his interests are personalistic and axiological. For him, love is the distinctive feature of the human person.[45] Some critics feel that von Hildebrand's general emphasis on Christian belief as a ground for ethics makes his thought a version of Catholic theology, rather than a moral philosophy.

A native of the United States, Leo R. Ward (1893–) of Notre Dame has made numerous contributions to the study of values and ethics. His *Philosophy of Value* (1930) is a pioneer Thomistic work in the field. Ward's recent *Ethics* (1965) makes use of much material from value theory and the social sciences to develop a modified version of Thomistic ethics. He has put more emphasis on special problems in ethics than the theoretical foundations of the subject. Leo Ward offers an excellent example of what might be called an "open" Thomistic ethics, developed under the influence of DeWitt H. Parker and R. B. Perry.

Much of the recent interest in axiological ethics in France is found in the work of the *philosophie de l'esprit* school, whose contributions we have noted already

(Chapter XII). Louis Lavelle and René Le Senne are primary examples of such a spiritual value approach to ethics. The outstanding recent authority on axiology in France is undoubtedly Raymond Polin (1910–), whose survey article on the "Philosophy of Values in France" (1950) is the best guide to French activity in axiology. Although Polin rejects the objectivity of values, his theory is existential: value is something given in concrete human experience. It has nothing to do, however, with "norms" in the sense of standards imposed on persons by the authorities. Norms are not as good as values. With this kind of axiology we have moved very far afield from the original school of Brentano.

In a sense value ethics has been too successful. Practically all ethicians now talk about values and mean many different things when they use the term. As a result, the notion of value has become so diluted that it is almost a transcendental term in contemporary ethics. Value enabled people to discuss the possibility of a rather ill-defined realm of moral standards without too clearly committing themselves on their status in being. And so, except for its usefulness as a general term, value is no longer a major item in strictly contemporary ethics.

Chapter XV

Self-Realization and Utilitarian Ethics

MANY ENGLISH-SPEAKING MORAL philosophers during the past century have felt that ethical judgment must include some appraisal of the consequences of moral activity. Theoretically this view is directly opposed to Kantian formalism: the teaching that a good motive prior to external action, or a pure will, is the only indicator of a morally good act or person. The broadest meaning of utilitarianism would include any kind of ethics that stresses the *results* of moral attitudes, volitions, and activities. If these results are chiefly viewed in relation to the total fulfillment of the powers and personality of the moral agent, then we have a self-realization version of consequence ethics. On the other hand, if the consequences mainly include the welfare and advantage of other persons, of the society in which the agent acts, we have social utilitarianism. We shall see that the contrast between formalism and utilitarianism has grown much less acute in recent Anglo-American ethics. Philosophers are beginning to think that a "good will" is hardly possible without some concern for the predictable results of moral decisions, and that factual consequences are of ethical importance to the extent that they do or can qualify the motivation and prior dispositions of the moral agent. Even more striking is the manner in which some recent versions of utilitarian ethics have turned to the idea of generalization as a method of determining the moral value of consequences.

Some of the most influential voices in British ethics at the end of the nineteenth century were idealists. Many of these thinkers combined Kantianism, or some later kind of German ethics, with a general acceptance of Christian morality. James Martineau (1805–1900) is a good example of a holder of this general position. His *Types of Ethical Theory* (2 vols., 1886–1891) classified the various schools as: Unpsychological Theories (Plato, Descartes, Malebranche, Spinoza—all basing their ethics on some prior metaphysics); Unpsychological Theories based on physical science (Auguste Comte): Idiopsychological Theories, which focus ethical attention on a man's own inner conscience (Bentham, Paley, and Martineau himself); Hetero-Psychological Theories, which are hedonistic and may be evolutionary types of ethics (Hobbes, Mill, Bain, Darwin, and Spencer); and Dianoetic Ethics, which employs some system of intellectual ideas or a moral sense (Cudworth, Clarke, Price, Shaftesbury, and Hutcheson). In point of fact, Martineau agreed with Kant that a person's inner awareness of his duty is the sole criterion of morality. His position is quite in keeping with that of his contemporaries, Bradley and Green, whom he classifies as ethical intuitionists, in the following text:

> Mr. F. H. Bradley tells us: "Morality has not to do immediately with the outer results of the Will:" "acts, so far as they spring from the good will, are good:" "what issues from a good character must likewise be morally good." And with equal distinctness, Professor Green insists that "it is not by the outward form that we know what moral action is. We know it, so to speak, on the inner side. We know what it is in relation to us, the agents; what it is as our expression. Only thus indeed do we know it at all."[1]

Instead of Kant's very formal imperative, Martineau takes as the basic axiom of his ethics: "Every action is RIGHT, which in presence of a lower principle, follows a higher: every action is WRONG, which in presence of a higher principle, follows a lower."[2] To illustrate, he gives the example of a son who decides to pay his father's large debt. Motivated by a "sense of justice," his act is morally good; if he had been motivated by a love of wealth and had decided otherwise, he would have been moved by the lower motive and his act would be bad. To provide criteria for the judgment of motivation, Martineau developed a table of "Springs of Action" that ranked thirteen different levels of motives, from low-grade passions of vindictiveness and suspicion to high-grade feelings of compassion and reverence.[3] His principle of ranking is obviously British social opinion in the nineteenth century.

British self-realization ethics reached its peak development in the writings of Thomas Hill Green (1836–1882). His general philosophical view was Kantian, although he never accepted Kant's teaching on the thing-in-itself. Green thought that there is an eternal consciousness in which the individual person shares. The awareness of moral duty is one aspect of this participation in the consciousness, which he sometimes calls divine. Essentially, then, Green's ethics is a working out of what is required for the development or realization within each self of the potentialities of this universal consciousness. This is how he expresses his position, in the *Prolegomena to Ethics:*

It is clearly of the very essence of the doctrine above advanced that the divine principle, which we suppose to be realising itself in man, should be supposed to realise itself in persons, as such. But for reflection on our personality, on our consciousness of ourselves as objects to ourselves, we could never dream of there being such a self-realising principle at all, whether as implied in the world or in ourselves.[4]

Earlier in the same work, Green had asked whether the working out of the destiny of eternal consciousness might simply be accomplished through some impersonal Humanity; in the passage just quoted, he made it clear that its realization is personal and individual. However, there is a social dimension to Green's ethics, because he insisted that many of the higher capacities of man depend on his status within his social group. The "common good" thus becomes a pivotal concept in Green's moral philosophy.[5]

Green's pupil Francis Herbert Bradley (1846–1924) was a quick realizer of his potentialities: he published his famous *Ethical Studies* in 1876, seven years before Green printed his *Prolegomena.* Bradley soon showed that he was a great metaphysician. His *Appearance and Reality* (1893) provided a theoretical background for his ethics. The opposition between good and evil is not absolute; it is overcome in the totality of the Absolute. Self-realization is the movement of the person from the condition of discrete and pluralized pleasures (hedonism) to a higher integration of the self in an infinite whole.

The best presentation of Bradley's ethics is in the famous Essay II, entitled "Why Should I Be Moral?"[6]

Here, he is inclined to minimize the notion of "moral consciousness" and to stress the effort to make one's personal will merge with the infinite whole. Two sentences in the essay make this clear:

> "Realize yourself as an infinite whole" means "Realize yourself as the self-conscious member of an infinite whole, by realizing that whole in yourself." When that whole is truly infinite, and when your personal will is wholly made one with it, then you also have reached the extreme of homogeneity and specification in one, and have attained a perfect self-realization.[7]

Another of Bradley's essays, "Duty for Duty's Sake," takes up the Kantian theme of the good will. This is not a departure from self-realization, as Bradley understands it, since a pure act of will is, to him, a fulfillment of the reality of the person. In this process, I become an end unto myself. In an effort to say more definitely what good will means, Bradley lists four special characteristics. First, the good will is *universal;* it is not the volition of particular men but a common standard above you and me. Second, it is *free* will: it is not conditioned or determined by anything other than itself. Third, it is *autonomous:* in willing what is valid for itself, it legislates for all. Fourth, it is *formal:* the good will acts not for the sake of some given content but for itself as without content or matter.[8] Nothing indicates better than the foregoing how basically Kantian is the self-realization ethics of Bradley.

Much the same sort of ethics is found in the many writings of Bernard Bosanquet (1848–1923). Two of his most influential works in this field are *The Principle of Individuality and Value* (1912) and *The Value and Destiny of the Individual* (1913). A series of fourteen articles by Bosanquet in the *International Journal of Ethics* made his teaching well known to American readers.[9] The "individual" is a very positive concept with Bosanquet, and its characteristics are integrity, completeness, and wholeness. Hence, the Absolute is an individual. Moreover, Bosanquet felt that the ethical theory of F. H. Bradley deserved to be better known. It interpreted Kantian ethics in a way that Kant "would have disowned" but, in Bosanquet's mind, Bradley's ethics really satisfies the theoretical demand which the *Critique of Practical Reason* had left unfulfilled.[10] This enthusiasm for Bradley's ethics was fully shared by J. H. Muirhead (1855–1940), who devoted much of his time to the job of making it better known.

The thinking of Hasting Rashdall (1858–1924) also falls within the scope of British self-realization ethics but with different emphases from the foregoing thinkers. Rashdall's *Theory of Good and Evil* (1907) is actually an example of ideal utilitarianism. Moral good is intuited through the faculty of reason. As a strong theist, Rashdall insists that God is needed in any theory of morality. His thinking is also much more dependent on teleology than are other versions of British idealist ethics. There is a sharp criticism of self-realization in the *Theory of Good and Evil,* where Rashdall points out that if to make the self real means to realize what is real, the view is nonsense.[11] If it means, on the other hand, to realize some potentiality of the self, then the theory is doubtless true but obscure. Certainly the point cannot be that one must realize all the capacities of human nature, for it is frequently necessary to choose between competing potentialities. Finally, if self-realization means developing one's whole nature—physical, intellectual, emotional—then this is simply impossible, as Rashdall sees it. To perfect one aspect of personality, say the intellectual, entails a certain depreciation of another side of one's nature, say the physical. Yet Rashdall thinks that self-realization is as good as any other approach to ethics; it is possible, he finally admits, that all attempts to define morality must move in a circle.[12]

A famous Plato scholar, A. E. Taylor (1869–1945), was critical of the self-realization theory of ethics but sympathized with the theistic approach of Rashdall. Taylor's *Problem of Conduct* (1901) and *The Faith of a Moralist* (1930) combine an idealistic value theory with certain elements of natural law ethics. Equally well known for his work in the field of Greek philosophy and also very active in the field of ethics, W. D. Ross (1877–1940) shared something of Taylor's idealism. Ross's *The Right and the Good* (1930) acknowledges a debt to H. A. Prichard and G. E. Moore but it is also strongly influenced by Kant. To Ross, right does not mean the same as good. This is clear, he thinks, from the fact that the words are not convertible; that is, one cannot be substituted for the other. When we say this act is "right," we mean that it ought to be done, or is morally obligatory. Eventually he suggests that moral rightness is intuited and that duties are of two general kinds: prima facie duties are certain types of activity (fidelity, reparation, gratitude, justice, beneficence, self-improvement, and nonmalevolence) that are generally right and obligatory unless some higher duty intervenes. Proper moral duties, on the other hand, apply in concrete situations and are the only guide that we have to what is morally right.[13] However, good is a quality of a thing, or action, or a character, that is connected with virtue, pleasure, or knowledge. Thus understood, moral good is probably indefinable.[14] Consequently, some acts may be right and not good, and vice versa.

In the *Foundations of Ethics* (1939), Ross makes some of these points more explicit. Right is a legalistic term suggesting obedience to law, while good suggests that which satisfies desire or obtains an end.[15] Both notions are important to ethics but that of right is more basic. Motives seem to determine goodness, whereas the suitability of an action is central to the notion of rightness.[16] In the final analysis, although most agents strive to achieve objective rightness, the ultimate obligation is determined by subjective rightness. That is, what a person thinks, or feels, that he must do is all-important. One's personal decision in the moral order rests on a comparison of prima facie duties.[17] For example, a policeman who finds that his mother is a habitual shoplifter is confronted by two prima facie duties, his obligation to secure obedience to the laws of his country, and his obligation to respect and honor his mother. His final decision, as moral judgment, rests on the resolution of the conflict of these types of duty. That one should decide in terms of promoting the most, or greatest, good is not always obvious. Intuition of what is right is often a surer guide.

A similar theory is advocated by H. A. Prichard (1871–1947) in a series of miscellaneous studies dating back as early as 1912 but published together under the title *Moral Obligation* (1949). Suspicious of utilitarian procedures, Prichard stated his view in a much reprinted article, "Does Moral Philosophy rest on a Mistake?" (1912). It was not that he doubted the value of ethical investigation but rather that he wondered whether ethics had been asking the right questions, for he felt that one cannot offer "proof" or reasons for a duty. It is there and one simply sees it. This is a radical example of ethical intuitionism.[18]

A popular version of self-realization ethics was made the theoretical basis for the ethical culture movement in nineteenth-century United States. It was a Cornell University professor, Felix Adler (1851–1933), who established the first Society for Ethical Culture, in 1876, at New York City. Other groups were founded elsewhere in the United States and an international organization came into being in 1887. W. M. Salter, Stanton Coit, and Percival Chubb took a prominent part in the spread of ethical culture. Aimed at improving the moral life of individual members and their communities, without regard for theological or philosophical opinions, this semireligious movement has not had a great impact on academic ethics but it is an example of a widespread effort to popularize the ideals of ethical self-realization.

The greatest name in idealistic ethics in the United States is that of Josiah Royce (1855–1916). With William James (whose views were very different) Royce attracted European interest to American thought, for the first time. His *Religious Aspect of Philosophy* (1885), *The World and the Individual* (1900–1901), *Studies of Good and Evil* (1902), *The Philosophy of Loyalty* (1908), and *The Hope of the Great Community* (1916) are all ethically oriented books. In general, Royce's philosophical position is an absolute idealism quite unlike the similarly named philosophy of his British contemporaries. Kant, Schelling, Lotze, and Schopenhauer are important in Royce's background, and Hegel, of course, is central in his great work, *The World and the Individual.*

In his study of knowledge and reality, Royce came to think that the real objects of thought cannot be outside consciousness; for, it they were completely so, they would never be known. Moreover, the possibility of intercommunication between persons, and the possibility of error within the thinking of one person, led him to conclude that there is an infinite Thought which contains all objects, all relations, and even all errors, that can be thought.[10] Thus, Royce's God is Absolute Experience, embracing all selves, all thoughts, and all volitions.[20] Ideas (viewed either within the consciousness of the individual man or in universal consciousness) have a sort of life of their own: they intend and will "objects," which are the external fulfillment of the internal idea. Such externality does not mean extraconsciousness but simply an independent reality within the realm of thought. As Royce states this idealistic theory: "To be, in the final sense, means to be just such a life, complete, present to experience, and conclusive of the search for perfection which every finite idea in its own measure undertakes when it seeks for any object."[21]

In the context of such a position, Royce's ethics is a type of self-realization, or better, self-perfectionism. A good moral life is to be guided neither by rules derived from the "facts of nature" (realism), nor from the codes of behavior current in actual societies (social relativism). Evolutionary ethics was coming into prominence in his day, and, confronted with the suggestion that man should act so as to achieve a higher state of evolution, Royce asked how we know that the later stages in evolution are any better morally than the earlier ones.[22] Instead, Royce based his ethics on an ideal moral order which embodied something of the Greek notion of living in accord with "reason," a good deal of the love-ethic of early Christian teaching, and much of Kant's theory of a kingdom of ends. As a young man, Royce's basic ethical imperative was: "In so far as in thee lies, act as if thou wert at once thy neighbor and thyself."[23]

A more distinctive teaching is developed in *The Philosophy of Loyalty*. There Royce treats "loyalty" as the fundamental moral experience and standard, and adds that loyalty means the willing and thorough devotion of an individual to a cause. As such, loyalty is for the individual person a supreme good. Two special features distinguish loyalty: decisiveness and fidelity. However, conflicts of causes or interests do arise and with them come conflicts of loyalties. A man may find that in taking a certain job he is depriving another person of work; a representative of one profession, or one state, or one school of thought, may find that his interest is in opposition to that of others; a patriot may discover that the citizens of an enemy nation are just as loyal to their country as he is to his own. In a famous lecture Royce proposed that the way to overcome these conflicts is to be "loyal to loyalty." What makes for conflict among the ideals or causes that people espouse is the limited way in which these causes are conceived. It is morally superior for the individual interested in his own welfare to think of a whole lifetime rather than a moment of pleasure. It is better to think in terms of the good of a larger group than a smaller one. Ultimately, one should strive to be loyal to all mankind; and this, Royce thinks, is to be loyal to God, and to loyalty itself. All special moral duties and all virtues are to be interpreted, then, in terms of loyalty to the whole duty of man.[24]

It was almost inevitable that Royce would go on to apply this ethical view to some of man's practical problems. *The Hope of the Great Community* (1916) expressed something close to the heart of American idealism in the social, political, and religious orders, when it proposed that all men should try to overcome petty differences in the total interest of humanity. The "great community" could be an international organization to promote peace, on one level; or, again, it might mean the community of all the faithful, which Royce took to be the essence of Christianity.[25] These high-minded ethical views did much to show other peoples that Royce's country was not solely devoted to material values.[26]

Royce's younger colleague in the famous Harvard department of philosophy, George Santayana (1863–1952), was an entirely different kind of thinker. Sometimes he was quite skeptical about the value of ethics. "Any feeling," he wrote, "nursed and kept close in the dark, may fester into a categorical imperative."[27] At other times Santayana took a naturalistic and somewhat hedonistic view of ethics. One must consider the consequences of our decisions and actions, and so, utilitarianism has some truth in it. Pleasure is obviously good and pain is evil. This was his position in *The Life of Reason: or the Phases of Human Progress* (1905–1906). As he put it, "Conduct that should not justify itself somehow by the satisfactions secured and the pains avoided would not justify itself at all."[28]

Later, Santayana came to his theory of "essences"—possibly under the influence of Plato.[29] Items like nature, history, and self are notions of things, images whose being is purely internal to them. These essences "possess no substance or hidden parts, but are all surface, all appearance." More generally expressed, Santayana's essences are "the characters possessed by such things as happen to exist, together with the characters which all different things would possess if they existed."[30] One might expect him to equate moral values with some of these essences but he does not; in themselves, essences are morally neutral. Value, both aesthetic and moral, is constituted by personal approval of some item in the realm of essences. "Values accrue to any part of the realm of essence by virtue of the interest which somebody takes in it."[31] So, from this point of view, Santayana's ethics (which he himself calls "naturalistic") is an example of psychological value theory.

In other places, Santayana's skepticism leads him to take a different attitude. Morality, he thinks, should mean actual allegiance to this or that ideal of life. Most of Royce's writing fell into this category and there is no doubt that Santayana respected Royce. On the other hand, ethics would be for Santayana a descriptive science recording the history of moral allegiances, the circumstances and effects involved in the historical shifts of moral perspective. In other words, Santayana sometimes treated ethics as the "science of manners" in the French sociological sense.[32] It might be just as well to admit that Santayana was not strongly committed to any ethic; he preserved an attitude of aristocratic disdain for ethical "enthusiasm" and was not especially loyal to anything.

The tradition of idealistic self-realization ethics was continued in the teaching of Hocking and Jordan. William Ernest Hocking (1873–1966) was Royce's most faithful follower at Harvard. *Human Nature and Its Remaking* (1918) shows that Hocking placed more emphasis on traditional theistic belief as a bulwark for ethical judgment. Moreover, Hocking was a very explicit defender of democracy and political freedom as ethical values. Elijah Jordan (1875–1953) never attracted the same amount of attention as Hocking, while he was alive, but Jordan's thought is now becoming better recognized as an important contribution to ethics and social theory in the United States. *The Good Life* (1949) offers a self-realization theory based on objective idealism. In it, Jordan opposed subjectivism in value theory and was particularly critical of the notion that moral value can be reduced to some sort of personal "interest."[33]

Academic philosophers have paid little attention to the writing of Albert Schweitzer (1875–1965), at least, in the field of ethics; yet to many people in the contemporary world he represented the personification of the ethical spirit. There are periods in the history of ethics when the key writers are anything but professors; at other times (and the twentieth century is one such), it is almost necessary to be affiliated with university work before one can get a hearing in ethics. In any case, Schweitzer's decision to abandon a promising medical career in Europe (the family was Alsatian) and to establish a hospital in Africa made him a universally esteemed figure. Not all of his admirers realized that he was an excellent scholar in philosophy and theology. Schweitzer's *Civilization and Ethics* (1922) was originally a series of lectures, delivered in French, at Mansfield College, Oxford, but published in German, as were the originals of his other books. Dr. Schweitzer did a great deal of reading as background for these talks and his book is the best short history of ethics that has appeared since Henry Sidgwick's *Outlines.*[34] Schweitzer's own ethical position is very simple: "Reverence for life affords me my fundamental principle of morality, namely that good consists in maintaining, assisting, and enhancing life, and that to destroy, to harm, or to hinder life is evil."[35] The term that he used in German is *Ehrfurcht,* which suggests both respect and awe for the living. Life was intended to include both its human and nonhuman examples.

Other than this vitalistic principle, Schweitzer's ethics has little to distinguish it from any other simple theory of self-realization.[36]

The most straightforward presentation of self-realization ethics is to be found in the writing of Henry W. Wright (1878–1959). His main publication is entitled *Self-Realization* (1913); he expounds his theory there in terms of the development of the individual self, the social self, and the universal self. The ends of the individual are pleasure and culture, of the social self they are altruism and humanitarianism, and of the universal self the goal is "universal progress," which involves resignation to the divine will and trust in divine wisdom.[37]

An Englishman who taught for many years at Princeton, Walter T. Stace (1886–) is a good example of the advocate of a refined hedonism. His chief work in ethics is *The Concept of Morals* (1937). Ethical relativism based on a hasty interpretation of data from the social sciences is subjected to very severe criticism by Stace, for he regards such an ethics as defeatism in morals. Stace has also insisted that without free will ethics is nonsense but that such freedom must admit of a certain amount of causal determinism.[38] His own ethics takes pleasure as the test of what is morally good and suggests that mental pleasures must rank above those of the body.

Another American thinker, Brand Blanshard (1892–), has been an outstanding critic of the noncognitivism and subjectivism of recent British ethics.

His *Reason and Goodness* (1961) represents a revision of the Gifford Lectures at St. Andrews and the Noble Lectures at Harvard. Blanshard has a broad knowledge of different types of ethics, and, in particular, is one of the few contemporary ethicians who knows anything about medieval ethics.[39] At times, Blanshard's own ethics comes very close to Kant, but he prefers to be known as a rationalist. Sometimes, Blanshard can sound positively classical in explaining the role of reason, as in the following sentence:

> Rationality, as we conceive it, does not lie merely in letting reason appoint one's beliefs, hard as that is; it means carrying a rational spirit into the ramifications of practice, making it permeate one's feelings and pervade all the decisions of one's will.[40]

Like Rousseau and Kant, Blanshard distinguishes between personal fluctuations of desire and volition (the actual will) and the rational will "which is what on reflection would commend itself as the greatest good."[41] In working out the features that constitute rationality, he presents a theory of human nature that is not far removed from Aristotelian ethics. It is not as close to Aristotle, of course, as the work of Henry B. Veatch (1911–), whose *Rational Man: A Modern Interpretation of Aristotelian Ethics* (1962) was written as a formal answer to the phenomenological work *Irrational Man,* by William Barrett.

Kantian deontology is combined with self-realization ethics in the work of A. C. Garnett (1894–). His *Ethics: A Critical Introduction* (1960) surveys all the main types of ethical theory and has been helpful at many points in the present history. Specifically expert contemporary scholarship in the ethics of Kant is represented in England by H. J. Paton (1887–) and in the United States by Lewis White Beck (1913–). Both have provided translations and interpretations of the practical works of Kant.

In the rest of the present chapter, it is proposed to offer a brief summary of two special trends in recent ethics which have some relation with consequence ethics. Oddly both provide a bridge between formalism and utilitarianism. The first is the theory of games as applied to ethics and the second is the development of "act" and "rule" utilitarianism.

Games theory goes back to the efforts of mathematicians to investigate the rules of strategy that govern the winning of table games such as chess. It is generally known that only a certain number and pattern of moves are required for success in such games and probability theory can be applied to this sort of problem. A pioneer article in this field was the German study "On the Theory of Playing Games" (1928), by J. von Neumann. With O. Morgenstern, von Neumann later applied this technique to the making of decisions in the sphere of economics. It is not a matter of going through a complicated calculus of all the possibilities that may be available for achieving a certain end. Nor is games theory anything like a calculation of the relative weights of pleasures that may result from a given action. As applied to decision-making, the method becomes rapidly simpler the nearer the agent is to his goal, since the number of possible moves diminishes rapidly, after the opening moves. It should be noted from the beginning, however, that this theory has nothing to offer in regard to opting for an end or goal of action. It is only after a moral agent has established his objective, that games theory may help him with the selection of the best means to that end.

The most discussed book applying the theory of games to ethics was written by R. B. Braithwaite (1900–) of Cambridge University. His *Theory of Games as a Tool for the Moral Philosopher* (1955, reissued 1963) was the inaugural lecture, delivered when he became professor of moral philosophy at Cambridge. This version of the theory is explained by discussing a definite problem that is moral, in a sense, but also somewhat like a game. The problem is later used in another context of ethical discussion by R. M. Hare.[42] Two men live in the same building: one plays piano and the other plays trumpet and the building is so constructed that one man's playing interferes with the other man's enjoyment. With this background (plus a few more details that are here omitted), Braithwaite asks:

> Can any plausible principle be devised stating how they should divide the proportion of days on which both of them play, Luke alone plays, Matthew alone plays, neither play, so as to obtain maximum production of satisfaction compatible with fair distribution?[43]

While it is impossible to summarize the mathematical steps used to suggest a solution, it may be noted that Braithwaite eventually decides that out of 43 evenings the piano player should play on 17, while the trumpet player should play on 26. That other solutions are theoretically possible, Braithwaite admits.

Two observations may be made concerning games theory and ethics. First, if one uses a teleological approach to ethics, such as this method implies, the really difficult problem centers on the option for ends, rather than the choice of means to secure these ends. This is generally recognized by people who work from the point of view of value theory: it is easy to set up proximate standards of worth but very hard to justify ultimate values. In other words, the theory of games may have some limited utility in helping people to make moral decisions, *if they already have an objective clearly in view.* Mathematical computation does not seem to help in determining such an ultimate objective for life. Second, while some moral decisions may be reducible to the competition-between-two-persons pattern, it does not seem that this is generally the case.

Some moral problems may not directly involve other persons at all; and other questions may include so many affected persons and so many variations of detail that the simplicity of Braithwaite's case may be deceptive. In any event, it is interesting to note how what looks like a very formal suggestion in recent ethics actually entails a consideration of ideal consequences, in the guise of what one means by "winning the game."

The other recent trend in utilitarian ethics has to do with the difference between using an appraisal of consequences to make a judgment of an *act* and of a *rule.* Act-utilitarians included most of the now classic thinkers in this school, notably Bentham and J. S. Mill. However, they may not have been entirely conscious of the point now under discussion. The act-utilitarian does not attempt to generalize; he asks, "What effect will *my* doing *this* act in *this* situation have on the general balance of good over evil?" On the other hand, the rule-utilitarian thinks that moral action should always be governed by a general rule that has been established by asking whether this general kind of action, if done by everyone, would result in general good or evil.[44]

An important contemporary representative of act-utilitarianism is the Australian J. J. C. Smart (1920–). His *Outline of a System of Utilitarian Ethics* (1961) discusses both kinds of consequence ethics and opts for the utilitarianism that concentrates on the act. The basic objection to rule-utilitarianism, according to Smart, is that it can lead to judgments that one should abide by a rule even in situations where it will not be beneficial to do so. Moreover, Smart insists that there is a difference between the person who thinks that all pleasures are equal in quality and the ethician who considers mental pleasures, for instance, superior to bodily ones. It is ideal utilitarianism that requires qualitative distinctions of pleasures.

Actually, Smart distinguishes two moments in the thinking of an act-utilitarian: he must first evaluate the consequences, and then he must judge the various acts that might lead to these consequences.[45] Admitting that there are difficulties in estimating the value of the consequences, Smart takes the example of the recent physiological experiments on rats which can be electrically stimulated so that they appear to enjoy almost endless feelings of pleasure. Whether humans thus artificially stimulated to feel pleasures on the sensual level might represent the ideal good which the ethician envisions, now becomes Smart's main query. It is indeed a question whether this sort of thing is true human happiness.[46]

As Smart sees the act-utilitarian teaching, the only reason for performing act A rather than act B is that doing A will make mankind happier than will doing act B. He feels that people who work in ethics and value general happiness will tend to agree that his is a most acceptable view.[47] Smart does not ask for altruism but simply for benevolence: the view of the agent who wishes others as much good as he gets himself.

There is always the problem of deciding whether one should promote the maximum of happiness for all men as a group, or whether one should strive for an equitable distribution of possibly lesser happiness to all men. Here Smart admits that one might need to use mathematical probability theory in order to secure complete equity. It is at this point that one realizes how thin the wall now is between a sophisticated utilitarian ethics and a formalism that shows some concern for the facts of life. In point of fact, as Smart notes, if one begins to think of possible rules in utilitarianism then one approaches the position of Kant.[48]

Another major contribution to this problem of ethical method has been made by Marcus G. Singer (1926–) in his *Generalization in Ethics* (1961). He has no use for act-utilitarianism—which he calls "direct" utilitarianism. Utility as traditionally understood is an ambiguous standard and leads to insurmountable ethical difficulties. However, Singer is willing to take a second look at what he calls "indirect" utilitarianism. This is the view that one may look to the consequences to evaluate various *kinds* of actions. "One thus considers the consequences that actions of that kind may generally be expected to have, and by such means directly determines the morality of that *kind* of action."[49] This indirect utilitarianism is, of course, but another version of rule-utilitarianism. That it is an improvement over act-utilitarianism but still subject to criticism is Singer's appraisal.

Singer's own ethical position is an attempt to refine the categorical imperative of Kant. It will be recalled that Kant said that one should act so that his very action could become a general rule of conduct. There is much ambiguity in this rule. Hence, Singer expands the generalization *argument* in these words: "If everyone were to do that, the consequences would be disastrous (or undesirable): therefore, no one ought to do that."[50] On the other hand, he phrases the generalization *principle* as follows: "what is right (or wrong) for one person must be right (or wrong) for any similar person in similar circumstances."[51] To Singer's mind, the categorical imperative can be interpreted so as to form an adequate guide for ethical judgment.[52] It is admitted that the consequences of an action—in the sense of the foreseeable results—are quite relevant to moral consideration. In fact no serious ethician would wish to exclude consequences from ethical discussions, and so Singer concludes with the odd suggestion that the major problem in "morals" is not one of theory but rather the difficulty of determining the facts in concrete cases. Surely no previous formal ethician has been this willing to grant a role to material morality.

This is something of what has happened, then, to recent thinking within the limits of classical ethical theories. What remains to be seen in our final chapters will be what is new in strictly contemporary ethics.

Chapter XVI
Naturalistic Ethics

WHEN G. E. Moore said that moral philosophers who attempt to define "good" in terms of anything else are committing the "naturalistic fallacy," he not only coined a phrase but also gave a name to a school of ethics. Naturalistic ethics has since come to mean that kind of theory which attempts to define the moral good in terms of certain elements of our ordinary experience of life. In the next chapter we shall see that Moore himself considered that the predicate "good" names a property that is not a natural quality or any grouping of such qualities. Good, Moore felt, is a nonnatural, specially intuited property. "Naturalism," Moore said, "offers no reason at all, far less any valid reason, for any ethical principle whatever."[1]

Since Moore wrote this, in 1903, many ethical philosophers have disagreed with him on this point and have taken considerable delight in committing the naturalistic fallacy. In the broad sense, then, any ethics is naturalistic that endeavors to define moral good by identifying it with well-being, pleasure, obedience to God's law, conformity with human nature, or with any principle other than good itself. Thus broadly understood, any ethics other than Moore's might be labeled "naturalism."[2]

There is, however, a more restricted meaning for naturalism in contemporary philosophy: this stresses an empirical, scientific, non-supernatural approach to the subject. To speak simply, the contemporary naturalist tries to couch his explanations in terms of what he experiences in the world about him. In this narrow sense, naturalistic ethics has four special features. First, all its explanations are expressed in terms of this world and it is opposed to the use of any transcendental principles, such as God or an ideal Absolute. Second, the data of ethical philosophy include not only the presentations of ordinary experience but also the findings of modern science, interpreted by the techniques of science, especially of the social sciences.[3] Third, naturalistic ethicians are dedicated to the notion of ongoing progress, of the continual advance of men and their institutions toward higher levels. This tends toward the view that any new change is an improvement.[4] And fourth, in opposition to analytical philosophers and positivists the nautralistic ethician maintains that ethical statements may be true and capable of verification.

Another way of stating the program of ethical naturalism is to say that it is possible to derive an *ought* from an *is*, or a value from a fact. We shall see in the next chapter that most British ethicians of the twentieth century are convinced that there is some sort of impassable gap between factual descriptions and moral prescriptions. American moral philosophers, until very recently, have tended to assume that there is a rather close connection between knowing what a problem is, what conditions surround it, what scientific experts think about it, and being able to discover what one should do about it. This is the naturalistic approach: get the facts, consult the experts, interpret the data with the help of scientific methods, if possible-then decide what ought to be done, without too much talk about God's law, a future life, or any sort of absolute standards or ideals.

In the present chapter we shall center our attention on American naturalistic ethics but will include some other types of naturalism that are either contributory to this kind of thought (such as evolutionary or psychological approbative ethics) or are tangential to it (such as some versions of natural law ethics).

When Charles Darwin (1809–1882) first published his famous *Origin of Species by Means of Natural Selection* (London, 1859), it was immediately apparent that his theory was pregnant with implications that went well beyond science into the area of religion and ethics. Its meaning is still a matter of speculation in the twentieth century.[5] Ethically, there was the initial tendency to identify moral improvement with biological change. Thus, Darwin spoke of "the rearing of the greatest number of individuals in full vigor and health under the conditions to which they are subjected."[6]

The leading philosopher of evolutionary theory was Herbert Spencer (1820–1903). His *Principles of Ethics* (2 vols., 1892–1893) assumes throughout that the more evolved man displays the better conduct. In Spencer's view, life is taken as a fundamental value. Human conduct requires "an improving adjustment of acts to ends, such as furthers the prolongation of life." Hence, it is good to preserve and strengthen the life of the individual and that of the race. Right and wrong have meaning only in relation to creatures capable of pleasures and pains.[7] Although he speaks of the possibility of an absolute morality, Spencer insists that the ethics that we now know is not absolutely right but only relatively so. Moral science (like "mechanical" science) has evolved from a primitive teaching developed by the Greeks, through a theological period, to its present incipient scientific state. As a consequence, moral perfection could not be attained by an individual man unless he existed in the environment of the ideal state.[8]

Oddly, Thomas Henry Huxley (1825–1895) took the opposite view. Admitting the importance of the evolutionary hypothesis in biological and related sciences, Huxley (in his Romanes Lecture of 1893 entitled *Evolution and Ethics)* argued that the law of the survival of the fit was not an ethical principle. Man, he felt, must do his best to overcome the law of the jungle and to establish his ethical ideals on a non-evolutionary basis.

> The practice of that which is ethically best—what we call goodness or virtue—involves a course of conduct which, in all respects, is opposed to that which leads to success in the cosmic struggle for existence. In place of ruthless self-assertion it demands self-restraint. . . .[9]

Still another version of evolutionary ethics is found in the writings of a Russian contemporary of Spencer and Huxley, Prince Pëtr Alekseevich Kropotkin (1842–1921). In a book entitled *Mutual Aid, a Factor of Evolution* (London: Heinemann, 1915) Kropotkin claimed that it is not competition but mutual assistance which is the law of evolutionary progress. He buttressed this idealistic version of evolutionary ethics in his *Etika,* where he offered a rather extensive survey of classical and modern ethical theories as support for his own ethics.[10] Kropotkin's own position is a type of naturalistic ethics that offers moral science as a substitute for religion, stresses the development of "social conscience" in mankind, but pays little attention to biological progress.[11] Thus, Kropotkin's ethics culminates in an altruistic form of social utilitarianism.

Outstanding among more recent works in evolutionary ethics is *A Modern Theory of Ethics* (1929) by Olaf Stapledon (1886–1950). In general, Stapledon attempted to put the theory of teleological order back into the interpretation of human conduct. Human activity is teleological in the sense that it shows definite tendencies toward some sort of completion in the future. Good designates such tendential activity, as free, fulfilling, or as instrumental in the ongoing perfection of cosmic processes. He does not reduce man to the purely mechanical or deterministic processes of physical nature, however, for Stapledon thinks that man can rise in "ecstasy" to the level of moral experience which is only a little lower than mysticism. However, "in the final ethical analysis it turns out that in *all* value-judgments, an objective situation, such as organic fulfilment or personal fulfilment, is simply judged good in and for itself."[12]

Very influential on the ethical attitudes of practical psychologists, psychiatrists, social scientists, and many writers of novels, has been the psychoanalytic teaching of Sigmund Freud (1856–1939). This Viennese medical doctor who spent the last part of his life in London was not really a theoretical ethician; yet the history of contemporary ethics would not be complete without some account of his teaching.[13] Freud admitted little debt to earlier philosophers but he did study under Franz Brentano and knew the general position of the Austrian value school.

Freudian psychoanalysis was initially a form of mental therapy developed to treat emotional disorders. It grew into a psychological view of man and his functions. Originally, moral attitudes played little part in Freud's work. His tendency was to ignore and even play down ethical considerations as factors in clinical practice. Thus Freud is frequently classified as an ethical skeptic.[14] However, as his theory of human endowments and functions grew broader, Freud took positions that have had profound ethical importance and influence. For instance, he opposed the "rationalism" of the Enlightenment and of nineteenth-century German idealism with the contention that men, in the concrete findings of the clinic, show themselves to be irrational and capricious.[15] This stress on the irrational has been picked up by contemporary existentialism. Moreover, as an ethic, Freud's later teaching adjures the supernatural, the otherworldly, the traditionally religious, the system-building of the idealists, and adheres to a rather simple naturalism. This is obvious throughout *Civilization and Its Discontents* (1939), Freud's key work in the field of ethics.

The basic analysis of the human psyche, on which Freudianism stands, is rather generally known. Freud distinguished the large and lower area of the unconscious from the smaller and upper field of consciousness.[16] Many instinctive impulses are thought to surge up from the unconscious and seek realization in conscious activities, and the main instinctual drives are sexual and aggressive.[17] To deal with these impulses, Freud postulated three functional levels within the human psyche: (1) the "id" is the unconscious considered as the seat of bodily appetites; (2) the "ego" is the middle level, the area of conscious and rational decision and activity; and (3) the "super-ego" is judgmental and critical, a sort of moral dictator, cruel and self-punishing.[18]

There is a partial similarity between the foregoing psychology and Plato's three parts of the human soul. Freud was well aware of this. He did not assign the highest role to reason, however, but put it in the middle as the field of mediation between lower instincts and higher tendencies toward inhibition. Unlike Plato, he denied that the lower impulses should be restrained at all costs; in fact, Freud felt that such restraint is the start of personality disorders. The dictates of the superego tend to be identified by Freud with the conventions of civilized society and the repressive teachings of traditional religion and ethics. What is good for man is an ethic of honesty in which the individual will strive to be open, frank, and uninhibited in speaking of and acting out his basic drives.[19] All secrecy, subterfuge, hypocrisy, and repression are bad. It is good to express oneself but one must learn to respect the interests of others in order to live peacefully in society.

During the same period, William James (1842–1910) was studying medicine, teaching psychology, and finally turning his attention to philosophy in the United States. He eventually became a member of the distinguished philosophy department at Harvard which included G. H. Palmer, Royce, and Santayana. There, James made numerous contributions to empirical and educational psychology and was one of the pioneers in the development of American pragmatism. There are naturalistic moments in William James's thought (for instance, his account of habit formation in humans as the "grooving of channels for nerve messages") but he is not anti-metaphysical in his general philosophy, nor is he inclined to reject entirely the values of theistic belief and traditional religion. Like Henri Bergson, James felt that the Christian saints are models of moral perfection.[20] We have several short studies of ethical significance from James's pen but the most important is his lecture "The Moral Philosopher and the Moral Life" (1891).

No great interest is shown by James in a ready-made ethical theory: "There can be no final truth in ethics any more than in physics, until the last man has had his experience and said his say."[21] In true pragmatic style, James views a realistic ethics in terms of three questions. The first is psychological: What is the historical origin of our moral notions? He reviews certain attempts to answer this but shows no fascination for the history of the subject. The second great question in James's ethics is metaphysical: What do key words in ethics, terms like good, evil, and obligation, mean? In considering this, James rejects absolutism and any suggestion that ethics might be grounded in metaphysics as a systematic construction. Since he sees good and obligation as the objects of feeling and desire, James concludes that they have no foothold in metaphysical being. His third question is "casuistic": What is the *measure* whereby good may be distinguished from evil? In answering this, he suggests that the morally good is simply that which satisfies demand, any demand. "That act must be the best act, accordingly, which makes for the *best whole,* in the sense of awakening the least sum of dissatisfactions."[22]

Among the people impressed by James's pragmatic ethics was the man who became the most prolific and best-known American ethician, John Dewey (1859–1952). He began his philosophical career as an idealist, strongly under the influence of German thought, and his early writings in ethics show this affiliation. However, Dewey soon adopted a more naturalistic and practical approach to moral philosophy. In the famous textbook *Ethics* (1908), which he wrote in collaboration with J. H. Tufts, the second part was written entirely by Dewey and has recently been separately published as *Theory of the Moral Life* (1960). It was already evident in this work that Dewey had reached, before 1910, his instrumentalist version of pragmatic ethics. Moral theory is only called for when some problem arises involving a practical conflict of ends or standards of conduct.[23] Thus, instrumentalist ethics is an attempt to offer a reflective answer to such a human problem. To this end, Dewey reviewed various historical theories concerning the supreme goals of human aspiration and concluded that they all have some partial validity as practical ideals, but he refused to draw up a table of such moral values, suggesting instead the importance of forming the habit of making wise and reflective judgments in ethics.[24] Eventually he proposed a delicate balance between the claims of egoism and altruism, with the preference going slightly to the latter because the social interest is more inclusive.

The next major ethical work by John Dewey is the seventh chapter of *Reconstruction in Philosophy* (1920), where the idea that serious reflection is central to the work of the ethician is further developed. Here, Dewey contrasts the position of those who base ethics on duty as deriving from some supreme law, with the theory that ethics seeks the moral good in self-realization, happiness, or some other ideal end. He now asserts that every moral situation is unique and cannot be judged by any ready-made law or rule. Each moral problem must be faced pragmatically. An intelligent and serious inquiry is required to come up with a judgment and choice concerning a given situation. These are to be the best that can be made in view of the predictable consequences of the proposed action.[25]

In *Human Nature and Conduct* (1922) Dewey reacts against the Freudian theory of unconscious instinctual drives. There is, as far as Dewey is concerned, no evidence that we have a distinct "psychic realm" for our instincts. Nor will he accept the notion of an original individual consciousness such as one finds described in Freud.[26] This is one of the most effective criticisms of Freudian psychology and through it John Dewey has influenced the modifications of psychoanalytic theory that have developed in the United States.[27] Dewey was then quite definite in his exclusion of any search for fixed standards of ethical judgment. He turned rather to the study of "ends-in-view" and endeavored to describe how these proximate goals arise and function within the field of human action. They are not final goals but function as "turning points" in activity. All ethics must devote some attention to the consequences of human action; even deontologists do this under the guise of "meaning well" or being properly motivated for moral decisions.[28] All ends-in-view may become means for other ends.

The *Quest for Certainty* (1929) shows Dewey's growing interest in value theory. In it, he clearly distinguished valuation from value: all values may be liked or enjoyed (that is a question of psychology) but not all acts of enjoyment are truly valuable. Since value judgments focus on the *objects* of our experiences, they constitute judgments about the *regulation* of "our desires, affections and enjoyments."[29] Psychological and scientific reports of human preferences have only "instrumental" utility in the discovery of value judgments. This is a revision of his earlier position and it distinguishes Dewey from the positivist who accepts social science data as the last word on ethical questions. On his part, Dewey always insisted on the need for reflective interpretation of all empirical materials, whether from science or from ordinary experience.

Further explanation of the important difference between acts of "prizing" and the values that are the objects of such actions is offered by Dewey in *Theory of Valuation* (1939). Now he is very critical of the positivist assertion that value judgments are unverifiable and thus without philosophic meaning.[30] To support his contention that such verification is possible, Dewey turned to modern experience in medical practice, where various means are clearly evaluated in terms of their fitness to achieve desired ends. Rather convincingly, he argued that value judgments as to the fitness of certain things for given purposes are practical generalizations and that they are justified in terms of the means-end relation. They can be tested rigorously by observing their actual results in comparison with their intended consequences.[31]

This kind of naturalistic ethics is still quite important in American thought, although not as popular as it was in the twenties and thirties. The influence of John Dewey in the moral judgments of social scientists and experts on educational theory is still strong. Noteworthy, also, is the growing number of sympathetic studies of Dewey's ethics written by American Catholic philosophers in the past two decades.

The view that reality is ever in process underlies Dewey's general philosophic position, and this same theme was strongly reinforced in the thought of Alfred North Whitehead (1861–1947). Although he did not develop a detailed theory of ethics he deserves to be remembered here because of the indirect influence of his thought on certain tendencies in contemporary ethics. As the author (with Bertrand Russell) of *Principia Mathematica* (1910–1913), Whitehead brought about a revolution in philosophic notions about logic and methodology. While it did not deal with the logic of ethical discourse, this work, in the view of many scholars, "dealt a blow" to faith in any sort of philosophic absolutes.[32] Another indirect influence stems from Whitehead's theory of a finite God.[33] This has impressed contemporary thought about the role of God's will in the moral area, particularly in the thinking of some recent Protestant Christian ethicians. We shall see in our final chapter that Christian ethics, which was formerly quite idealistic and absolutistic, has now become aligned with existentialism. This is true of only one branch of Protestant ethics, of course, that which is now identified as situationism. The expositions of Whitehead's philosophy of God by followers such as Charles Hartshorne (1897–) and Henry Nelson Wieman (1884–) have been especially influential in the thinking of recent Christian ethicians.

As we saw earlier, value ethics has frequently adopted a naturalistic stance. It was Ralph Barton Perry (1876–1957) who provided the generic definition of value from which later naturalistic ethicians took their starting point. In his *General Theory of Value* (1926) Perry defined value as "any object of any interest."[34] Thus used, interest is any "organization that consistently acts for its own preservation" while moral good consists in the fulfillment of any organization of interests.[35] To Perry, duty consists in the enlightened recognition of the good. For the ranking of values, Perry proposed four criteria: correctness, intensity, preference, and inclusiveness. Actually, the last three have to do with degrees of value, whereas the first is the test of whether something is a value or not.[36] In the final analysis, Perry's basic moral imperative becomes: "Cultivate that kind of will that is qualified to bring harmony through its universal adoption."[37]

Some moral philosophers have continued to base their views on various versions of the general theory of evolution. The biologist Samuel Jackson Holmes (1868–) equated moral goodness with that which promoted the preservation of the life of the individual or of the species. In his turn, Julian Huxley (1887–), the grandson of Thomas Huxley, delivered the Romanes Lecture in 1943 and took the occasion to correct his grandfather. Julian's *Evolutionary Ethics* insists that the development of moral consciousness *is* a part of the general process of evolution, and he ties in the growth of awareness of moral values with the level of civilization in which a person lives.[38] It is well known that Julian Huxley has had a considerable influence on the philosophic outlook of the UNESCO program.

In Europe, naturalism was not lacking in twentieth-century supporters. A remarkable Jesuit scientist, Pierre Teilhard de Chardin (1881–1955), shared many of Julian Huxley's naturalistic views but assimilated them to a theistic account of man and the universe. Teilhard's *Phenomenon of Man* (posthumously published, in French in 1956, in English in 1959) pictures the evolution of man from physical nature as a continuous process, springing from the presence of psychic energies in even the lower levels of bodily nature. As things evolve they become more complex; we are now in the stage of the "noosphere," at which mind has appeared. Optimistically, Teilhard saw evolution as an upward process toward ever higher and better things. The whole movement is tending toward an ultimate stage, the omega point, which will be the climax of the development of the noosphere. Although infinite and transcendent, nevertheless the omega point will remain in immanent continuity with the ongoing process of nature.

There are ethical and religious implications in the *Phenomenon of Man* but the most interesting of Teilhard's published works, from the point of view of moral philosophy, is *The Divine Milieu* (1960). This work stands out as a highly spiritual account of the natural environment (the *milieu)* of man as transfused by charity (divine love) which becomes the stable principle of natures and powers.[39] Through Christ humanity is to be "divinized" in the love of God. This involves the concerted union of all human spirits in moving toward God as the "ultimate point" at which all realities converge.[40] There are similarities between the evolutionary thinking of Teilhard de Chardin and the ethics of Julian Huxley (they were quite friendly) but most commentators see Teilhard as close to the views of Bergson in the *Two Sources of Morality and Religion.*[41] It has even been suggested that Teilhard's ethic of divine love takes us one step beyond existentialism.[42]

In England, a noteworthy attempt to gather the resources of anthropology and ethnology in the service of ethics has been made by Alexander Macbeath (1888–1964). His *Experiments in Living* (1952) is a serious attempt to test the claim of ethical intuitionists, like G. E. Moore and Henry Sidgwick, that there are certain "deliverances of moral consciousness" that are self-evident to all men. Among other things which Macbeath notes in his first lecture, are the lack of precision and ambiguity of the propositions usually offered as ethically self-evident. He also points to the lack of agreement among people like Sidgwick, Moore, and Ross as to the precise nature of these initial judgments of intuitionist ethics. However, the major part of *Experiments in Living* is given over to the examination of published reports on the moral convictions of primitive peoples in many parts of the world. At the end Macbeath offers five conclusions: (1) He finds few, if any, primitives who consider that their moral rules apply to all men. (2) Although there are similarities among the general formulations of rules of life in various tribes, the concrete interpretations of these vary among different peoples. (3) Some of the prima facie duties known to British intuitionists are quite unknown to primitive peoples. (4) These various tribes think of their rules of living as limited to the conditions of their own life. (5) There are some rules recognized by primitive peoples that we would not approve on a moral basis at all.[43] It is only fair to note that Macbeath's rather negative findings are partly contradicted by other competent anthropologists with an interest in the moral significance of their work.[44]

The "social adjustment theory" of Stephen C. Pepper (1891–) is one of the most important recent American efforts to work out an axiological approach to naturalistic ethics. His *Sources of Value* (1958) is the best study since Perry's *General Theory*. In his *Ethics* (1960), Pepper devotes a dozen chapters to a thorough survey of all the great empirical theories of ethics. At the end, he suggests that each of these theories uses a "selective system" of evidences for its teachings on moral values. Each is limited by its particular point of view. Pepper lists the selective systems used in the important empirical types of ethics: *individual value* systems (hedonists use purposive structures and stress the work of prudence; self-realizationists use personality structure and the harmonious integration of the person); *social values* (pragmatists use the social situation and aim at the reduction of social tensions; cultural relativists concentrate on the cultural pattern and stress positive conformity to this structure); *biological values* (evolutionary ethicians emphasize progress in accord with natural selection). From this survey of naturalistic values, Pepper concludes that natural ethical norms do exist.[45] His own social adjustment theory has two main conclusions. When no special problem of social adjustment arises, then the ordinarily recognized naturalistic norms work alone. However, in cases of conflict, one's decision may depend on the degree of social pressure in a given society. Ethics, according to Pepper, is the "study of the structure and operation of selective systems bearing on human activity and the lines of legislation running through them."[46]

In the broad meaning of "naturalism" most of the ethics that has been developed by Roman Catholic thinkers in recent times is naturalistic. That is to say, they do feel that one may derive an "ought" from an "is." It is usual in Catholic writings to distinguish moral theology (the study of most of the traditional problems of ethics from the point of view of divine revelation, Biblical teaching, Christian traditions, and ecclesiastical law) from moral philosophy or ethics (which is restricted to information gained from ordinary experience and interpreted philosophically). In practice, of course, the views and positions taken in ethics by some Catholic philosophers may be indirectly influenced by their religious commitment, as is doubtless the case with all thinkers having either pro or con attitudes toward traditional religion.

One of the best-known Catholic philosophers in the twentieth century is Jacques Maritain (1882–). His efforts to make Thomism known and respected in contemporary circles are widely recognized. One of his books, *Science and Wisdom* (1935), takes a somewhat different position concerning the relation of moral theology and ethics from the view just stated above. In it, Maritain argues that a Christian thinker may, and can, borrow certain items of information from what he believes, in order to produce a more adequate ethics. That is to say, if one believes in original sin and its debilitating effects on mankind, and if one believes that men have been raised by God's special grace so that they may aspire to a future vision of God in heaven provided they live well on earth, then one's ethics may be more completely and practically developed under the influence of these Christian teachings. Such a "Christian ethics," as Maritain sees it, would be better and more practical than an abstract version of purely philosophical ethics. Thus envisioned, Maritain's ethics would be "subalternated" to moral theology.[47] Such an approach to a Catholic Christian ethics is not the usual view of Catholic ethicians, as is indicated by the rather severe criticisms aimed at Maritain by J. M. Ramirez and others.

The *Nine Lectures on the First Notions of Moral Philosophy* (1951) have not been translated into English, although this book is Maritain's most noteworthy effort to treat some of the central problems in ethics. The relation of good and value, the final end of man, the concept of moral obligation, and the role of moral sanctions are discussed. Most distinctive in this and later writings of Maritain is his theory of "connatural knowledge." This implies that, in the area of practical philosophy, man's initial judgments are preconceptual and are guided by certain affective inclinations. Consequently, ethical propositions are not purely cognitive but involve certain natural tendencies stemming from human appetites. Maritain professes to find some basis for this teaching in Thomas Aquinas' doctrine on man's natural desire to see God. Many readers think that Gabriel Marcel, the Catholic existentialist, has influenced this tendency in Maritain to stress affectivity in the context of ethical judgment.

In 1960 Maritain published the first volume of his large work entitled *Moral Philosophy.* (The second volume, subtitled "Doctrinal Examination of the Great Problems," has not appeared.) This first volume surveys many of the great theories in the history of ethics, from Socrates to Bergson, but it exhibits two important lacunae: no effort is made to treat the ethics of the Middle Ages—and British ethics is completely ignored! Except for certain tangential remarks and the various criticisms which Maritain offers, this *Moral Philosophy* does not expound his own ethics.

Much more open to the use of scientific data (and so, more naturalistic in the narrow sense) is the ethics of the Austrian Catholic scholar Johannes Messner (1891–). His treatise *Ethics and Facts* (1952) discusses five basic problems or tendencies in human life: the impulse toward sexual satisfaction, toward general happiness, toward freedom in choice and action, toward society, and toward the satisfaction of intellectual curiosity. Messner's openness to empirical information and all types of contemporary ethics is striking. On the last page of this book, he restates his solution to the fact-value, or is-ought, problem. Briefly, Messner does not think that ethical judgments can be verified by a simple appeal to the facts of sense experience. What he does claim, however, is that "the consequences of moral principles" can be tested in the life of each man and of society. For people who would like to know what contemporary Thomistic ethics stands for, reading Johannes nes Messner can help to balance the more theology-oriented thought of Maritain. Interestingly enough, Messner is a priest and Maritain is not.

Natural law ethics still holds the attention of many modern Catholic thinkers, and of a good many who are not Catholics. Of course, there are many variations in the explanations of what natural law is and requires. One prominent Belgian Catholic writer, Jacques Leclercq, quite frankly admits that "natural law has never been systematically studied."[48] In his French study of natural law and sociology (1960),

Leclercq adopts a surprisingly naturalistic and even relativistic view of morality. He admits, for instance, that poor children who grow up in an economically deprived area are almost inevitably driven by the force of circumstances into crime. To talk about what such children "ought to do" is next door to nonsense: their moral freedom is very much limited by the conditions of their lives.[49] There is still a good deal of talk among natural law ethicians about the obligations of human nature, the need to work for an ultimate end, and the importance of somewhat abstract principles, but few advocates of this kind of ethics now claim that its rules are absolute and unchanging (except for very formal imperatives such as: "The good should be done and evil should be avoided"). Nor are there many natural law thinkers today who would suggest that there is a ready-made code of natural moral laws.

Still other forms of naturalism look to studies related to psychology for guidance. Psychoanalysis, psychiatry, and clinical psychology continue to provide both data and problems for contemporary ethics. In France, the Swiss scholar H. Baruk (1897–) has made studies of the relation between delinquency and the level of moral judgment. He is the editor of a new Swiss journal devoted to the relation between science and ethics. The best-known name in the field of psychology and ethics is, of course, that of Erich Fromm (1900–), but his position is complicated by an interest in Marxism which introduces a third factor into an already difficult relationship. Fromm's *Escape from Freedom* (1941) illustrates very well his rather facile ability to make striking generalizations and popular summaries of the moral implications of science. For instance, a negative way of looking at freedom sees it as a separation from mother, a breaking of the ties to immediate community, church, and social caste.[50] Later, he suggests that Protestantism and the growth of capitalism have favored the development of another and more positive freedom in the moral person. Commenting on selfishness, Fromm says: "To love others is a virtue, to love oneself is a sin."[51] It is not always clear how he grounds these insights in the data of psychology.

Man for Himself (1947) is Fromm's most serious attempt to give his ethical views. Chapter four is a famous criticism of the "authoritarian conscience" as the voice of external authority (parents, state, or other authorities) represented within the feelings of the moral agent. This version of moral conscience he identifies with Freud's superego. Although affectively internalized (that is, presented by moral feelings within the person), the authoritarian conscience actually rejects the possibility that the agent himself can *know* what is right or wrong for himself.[52] When it occurs as fear of the authorities such conscience is called bad; when it is the awareness of pleasing the authorities it is good. Psychoanalytic therapy will cure a person of these feelings of guilt and self-approval. In Fromm's ethics, man is a different sort of agent, however, from what he was in the original Freudian psychology. Perhaps the chief difference lies in Fromm's more extended role for human love.

Fromm calls his own position "humanistic" ethics, because he makes *man* the sole judge of his own ethical welfare and sets up man's personal development as the criterion of moral judgment. For Fromm self-interest does not exclude altruism and is not equivalent to selfishness.[53] Distinctive in this version of psychological ethics is Fromm's insistence on the "objectivity" of ethical principles: most psychological approbative ethicians adopt a relativistic and subjectivistic account of ethical judgment but Fromm always insists that the conclusions of his ethics are objective norms, open to public verification by the study of their consequences and by deductive reasoning.[54]

The *Sane Society* (1955) maintains the theme of "humanistic psychoanalysis." Fromm's naturalism is now evident in his discussion of man as an animal and as part of the evolutionary process. But man also rises above "nature" and, as thus separated, displays the functions of reasoning, self-consciousness, and moral conscience. Human needs and consequent rules of behavior become different from those of the brute animal.[55] This is the theme of the "human situation." Fromm now uses the concept of the "total needs of man" as his criterion of moral value: in facing a moral problem one finds that "one answer corresponds more to the total needs of man, and hence is more conducive to the unfolding of his powers and to his happiness than the other." At points, Fromm sounds like a natural law ethician, for he says that ethical judgment must be based on "our knowledge of man's nature and the laws which govern its growth."[56] In this book, also, Fromm points to growth in "creative love" as the positive ideal of higher human aspirations.

A similar approach is found in *The Morality of Self-Interest* (1965) by Robert G. Olson (1924–). Somewhat more insistent than Fromm on the welfare of society as a norm of judgment, Olson openly accuses "prevailing religious views" of undermining the practice of morality.[57] What Olson advocates is "religious naturalism"—a view that combines the left-wing naturalism of Bertrand Russell's "A Free Man's Worship"[58] with the right-wing religious optimism of John Dewey's *A Common Faith* (1934). Religious naturalism, in this formulation, takes a middle path between Russell's pessimism and Dewey's optimism.[59]

One of the leaders of a similar "humanist" movement in ethics is Corliss Lamont (1902–). Much of his effort is given to criticism of traditional religious views (such as the belief in personal immortality) that have some bearing on ethics and the conduct of life. Thus, Lamont's *Humanism as a Philosophy* (1949) has a section devoted to the ethics of this form of thought.[60] As a sort of antidote to religion, humanist ethics is more a semi-popular substitute for religion than a type of academic ethics.

American naturalistic ethics has received quite diverse presentations since the initial impact of John Dewey's instrumentalist ethics was felt in the United States. William R. Dennes (1898–), for instance, has directed attention to a certain basic similarity in the manifestations of human drives and needs in diverse cultures. *Some Dilemmas of Naturalism* (1960) is Dennes' eloquent plea for the reinstating of some sort of objective values as a basis for "oughtness" in the naturalistic enterprise. Sharing such a view is Eliseo Vivas (1901–), who began his career as a naturalist, changed his views, and then wrote a severely critical appraisal of this type of ethics, in *The Moral Life and the Ethical Life* (1950). Calling his own view "axiological realism" (under the influence of Nicolai Hartmann), Vivas complains of the naturalists' insensitivity to the tragic dimensions of twentieth-century existence. In particular, Vivas points to three errors of naturalism: (1) the belief that psychological data are logically prior to the definition of value; (2) the formation of a view of man that is a thin abstraction, paying lip service to scientific facts; and (3) "scientism," the notion that the method of the physicist is primary in philosophy.[61] Naturalistic ethics, according to Vivas, has thus neglected the "primacy of the person."[62] His criticism has been resented by some naturalists but it has elicited new clarifications of the naturalist position in ethics.

A thoughtful and important revision of naturalistic ethics has been propounded in the book *On the*

Knowledge of Good and Evil (1955), by Philip Blair Rice (1904–). His first four chapters review the chief theories of ethics in twentieth-century British and American thought but, the remainder of the book develops Rice's notions on how naturalism and emotivism (on which, see *infra,* Chapter XVII) may be related. Throughout, Rice maintains that value judgments have both descriptive and prescriptive parts. When one expresses a personal "ought," this indicates "the fact that a choice has been made, and serves as a signal to release the action."[63] Without some cognitive content, an ethical judgment is "empty and blind." So, certain "identifying properties" are required and they must be natural rather than nonnatural. Thus, Rice's basic imperative limits one's judgment to a definite state of affairs: "This is good means 'This has the Identifying Property of goodness; do or seek this under conditions C!' "[64] Such a justification of ethical principles appeals to "normativeness" in human nature and to man's goal-seeking tendencies. Rice admits that this is somewhat a priori. Empirically, Rice speaks of the observable development in man of a "second nature" that carries a sense of well-being and is somewhat like conscience. At another point it is called "an operative sense of rationality."[65] In a work such as this, we see a naturalistic approximation of a religiously neutral natural law ethics.

A valiant effort has been made by Abraham Edel (1908–) to work out some special methodology that would enable the naturalistic ethician to convert the data of social science to moral use. His *Ethical Judgment: The Use of Science in Ethics* (1955) and *Method in Ethical Theory* (1963) review the various techniques available in the field of sociology and statistical interpretation. Well aware of the difficulty of moving from *is* to *ought,* Edel has suggested, in a survey of the ethics of naturalism, that the ethician should take as his guidelines certain "fundamental global needs," things like peace, increased world productivity, and freedom for all men.[66] These, according to Edel, cannot be logically or scientifically justified, except in the sense that they are as obviously good as is the conclusion that health is better than sickness.

Taking a more critical approach, Patrick Romanell (1912–) has written an important reformulation of the naturalistic program in ethics, in his book *Toward a Critical Naturalism* (1958). He thinks that Dewey was wrong in requiring ethics to use the same *methods* as the empirical sciences; experimental verification works, according to Romanell, only for questions of fact. It is "not good for ethics proper, which deals with questions of norms or *what-ought-to-be-so.*"[67] Admittedly, the justification of ethical norms is difficult. Traditional utilitarianism has some validity in its study of consequences but Romanell does not see it as a "mature form of naturalistic ethics." Like Vivas, Romanell thinks we need to become more aware of the "tragic" dimensions of modern life, and to pay more attention to the meaning of the human person. These, of course, are ever-present themes in the personalistic and quasi-existential writings of Spanish and Italian philosophers, with which literature both Vivas and Romanell are well acquainted.

There has been some recent tendency to combine the position of British noncognitive ethics (emotivism) with a modified naturalism. Mrs. Philippa R. Foot has published a series of articles in British journals which maintain that there is more validity to naturalistic ethics than is usually granted in present-day England. One of her articles says some things that needed to be said about the rather dogmatic rejection of naturalism in British ethics, from G. E. Moore onward.[68] In reasoning from facts to values, according to this article, some things do "count in favor of a moral conclusion." She seriously questions the whole claim that an evaluative conclusion requires evaluative premises and bluntly asks how such a generalization can be proved. This is Humean heresy, of course, but Mrs. Foot suggests that present-day ethics should take a more careful look at the rules of evidence and should avoid the assumption that there is no possible proof for ethical conclusions.

A modified naturalism is combined with emotive ethics in Paul Edwards' (1923–) *The Logic of Moral Discourse* (1955). While Edwards agrees with the emotivists that moral judgments express attitudes of approval or disapproval, he does not limit them to what is merely subjective. There is an objective side to moral thinking, and moral disputes are capable of resolution, within certain limits, by an appeal to the facts of the case. He feels that it is wrong to exclude, arbitrarily, the observable facts of a moral situation from a reflective attempt to reach ethical conclusions.[69] Thus, moral disagreements are more than verbal disagreements. This is a great concession for an emotivist to make, as we shall see in the next chapter.

In spite of its indefiniteness concerning even pragmatic standards of ethical judgment, and its vulnerability to criticism (see the impressive work of E. M. Adams),[70] naturalistic ethics is a most promising approach to this subject. It is not limited to as narrow a method as British analytic ethics (which we shall examine next); nor is naturalism as antithetic to ethical *theory* as existential ethics seems to be. Doubtless the very narrow, positive-science view of ethics which characterized the work of some naturalists early in this century is too restricted to produce useful results. Yet there is a present anticipation in many quarters that much of the future of this subject rests on the shoulders of those who will perfect the methodology of naturalism.

Chapter XVII
Analytic Ethics

BRITISH PHILOSOPHY IN the twentieth century has emphasized the analysis of language. In part this approach has been a reaction against the idealism of T. H. Green and F. H. Bradley, which was couched in grandiloquent terminology and contained a good many obscure notions. Primarily, language analysis stemmed from a desire for clarity of meaning. A realistic and down-to-earth point of view was advocated early in the century by G. E. Moore and others who felt that philosophy should make its terminology understandable; many questions are hard to answer, because the questions are not clearly expressed. Eventually, many British philosophers came to think that this is the central activity of the philosopher: to examine critically the logic of linguistic discourse and to work out an explanation of how various meanings are best expressed in linguistic communication. This program was reinforced by the rapid growth of modern logics, in which the formal patterns of various types of rigorous thinking were examined. For a time after the publication of Russell and Whitehead's *Principia Mathematica* (1910–1913) hopes were high that an entirely new method of philosophizing would soon be discovered. Some thought that philosophy would eventually be carried on in a special symbolic language; others felt that the ordinary language of human intercourse was quite adequate and, indeed, that it was pregnant with the accumulated wisdom of the ages.

David Hume had set the stage for the application of this program of language analysis to ethics when he complained about the sudden way in which all moral philosophers shift from statements about what *is* so (God is a perfect being; or, man is rational, or immortal, or free) to *ought* statements (a man ought to keep his promises, he ought to avoid injuring others). This change from *is* to *ought,* as Hume saw it, requires justification or, at least, some explanation.[1] There is obviously a language problem here, for the difficulty may be expressed as the unexplained transition from the simple indicative mood to some oblique grammatical mood. How does the moral philosopher move from the indicative (which states facts) to the subjunctive, the optative, the hortatory, and the imperative (which express wishes, aspirations, encouragement, choices, and commands)?

A great deal of British ethics in this century has been devoted to Hume's problem. The consequent preoccupation with the analysis of language, on the part of the British, has been a puzzlement to other Europeans (with the exception of the Scandinavians, who have been speculative grammarians since the Middle Ages and share this interest in linguistic analysis) and it has set British ethicians apart from the main stream of continental thinking on the subject. The British do not "do philosophy" the way that others do. The feeling of exclusion is mutual. Jacques Maritain once remarked concerning the ethics to be examined in this chapter: "Je la tiens pour absurde!"[2]

In most versions of analytic ethics, it has become customary to speak of three levels of practical discourse. This helps one to understand the main thrust of British ethics. There is, first of all, the practical thinking of the agent trying to work out his own personal problems: this is the level of *moral* discourse. Few analytic ethicians write about such problems: the level would be that of advice to the lovelorn. In the second place, there is philosophic thinking about the principles, patterns, and methods of making decisions in regard to moral problems: this reflective examination of practical thinking is the level of *ethical* discourse. Finally, there is the study of what might be called the logic and epistemology of ethics, the consideration of some very general problems which go beyond the scope of ethical reasoning (such as the difference between ethical and nonethical judgments, the nature and relation of freedom to ethics, the comparison of empirical science and ethics): this third level is that of *meta-ethical* discourse.[3] Analytic ethics moves chiefly on the third level, that of meta-ethics. It does not attempt to tell you how to live well, or even to provide the rules whereby you might decide for yourself. Analytic ethics attempts to find and explicate the logic of ethical discourse, but it sometimes goes into ethical (second-level) views and problems, in order to illustrate its points and show its applicability. To work out a complete ethical theory, without first dealing with some of the problems of meta-ethics, would seem to the analyst to be foolish.

At Cambridge University, George Edward Moore (1873–1958) initiated the new approach to philosophy with the publication (in 1903) of his "Refutation of Idealism" and the book entitled *Principa Ethi*ca. It is the first chapter of the latter that has occasioned a sort of Copernican revolution in British ethics. Moore starts off with an ordinary definition of ethics as the study of what is good or bad in human conduct. In the first chapter, he asks what "good" means in such a usage. It cannot be defined, he thinks, because if you say that it is anything else other than good then you are shifting its meaning. To explain this he takes the example of "yellow"—it is also a simple indefinable qualitv. You either know it or you do not know it. Hence, good may be taken to mean some quality that belongs to a thing (this sort of realism of sensory qualities is defended in Moore's "Refutation of Idealism") in much the same way that yellow is known to belong to a thing. Good cannot mean what is pleasurable, or that which promotes happiness, or any such natural property or complex of properties. To identify "good" with a natural property is to commit the "naturalistic fallacy." Moore concludes that in the intrinsic ethical sense "good" is a simple, indefinable quality, which is unique and nonnatural, and which must be known directly in itself. There is a ditterence between this "good in itself" and "good as a means"; the first is the intrinsically good and that is what Moore finds most interesting.

In the Preface to *Principia Ethica* two questions asked by moral philosophers are stated: (1) What kind of things ought to exist for their own sakes? and (2) What kind of actions ought we to perform? The first is treated by Moore in his famous discussion of "good" and that is the part of his ethics that has had the most influence—positive and negative. Many people have failed to note that, in answering the second question, Moore argued that such queries can be treated empirically. To determine what kind of actions we should do, we may certainly consider which ones will produce the most good.[4] As far as he is concerned, all moral laws "are merely statements that certain kinds of actions will have good effects." Hence, in the concrete, each moral duty is the action that will cause more good to exist in the universe than any other alternative.[5]

Moore's shorter *Ethics* (1912) is an obvious attempt to make his views understandable to a larger audience. He devotes two chapters to utilitarianism, then argues that moral judgments are objective in the sense that "one and the same action cannot be both right and wrong," and finally he restates his views on duty and right and wrong actions.[6] Quite plainly, Moore now states that whether an action is right or wrong "*always* depends on its *actual* consequences."[7] While Moore admits that our awareness of duty has a certain element of feeling as well as of cognitive consciousness, he will not accept the claim that an action is right or wrong because "his society has some particular feeling towards actions of that class, nor yet that *some* man has."[8] Such a criterion (as social or subjectively personal attitudes) will not enable one to make an objective moral judgment. As far as Moore's teaching on the meaning of moral good is concerned, the *Ethics* of 1912 only modifies one major point in *Principia Ethi*ca. He is now ready to assert that pleasure is the only "ultimate good" but hastens to add that the ultimate good is different from the intrinsically good. The latter will involve a great deal more than pleasure.[9]

Two points are clarified in Moore's contribution to the volume entitled *The Philosophy of G. E. Moore* (1942). First of all, in his "Reply to My Critics," Moore discusses the pro and con arguments for Charles Stevenson's "emotive" meaning for good (which Moore knew through Stevenson's article in the 1937 issue of

Mind). At first it seems that Moore is going to accept the emotive position but he finally rejects it as untenable.[10] This is in keeping with his earlier decision that feeling alone cannot lead to objectivity in judgment. The second thing that Moore tries to develop in this "Reply" is the meaning of natural and nonnatural, since neither is very clear in his earlier writing. Now he maintains that a natural property must be "descriptive" of the object to which it belongs.[11] However, Moore continues to insist that the nonnatural property ("good") is not perceptible to the senses and is not part of the description of the object.

There are obvious difficulties and lacunae in Moore's account of the meaning of good and right. He seems to need an intuition of the nonnatural quality which is good, yet he cannot accept Sidgwick's theory of intuitionalism. Of what the intrinsic good is a property is never entirely clear: most frequently, conscious states or attitudes are viewed by Moore as the bearers of the quality of being good, but the last chapter of *Principia Ethica* suggests that things like "Art or Nature" are also good in this intrinsic sense. In any event, after reading this epoch-making English treatise, moral philosophers divided into naturalists and nonnaturalists.

In 1910 Bertrand Russell (1872–) wrote a series of articles for various journals, and they have been gathered under the title "The Elements of Ethics." If one has any doubt about the influence of G. E. Moore, he should read this little work of Russell's, for it is a very precise summary of *Principia Ethi*ca. At some later date, Russell wrote a note[12] in which he acknowledged his debt to his Cambridge colleague and added that he had changed his mind about the indefinability of good. Russell also came to think that the only objectivity that good possesses is "political," a notion which he claims to have found in Santayana. In this note Russell adds that he finds it difficult to work out any satisfactory view of ethics and, henceforth, he is refraining from further writing in the field.

Of course, it was not in Russell's temperament to remain silent on ethics for the rest of his life. Although he has not produced a major treatise on moral philosophy, Bertrand Russell has been a vocal member of the Cambridge school. In "A Free Man's Worship" (1903), he had looked upon morality as something imposed by traditional religious beliefs and suggested that "the world of fact, after all, is not good."[13] The free man's worship depends on emancipation from personal desire and a burning passion for eternal things.

By 1935, in the ninth chapter of his *Religion and Science,*[14] Russell is saying that questions of "good" and "values" are beyond the reach of science and, indeed, lie "outside the domain of knowledge." Hence, my statement that something has value is simply an expression of my own emotion. Ethics, in this period of Russell's thought, is an unsuccessful attempt to escape the subjectivity of emotional preferences.[15] It is this type of ethical skepticism that is usually associated with Russell's later views.[16]

The contribution of another Cambridge thinker, Ludwig Wittgenstein (1889–1951), to ethical theory is equally difficult to estimate. Yet he has had an impact in the field. A Viennese, Wittgenstein first (1908) studied engineering at Manchester University in England, read the first volume of *Principia Mathematica,* and went to study philosophy with Russell at Cambridge. The early twenties found him back in Vienna (living for a time on the grounds of a Benedictine monastery and considering entrance into this Catholic religious community) where he had some contacts with Moritz Schlick and other members of the Vienna Circle of positivists but never became a member of their famous group. At this time he published the first German version of the meditations which became known later (1922) as the *Tractatus Logico-Philosophicus.* Returning to Cambridge in 1929 as an advanced student in philosophy, Wittgenstein soon gathered about him a group of admirers and began to function as a master. Something very much like a personality cult developed about him, in which G. E. Moore oddly participated, and this mystique persists, even after Wittgenstein's death. It is necessary to understand this, that many people feel that he was a man of great wisdom, before one can grasp the impact that he had on British philosophy. In 1929 Wittgenstein succeeded Moore as professor of philosophy at Cambridge.

Wittgenstein's writings (along with the work of John Wisdom at Cambridge) are central to the whole movement of language analysis. Unlike many others (including Moore), Wittgenstein did not see words functioning primarily as symbols of things or of internal acts of consciousness. For him, words are more like dominoes with which people play different games. (He is not without responsibility for certain recent notions popularized by Marshall McLuhan to the effect that "communications theory" has to do with the manipulation of media.) As a result, Wittgenstein convinced many English philosophers that the main work of philosophy is simply to get things straight in regard to the use of language.[17] From logical positivism he brought the theory that propositions can be verified only if they are tautologous or if they accord with the direct evidence of sense perception. This makes nonsense of metaphysics, of religion as a creedal institution, and of theoretical ethics.

In his *Tractatus* Wittgenstein had ruled out ethical propositions.[18] At this time (1921), he admitted that one could speak of good and evil in concrete circumstances but he objected to ought-statements as meaningless.[10] So, the *Tractatus* teaches that we may express judgments of value in circumstances which make it sense to do so. For Wittgenstein, this does not suggest that ethics should be equated with the social sciences; indeed, in 1942 he said that he did not consider the description of "the ways and customs of various tribes" to be ethics.[20]

We now have a published (1965) "Lecture on Ethics" which was written and read in English (he was always more at home in German) by Wittgenstein for some group at Cambridge, at some time between September, 1929, and December, 1930. The talk begins with Moore's definition: "Ethics is the general enquiry into what is good."[21] To provide a sort of composite picture of the meaning of ethics, Wittgenstein next offers a series of "synonymous expressions." Thus, ethics is the enquiry into what is valuable; into what is really important; into the meaning of life; into what makes life worth living; or into the right way of living. "If you look at all these phrases you will get a rough idea as to what it is that ethics is concerned with," explains Wittgenstein.[22]

Two ways in which "good" or any value word may be used are now distinguished: trivial or relative usage simply means that something comes up to a predetermined standard (this man is a *good* pianist; this is the *right* road); ethical or absolute usage is different and can be exemplified as follows. I tell a preposterous lie; a listener says to me, "You're behaving like a beast"; I reply, "I know, but I don't want to behave any better"; he answers, "Well, you *ought* to want to behave better." Wittgenstein ends this bit of dialogue with the observation: "Here you have an absolute judgment of value."[23]

All relative judgments of value are mere statements of facts, the lecture adds, but there is no way in which an absolute judgment of value can be grounded in statements of facts. Even an omniscient mind writing a complete factual account of the whole universe and of all men and their states of mind, "would contain nothing that we would call an *ethical* judgment or anything that would logically imply such a judgment." If this suggests that there is no ethics, for Wittgenstein, that is not what he means. Characteristically, he now suggests that if someone could write an ethics "which really was a book on Ethics," this would explode and destroy all the other books in the world! Ethics is supernatural (sic) and our words will only express facts.[24] The remainder of Wittgenstein's talk is devoted to an expansion of the theme of the inexpressibility of ethical judgments. His final summary is this:

Ethics so far as it springs from the desire to say something about the ultimate meaning of life, the absolute good, the absolute valuable, can be no science. What it says does not add to our knowledge in any sense. But it is a document of a tendency in the human mind which I personally cannot help respecting deeply and I would not for my life ridicule it.[25]

One additional point should be noted before we leave Wittgenstein. In his "Notes on Talks with Wittgenstein,"[26] Friedrich Waismann recorded some comments that Wittgenstein made concerning the ethics of Moritz Schlick. Among other things mentioned is Schlick's statement of two conceptions of ethics: (1) the good is good because God wills it; and (2) God wills the good because it is good. Wittgenstein then says that he prefers the first view: "Good is what God orders."[27] This indicates that, in the ultimate analysis, Wittgenstein opted for divine voluntarism. His explanation for this preference is that it cuts off any rationalistic attempt to explain why something is ethically good. "A theory gives me nothing" either in ethics or in religion, adds Wittgenstein, and this is probably his last word on the matter.

What Wittgenstein was saying was not some novel personal discovery that he had made; it was standard teaching in the Vienna Circle. One of the main figures in this group, Rudolf Carnap (1891–), has written very little about ethics, but in *Philosophy and Logical Syntax* (1935) he included a passage which flatly states that the propositions of normative ethics have no "theoretical meaning" and are not scientific (i.e. verifiable) propositions.[28] In another sense, Carnap explained, ethical statements may be taken as expressions of emotions or wishes within the speaker. Furthermore, these feelings may be investigated empirically in psychology, or if you wish, in psychological ethics. Moritz Schlick was another member of the Vienna Circle who held these same views. It is an early version of the emotive meaning of ethical statements.

Not all the philosophers at Cambridge fell victim to the spell of Wittgenstein. Alfred Cyril Ewing (1899–) has staunchly defended intuitional ethics against all opponents, and his *The Definition of Good* (1947) is probably the outstanding book on intuitionism in recent ethics. Ewing rejects (in this work) both naturalism and subjectivism and also dissociates himself from ideal utilitarians (who would otherwise seem his closest allies). That Moore's "intrinsic good" is basic to all ethical theory and that this good is known in itself, objectively, by right-minded people, is assumed throughout by Ewing.[29] Concerning ought-judgments, Ewing is a deontologist with theistic commitments. To say, "A ought to be done," is equivalent to saying, "A is commanded by God."[30] However, Ewing does not agree with Wittgenstein that this is the end of the matter. What God commands is obligatory, Ewing thinks, because God is good. It is "goodness" in the objective and metaphysical sense that is the ground for ethical commands.[31] For many years Ewing has stood almost alone in England in supporting such views. Vigorously attacked by A. J. Ayer (whose own position we shall examine shortly), he has been forced, since 1958 or so, to modify his ethical position. *Second Thoughts in Moral Philosophy* (1959) shows Ewing open to the sort of "reasoning" about duties and goods that is carried on by younger British thinkers in the "good reasons" school. Moreover, in a paper delivered in 1958,[32] Ewing listed naturalism, intuitive nonnaturalism, and subjectivism as the main divisions of contemporary ethics and then suggested that he could see the possibility of fusing the three into a single position. Willing now to abandon the indefinability of "good," Ewing still insists that "ought" is beyond definition. He agrees that ought-judgments express subjective feelings for or against something. However, what he now emphasizes is that ethical judgments must be "rationally justified and indeed imposed on us by the objective situation."[33] Ultimate justification can only be achieved by an appeal to empirical facts. But he still thinks that the main concepts of ethics are nonnatural. Ewing's ethics present many difficulties, even to those who are inclined to agree with his basic assumptions.[34]

Philosophers at Oxford University eventually took up language analysis and made it their own. Central to this movement was John Austin (1911–1960), who became professor of moral philosophy at Oxford in 1952. He published no books during his lifetime and the two issued posthumously *(Philosophical Papers,* 1961; and *How to Do Things with Words,* 1962) are only indirectly related to ethics. Being editions of two series of lectures, they show that Austin made the study of words and meanings central to his work at Oxford. One of his editors, James O. Urmson (1905–) has written *Philosophical Analysis* (1956), which is a valuable study of the whole movement. Urmson's most discussed contribution to ethics is a little paper "On Grading"[35] where he talks about the experienced appraisal of the relative rank of various items (such as apples) in terms of "grading." In discussing various examples of grades, including the academic lists of "excellent, very good, good, fair, etc.," Urmson calls such classifications, into higher and lower, "grading labels." Naturalism, intuitionism, and emotivism (and also subjectivism and utilitarianism)—all have something to contribute, according to Urmson, to the understanding of ethical grading. At least we now know that to describe is one thing and to grade is quite another.[36] Moral choice is much closer to a grading judgment than to a description but no one set of grading criteria for ethics imposes itself. Urmson ends with the suggestion that one might grade ethical criteria from the viewpoint of the ultimate grades, "enlightened and unenlightened." This is a good example of the sort of thing that Oxford analysts do from the "ordinary language" approach to ethics.

Eventually a philosopher from the United States joined the analysts. This was Charles L. Stevenson (1908–), who studied at both Harvard and Cambridge. In 1937 he published an article in *Mind* that was entitled "The Emotive Meaning of Ethical Terms."[37] This is a key statement of the emotive theory of ethics. In it, Stevenson listed three requirements for the meaning of "good" which is important in ethics: (1) it must be open to intelligent disagreement; (2) it must be "magnetic" (the quotation marks are Stevenson's); and (3) it must not be discoverable solely through scientific method. Two main uses of language are distinguished by Stevenson: first, to communicate beliefs and to express our feelings, or create moods (as in poetry); or second, to incite people to actions (as in oratory). The first usage is "descriptive" and the second "dynamic." Emotive meaning (as employed by C. K. Ogden and

I. A. Richards in a noted book on literary meaning)[38] seemed to Stevenson to designate this second usage, as a tendency of words to produce affective responses in people. So his general contention has been that ethical sentences are best understood in terms of such emotive meaning.

Stevenson's first book, *Ethics and Language* (1944), expands this same basic theme, but he now insists that emotive meanings are not devices for pushing aside ethics from the serious consideration of philosophers but are precisely what the ethician must investigate.[39] For Stevenson it is very important to clarify two kinds of disagreement: a) in attitude, b) in belief. Since beliefs about facts may influence attitudes, there is a sense in which ethical statements may be true or false. If one will grant one basic assumption to Stevenson (that "all disagreement in attitude is rooted in disagreement in belief"), then he feels that he may investigate the reasons that lie behind ethical judgments.[40] Discussion of this contention has led to the more recent versions of good reasons ethics, as we shall note later.

Facts and Values, Studies in Ethical Analysis (1963) does not represent a rethinking of Stevenson's ethics but it is a useful collection of periodical articles and addresses (beginning with the *Mind* article of 1937) on emotive ethics and other theories, such as John Dewey's. It is worth noting that the two American philosophers who most affected Stevenson were R. B. Perry and Dewey. Perry's notion of value as any object of any interest is always a point of departure for the presentation of the emotive theory, as Stevenson understands it. From Dewey he took the important distinction between a psychological description of the way in which ethical decisions are made and the authentically ethical study of "how we ought to proceed"[41] Stevenson's Preface (dated 1962) states three questions: one asks for the kind of reasons that can be offered for normative conclusions; a second asks how the problems of normative ethics are different from those of the sciences; the third asks how the key terms used in ethics differ meaningtully rrom scientific terms. As he sees the situation, analytic ethics deals with these three questions.[42]

Contemporary with Stevenson is the British philosopher, Alfred Jules Ayer (1910–), who is also a pioneer in emotive ethics. Ayer knew and shared in the discussions of the men who constituted the Vienna Circle. Besides Schlick and Carnap, this group of logical positivists included Herbert Feigl, Philipp Frank and Kurt Gödel. Interested in applying scientific method to philosophy, they tried to find some one version of this method that would be suitable for all parts of the philosophic enterprise. Furthermore, they insisted on the verification principle: that all scientifically meaningful propositions must be either tautologies or tested by empirical reference to sense data. Ayer shared these views. In the sixth chapter of *Language, Truth, and Logic* (1936), he explained that ethical philosophers put four kinds of propositions into their writings: (1) definitions of ethical terms, (2) descriptions of moral experiences and their causes, (3) exhortations to live virtuously, and (4) some actual ethical judgments. Ayer felt that only the first kind of propositions really belong in ethical philosophy.[43] As he sees it, propositions of type (2) belong in psychology or sociology, type (3) do not belong in any science, and type (4) defy classification but do not belong in ethics. Ayer's main conclusion is that ethics should "make no ethical pronouncements" but should give "an analysis of ethical terms."

At the end of this chapter, Ayer offered to "define the nature of all ethical enquiries." Eventually, it must be recognized that all concepts in ethics are pseudo-concepts and defy analysis, for ethical statements simply express the feelings of the speaker. They are completely subjective and it is nonsense to ask whether they are true.[44] This version of emotive ethics differs from Stevenson's in excluding ethics from the category of philosophical sciences. It goes without saying, that Ayer's subjectivism has been severely criticized—especially by C. E. M. Joad, who summarizes his objections in these words:

> If I consistently believe that the statement, "stealing is wrong," does no more than express an emotion of horror at stealing, it will presently cease to express the emotion of horror. Not to put too fine a point on it, I shall cease to believe that stealing is wrong.[45]

On the other hand, Mary Warnock writes, in her survey of contemporary ethics, that Ayer's formulation of the emotive theory "has great plausibility and appeal for any empiricist."[46]

For the second edition of his book, Ayer wrote in 1946 a rather lengthy new Introduction. Although he defends his earlier views on ethics, he now states that, when actions are called right or wrong in ethics, *types* of actions and not particular actions are the objects under discussion.[47] This is an important point, for it opens Ayer's thinking to the possibility of universal ethical judgments. Also, in regard to Moore's argument that ethical subjectivism would make all disagreement about ethical statements impossible, Ayer now says that disputes about matters of fact are always possible (and he now admits that some ethical statements include factual elements) but no disagreements concerning questions of value are possible. While Ayer still denies theoretical meaning to ethical propositions, he admits that they may have some utility as means to influence the conduct of other persons. But Ayer continues to maintain that ethical expressions cannot be true or false: they simply express one's own feelings.

There has been some polite disagreement among British and American commentators as to who was first in the field of emotive ethics. Actually, neither Ayer nor Stevenson can claim this honor. In 1911 the Swedish philosopher Axel Hägerström (1868–1939) first suggested that ethical norms are not propositions but expressions of feelings, and that they cannot be verified empirically and so are neither true nor false.[48] We have a collection of Hägerström's studies, translated into English by C. D. Broad, under the title *Inquiries into the Nature of Law and Morals* (1953). The second essay, dated 1916, deals with "Law as an Expression of Will"; and the third essay, from 1917, treats "The Notion of Law." In both of these early studies, Hägerström takes an emotive position. Duty, he explains, involves a "feeling" of compulsion similar to what is found in a person who receives a command.[49] To Hägerström, the objectification of value or duty is associated with the "indicative form of expression for the simultaneous association which is present, while the expressions 'value' and 'duty' . . . refer primarily to a background of feelings." Moral imperatives stem from emotions usually expressed in the form: "that must (not) be done." Such commands are not self-explanatory.[50]

Hägerström was not the only Scandinavian to hold such views. Alf Ross was another Swedish philosopher of law who quite early took a positivistic approach to ethical norms.[51] In 1945 Ross was saying that the assertion that an ethical norm is "objectively valid" means that it can be verified (1) by immediate observation, or (2) by its coincidence with a wide experience not possessed by the immediate observer. Statements of value cannot pass these tests, according to Ross, so he concludes that propositions of value and oughtness are unverifiable and without logical meaning. In his book *On Law and Jus-*

tice (the original was published in 1953), Ross says: "To invoke justice is the same thing as banging on the table: an emotional expression which turns one's demand into an absolute postulate."[52] On questions of value, goodness, and duty, Alf Ross is a thorough positivist.

A widely esteemed book written from a modified analytic viewpoint is the *Ethics* (1954) by P. H. Nowell-Smith (1914–), who studied at Oxford. Here, he takes the position that intuitionists have distorted the ethical situation by treating moral discourse as if it were descriptive.[53] Their constant talk about ethical "qualities" is, to say the least, misleading. If they were correct (W. D. Ross is the intuitionist that he has particularly in mind), then ethics would be a sort of implausible empirical psychology.[54]

After his critique of intuitionism, Nowell-Smith proceeds to examine the language in which ethical judgments are expressed. He insists on the major distinction between linguistic expression of *what is* and the expression of what *looks* or *feels* in a certain way.[55] In moral matters it is important to see that what is right may contrast with what seems right. We are asked to notice how adjectives have a variety of usages. A dress may be red, comfortable, and indecent. Red is a D-word, simply descriptive. Comfortable is an A-word, expressing aptness to arouse certain emotions pro or con. Indecent is a G-word, a gerundive usage, capable of inciting to action.[56] Not only single words but also sentences are used in these three ways. Often the usage is indicated by the context in which something is said. Hence, three rules of "contextual implication" are required. First, when a speaker states something in a sentence, it is contextually implied that he believes it to be true. Second, it is contextually implied that a speaker has good reasons for his statement. Third, what a speaker says is assumed to be relevant to the interests of his audience. The importance of these seemingly elementary rules lies in Nowell-Smith's contention that the work of the ethician is "to map the mutual relationships of moral words, sentences, and arguments."[57]

A key chapter is devoted by Nowell-Smith to "Reasons for Choosing."[58] This section has helped to stimulate recent formulations of "good reasons" ethics. Nowell-Smith here agrees with the subjectivists that pro- and con-attitudes are basic motives for decision. An apparent exception is the choice of certain things as means to ends, rather than for their own sake (i.e. because we have a pro-attitude toward the means itself). Sometimes statements of fact function as motives: thus, if asked why I helped a man across a road, I could answer, "Because he is blind." Moreover, aptness sentences may similarly function in lieu of motives. The whole problem of motivation is seen by Nowell-Smith as linguistically complicated. This is not a mere problem of psychology, for he claims that "a motive is not an event or force inside you which functions as an antecedent cause; but is a disposition or tendency to behave in a certain way when certain events occur."[59] Here, too, Nowell-Smith stresses the relevance of the context of a problem, and because of this emphasis his ethics is sometimes called contextualism. Most of the latter part of his book is taken up with the practical problem of bridging the gap between the question, "What is the best thing to do?" and the even more practical query, "What shall I do?"[60]

It is apparent that Nowell-Smith knows a good deal about the history of ethics. Aristotle's theory of "voluntary" action figures prominently in his book, for instance. At one point, after talking about the ethics of the great philosophers, Nowell-Smith takes an almost traditional stand on the importance of human nature. These great philosophers, he says,

> do not seem to have been mistaken in their basic assumptions that the language of obligation is intelligible only in connexion with the language of purpose and choice, that men choose to do what they do because they are what they are, and that moral theories which attempt to exclude all considerations of human nature as it is do not even begin to be moral theories.[61]

A group of moral philosophers working from somewhat the same approach that we have seen in Nowell-Smith take what is now called the "good reasons" way of dealing with ethical questions. Admitting that formal verification of value judgments is not possible, they claim that such rigorous procedure is not necessary. It is enough, they think, to find or state some acceptable practical justification for one's choice or action. Simple intuitionalism is rejected by this group, mainly because they find no convincing evidence for the objectivity of moral properties such as goodness, or meekness, or Tightness. Nor do the good reasons ethicians agree with the emotive analysis of ethical propositions; for if moral utterances merely express emotion and encouragement to others, it is very difficult to explain why so much time and paper have been devoted to ethical discussion. In the positive sense, what the good reasons school has done is to turn the attention of moral philosophers from the job of isolating and describing nonnatural properties to the more concrete task of explaining how one thinks through to a morally good action. They are concerned with somewhat the same type of problem as that which Aristotle handled with his theory of the practical syllogism culminating in a conclusion that is not a judgment but a right action.[62]

A leading exponent of the good reasons view is Stuart Hampshire (1914–) who, like most of the thinkers in this group, represents the Oxford type of ordinary language analysis. Hampshire's article "Fallacies in Moral Philosophy" is a good introduction to the position.[63] In this article, two quite different questions are stated. First, there is the metaethical query: "What are the distinguishing characteristics of sentences expressing moral praise or blame?" (This is somewhat analogous to the work of the art critic in passing judgment on an artist's work.) Second, there is the moral question: "What are the distinguishing characteristics of moral problems as they present themselves to us as practical agents?" (This is somewhat like the problem of the artist facing a job that he proposes to do.) Now, Stuart Hampshire argues that the work of ethics is more closely allied with the second question than with the first.[64] The main problem of ethics then becomes the determination of the procedure of practical deliberation. According to Hampshire, it is not necessary that such practical reasoning be logically conclusive in a strictly demonstrative sense. As he sees it, "All argument is not deduction, and giving reasons in support of a judgment or statement is not necessarily, or even generally, giving logically conclusive reasons."[65] Hampshire's book *Thought and Action* (1959) is thus an expansion of this program of good reasons ethics.

Another advocate of good reasons ethics who now teaches in the United States is Kurt Baier (1917–). In a significant address, "The Meaning of Life," delivered in 1957 at the Australian National University, Baier compared the views of traditional religion concerning the meaning and purpose of human life with the testimony of modern science on the same subject and suggested that the otherworldly attitude of much religious teaching is impractical today. To Baier, at this point, the Christian standard of perfection seemed unjustified.[66] So, what men need to do is to identify some "everyday" standard for making their moral decisions on earth. Baier's book *The Moral Point of View* (1958) is an effort to fill this need, and it has become much discussed and cited in recent ethical writing. In it he criticizes emotivism (which he calls the "impact theory"), because he feels that it implies that there are really no moral questions. Less interested than Hampshire in directing ethical attention to the purely practical problem of translating good thinking into action, Baier strongly supports the idea that moral "reasons" do not have to be proofs. Rather, these reasons involve the presentation of facts which will move a person to act in a certain way.[67]

As we have seen, one part of the good reasons program in ethics involves the rejection of objective, nonnatural moral qualities. This sort of criticism is exemplified in an article by Peter F. Strawson (1919–) entitled "Ethical Intuitionism" (1949), which simply denies that there are such objects. A rather different approach is taken by R. M. Hare (1919–) in his first book, *The Language of Morals* (1952), where he conducts a very general discussion of the difference between the "descriptive" and "prescriptive" use of language. For Hare, value judgments are prescriptive and, if they are calculated to influence action, they must contain some imperative. In turn, moral judgments are one type of value judgments.[68] In a rather abstract way, Hare then tries to show that various logical relations of implication, entailment, consistency, and so on, do hold among imperatives.

In a more recent book, *Freedom and Reason* (1963), Hare stresses three main points that he wished to make in *The Language of Morals.* The first claim is that moral judgments are one type of prescriptive judgments. Second, moral judgments differ from other prescriptive judgments in being universalizable. Third, as we have just seen, there are logical relations between prescriptive judgments, including imperatives.[69] Much of the burden of Hare's second book goes to show that his theory is practical and applicable to problems of action. Thus, the first sentence of his Preface states that the work of ethics "is that of helping us to think better about moral questions by exposing the logical structure of the language in which this thought is expressed." In spite of his new emphasis on the "practicality" of ethics, it is rather obvious that Hare is not as interested in actual moral deliberation as Hampshire. Part II of *Freedom and Reason* is devoted to "Moral Reasoning" but the exposition remains rather abstract.[70]

Many students of contemporary ethics would regard *An Examination of the Place of Reason in Ethics* (1950) by Stephen E. Toulmin (1922–) as the most important exposition of good reasons ethics. Perhaps his most significant contribution is found in the eleventh chapter, where Toulmin describes two kinds of moral reasoning. One type simply takes an accepted moral code, asks whether an action that is in question comes under one of the provisions of this code, and then decides that the action is right or wrong. This gives a good reason for doing or avoiding many actions. However, there is a second kind of practical reasoning that is used where the first is not applicable. In some cases one has to make an estimate of the social value of the consequences of a proposed action. (Here Toulmin is not far removed from Dewey's instrumentalism.) This sort of reasoning does not provide an absolutely certain solution but it is the best thing that one can appeal to in cases of conflict of duties; and in the final analysis, social harmony is the ideal on which such thinking is based.[71] Modestly, Toulmin makes no claim that he thereby discovers *the* right way to act: he merely finds a good reason for so acting. As a consequence it is not always clear whether the good reasons approach is an ethical procedure or a method of moralizing.[72]

Analytic ethics has been chiefly a British phenomenon but it is spreading rapidly in the United States, where many of the previously mentioned moral philosophers are teaching or have taught on a temporary basis. Few native Americans, other than Stevenson, have, as yet, become adept in this kind of ethics. Perhaps John Rawls (1921–), who studied at Oxford, would be a leading exception. Paul Edwards shares many of the views of the analysts but he was originally an Austrian who did a good part of his philosophical studies in Australia, where the method of language analysis has been much cultivated. Canada has not shown much interest in the theory. F. E. Sparshott (Toronto) has published *An Enquiry into Goodness*

(1958), of course, but he is a native of England and a product of Oxford.

It is very difficult to offer any appraisal of the value and the future expectancy of analytic ethics, since, of late years, the efforts of the ordinary language school have branched off in many directions. Perhaps the most helpful thing that one can say is that analytic ethics is productive of more books and articles than any other kind of moral philosophy that is being cultivated in English. This means that its influence has been very extensive in many parts of the world, although it is not important in continental Europe, except for the Scandinavian countries. From the point of view of its content, analytic ethics has contributed most through its insistence on clarity. These twentieth-century British thinkers have continually stressed the supreme importance of understanding the meaning of, and the evidence for, ethical statements. Doubtless, this is a valuable lesson for any kind of ethician.

Chapter XVIII

Existential and Phenomenological Ethics

THE MORAL PHILOSOPHY to be examined in this final chapter is generically different from almost all the theories of ethics that we have considered in this *History*. It is not really a "theory" but an attitude (or set of attitudes) toward human life and its problems. What we are now to review cannot be called an ethics in the formal philosophical sense, yet it is ethically important to contemporary man. Some informed readers would claim that the existential point of view is the key to what is most significant in life today.[1]

We shall consider both existential and phenomenological ethics. Phenomenology is not identical with existentialism but most existentialists use some version of the phenomenological method. From the teaching of Franz Brentano in Vienna, one line of thinkers developed the Austrian theory of values (whose ethics we saw in Chapter XIV) and another group of philosophers worked out the program of phenomenology. In the early phenomenological school, Edmund Husserl was the leading philosopher. For our present purposes we may state the method of phenomenology under two points. First it. starts. with the facts of personal consciousness, with things as objects of knowledge and feeling, and it tries to make a very careful "description" of what is so given in consciousness. Whatever is thus given is a *phenomenon,* something that appears, hence the name phenomenology. Second, it seeks essential knowledge of what is, of the *essence* of the appearance and of the object which thus appears. As Husserl put it, phenomenology "will be nothing less than a theory of essence contained in pure intuition."[2] We have already looked at two great German philosophers who made some use of phenomenological method in their ethics: Max Scheler and Nicolai Hartmann. Indeed, it is quite possible to interpret G. E. Moore's realistic theory of ethical qualities as but another version of phenomenology.[3]

Existentialism, on the other hand, names a reaction against the traditional philosophies which tended to stress *essences* as the most important aspects of reality. Hegel's absolute idealism, a system in which everything is rational, everything has an understandable explanation, everything occurs according to a fixed pattern—this is the bête noire of all existentialists. One might think that existentialists would have no use for phenomenology, since it gives an important place to "essences"; but the point is that phenomenology was also born out of resentment to Hegelianism and is quite opposed to his rationalistic account of immutable essences. Both phenomenology and existentialism also owe a good deal to Descartes's *cogito;* his notion that the human mind is a "thinking thing" *(res cogitans)* in which occur not only cognitions but doubts, affirmations, denials, willings, refusals, imaginations, and perceptions *(Meditationes,* II)—this constitutes a point of departure for both phenomenology and existentialism.

The man who is generally regarded as the first modern existentialist, Søren Kierkegaard (1813–1855), preceded the phenomenological movement. A Danish Protestant with deep religious convictions, Kierkegaard protested against the established Church, the clergy, the professors, academic philosophy (Hegelianism), and all hypocrites. In his short lifetime he wrote a large number of passionate and moving books, most of which have now been put into English. The very titles-*Either/Or* (1843), *Fear and Trembling* (1843), *The Concept of Dread* (1844), *The Sickness unto Death* (1849), *Purity of Heart Is to Will One Thing* (n.d.)—suggest the nonacademic character of his writing.

In *Either/Or,* one of Kierkegaard's first works, we meet the characteristic theme of *choice.* Unlike Hegel, whose dialectic was a both/and affair, Kierkegaard insisted that the moral agent must take sides."Both-and is the way to hell," was his, blunt warning.[4] This is the idea that will run through most subsequent existentialism: to be a free and real person one must commit oneself, make a choice at the major crossroads of life.

Kierkegaard felt that there are three levels at which a person may live: the aesthetic, the ethical, and the religious. The aesthetic man is devoted to cognitive perception, to the cultivation of the life of the senses, even to sensual pleasure. He lives, as it were, on the surface of reality. The ethical man fights and struggles with himself; his victory consists in putting off the lust for pleasure for one hour.[5] In knowing himself he sees his duty. Most of the second part of *Either/Or* is concerned with this ethical level of existence, and Socrates becomes the personification of the ethical person. This, however, is not the highest level of human life. The *Concluding Unscientific Postscript* (1846) deals with how to become a Christian. The truly religious man lives the highest form of existence. Suffering is the keynote here; without some anguish no one can be a religious person. The "leap" of faith brings one to an awareness of subjectivity, and of God's inward presence within the subject. Where Hegel worshiped totality, Kierkegaard revered individuality. "Had I to carve an inscription on my grave I would ask for none other than 'the individual," he wrote in his *Journals.*[6]

It is rather clear, then, that ethics cannot be an ultimate view of life, for Kierkegaard. Sin is more important than any ethical category and if ethics begins to pay attention to sin it goes beyond itself.[7] Like the Neoplatonists and Augustine, Kierkegaard thought that man is balanced on a precarious line between pleasure or suffering, between the lower and the higher; for the life decisions that he must make, academic ethics is of little avail.[8] Whatever the high religious significance of Kierkegaard's message, it must be recognized that he offers us not an ethics but an anti-ethics. Yet he continues to influence existential ethics.

Another personality in the early existentialist school was Friedrich Nietzsche (1844–1900), and he, too, was quite apart from the phenomenological movement. Like Kierkegaard (with whom he had, apparently, no contacts), Nietzsche was violently critical of Church and university. He also hated Hegelianism and other systematic kinds of German idealism, but it is doubtful whether Nietzsche shared the profound religious commitment of Kierkegaard. Some interpreters treat him as an "immoralist," while others defend him as a supporter of a higher morality.[9] Something which makes it more difficult to reach the real Nietzsche is the fact that his sister, Elisabeth Förster-Nietzsche, edited the famous (or infamous) *Will to Power (Der Wille zur Macht),* from fragmentary materials and alleged private conversations, in such a way as to make Friedrich

Nietzsche appear a Nazi before the fact.[10] The expression "will to power" does occur in the authentic writings of Nietzsche but it is not as much emphasized as many commentators think. His ethical views (which are far from orderly) are best seen in *The Birth of Tragedy* (1872), *Thus Spake Zarathustra* (1883), *Beyond Good and Evil* (1886), and *Toward a Genealogy of Morals* (1887).

Coming down from the mountains, Nietzsche's sage, Zarathustra, meets a traditional saint who asks for gifts. Zarathustra hurries away from him, saying within himself: "Could it be possible! This old saint in the forest has not yet heard of it, that *God is dead!*"[11] This theme of the death of God runs through many of Nietzsche's works.[12] What it means is debatable. Possibly Nietzsche is saying that men have lost their contact with, and awareness of, the real God: in this sense, God has died within the awareness of mankind. (As we shall see, this is the way the "death of God" is understood in present-day "process theology.") On the other hand, Nietzsche may be taken as meaning precisely what he says, that there is no God, and this would be the core of his atheism. Following the second interpretation, it is usual to think of Kierkegaard as the pioneer in theistic existentialism and Nietzsche as the originator of the atheistic school.

Another key theme in Nietzsche's ethical outlook is that of the devaluation of all values (*Umwertung aller Werte*). The traditional moralities stemmed from social and religious cultures that distorted man's ethical potential, according to Nietzsche. The Jews, for instance, are blamed for exalting the moral value of slaves and the poor, for saying that the noble virtues of power, courage, and joy are to be replaced with weakness, humility, and suffering as moral ideals.[13] Christianity, too, is an "old ladies' morality." What is needed Nietzsche says, is a reversal an overturning, of this perverted sense of traditional values. The ideal person is the "superman" *(Ubermensch)* who can rise above the petty limitations of ordinary morality. This aristocrat makes his own ethical values. Thus, "one has duties only toward one's equals; toward beings of a lower rank, toward everything foreign to one, one may act as one sees fit, 'as one's heart dictates'—in any event, 'beyond good and evil.'"[14]

To determine what Nietzsche really stands for, in ethics, is not easy. In the *Genealogy of Morals* (which is the best source of information), he attacks and condemns the whole "ascetic" trend of Christian morality. But he also bitterly castigates those "freethinkers and scientists" who are "anti-idealists."[15] In any event, the antitraditionalism of Nietzsche has certainly had its influence on present-day existentialism. Positively, perhaps the chief thing that he had to say was that the ethical person must assert himself, make his own choices, determine his own future.

Feodor Dostoyevsky (1821–1881) is another figure in the prehistory of existentialist ethics. Popularly known as a novelist fascinated with the problem of evil, Dostoyevsky concentrated on this theme, with which academic ethics has, perhaps, been too little concerned. *Crime and Punishment, The Idiot, The Brothers Karamazov,* and Dostoyevsky's other stories have taken their place among the great works in world literature and they all deal with moral evil. For his anticipation of many of the themes of recent existentialism, Dostoyevsky's *Notes from the Underground* (originally published in 1864) is the important source.[16] Dostoyevsky's "hero" is an unlikable, sick, unfortunate man. Fascinated with the "absurdity" of life, every sort of consciousness is for Dostoyevsky, "a disease." He feels some inner "gnawing" as a result of some hateful action and eventually finds a shameful sweetness in it. This anti-hero tends to think of himself as a mouse rather than a man. Yet he prizes his "own free unfettered choice" above all else.[17] Reason satisfies on man's rational side, but it is will that manifests life as a whole, in the view of Dostoyevsky.

Dostoyevsky may not technically be an existentialist; but, if that is the case, then "Part One of *Notes from the Underground* is the best overture for existentialism ever written."[18] The character Raskolnikov, in *Crime and Punishment,* is like Nietzsche's superman in determining his own values, and he commits a completely absurd murder, like a person in a novel by Albert Camus. Thus, we find both the cult of unreason and of absurdity in Dostoyevsky.[19]

It is with Edmund Husserl (1859–1938) that we come to the beginning of the phenomenological school. We have seen that his *Ideas: General Introduction to Pure Phenomenology* (1913) introduced the theory of description of the presentations of consciousness and the notion that these phenomena are essences. He did not work out an ethical theory himself. What he did offer, apart from the phenomenological method, was the suggestion that persons meet and intercommunicate *as subjects:* not simply as one person viewing another as an object but in something of a sharing in the subjective experience of the other person.[20]

Of the followers of Husserl, Max Scheler was the most prominent in the history of ethics. We have looked at his work in Chapter XIV. Apart from Scheler, perhaps Alexander Pfänder (1870–1941) is the outstanding writer on the psychology of moral consciousness. His *Phänomenologie des Wollens* (1930) is a valuable study of ethical motivation. Another member of the Husserlian School, Herbert Spiegelberg (1904–), the well-known historian of the phenomenological movement, has published a set of studies preliminary to a truly phenomenological ethics in his *Gesetz und Sittengesetz. Strukturanalytische und historische Vorstudien zu einer gesetzfreien Ethik* (1935).

Also falling within the broad category of phenomenological ethics was the greatest figure in contemporary Jewish thought, Martin Buber (1878–1965). His main contribution was to have worked out in the setting of religious ethics the implications of intersubjectivity. In this field Buber's most influential writings are *I and Thou* (1923) and *Good and Evil* (English version, 1953). A long-time professor at the Hebrew University in Jerusalem, Buber was respected throughout the world as an outstanding proponent of religious existentialism. Buber's basic contention is that we should leam to know, and feel toward, and treat, the other person as a "Thou" and not as an impersonal "It." As he expressed the point: "Without *It* man cannot live. But he who lives with *It* alone is not a man."[21]

One of the comparable personalities in Christian ethics is Paul Tillich (1886–1965), who is also frequently called an existentialist; but his thought is not that simple. Tillich's background combines Kantian ethics with Christian theology and moral relativism. Among his ethical writings are *The Courage to Be* (1952), *Love, Power, and Justice* (1960), and *Morality and Beyond* (1963). Of course, the *Systematic Theology* (3 vols., 1951–1963) is necessary for the understanding of Tillich's thought, for he is convinced that the attempt to separate theological ethics from philosophical ethics is a bad thing; it smacks of a "double truth" approach.[22] Tillich calls his own position a "theonomous" ethics.

From the philosophical side (here Kant is very important), Tillich insists on an ontological basis for ethical judgment: "There is no answer in ethics without an explicit or implicit assertion about the nature of being."[23] On the religious side, he draws together the act of faith and obedience to the moral imperative: they are but one and the same act.[24] It is in this sense that his ethics is theonomous. Practical understanding is not enough; we must shift from reason to the *person* as the source of ethical decision.[25] Courage is a basic virtue and value. It is a universal self-affirmation, a positive assertion of one's being.

Tillich's existentialism stands out particularly in his rejection of eternal and immutable norms of moral behavior.[26] It is in this spirit that he criticizes rationalized laws and makes love (*agape*) the fundamental ethical principle. This affirmation of the primacy of "love" is the outstanding feature of theistic existential ethics. It is basic to the emphasis on the person-to-person encounter—which is almost as much stressed in Tillich as in Buber. The "other" can only be loved when he is recognized as an "I."[27] The claims of personal morality, religion, and social culture merge and even conflict within the human spirit, producing a situation of ambiguity and tension. With this ambiguous background, the ethical person makes his own resolution of each moral situation.[28] A man's decisions must be the best that he can make but they have only relative value.

Very important in Protestant Christian ethics on the American scene has been the thought of the two Niebuhr brothers. Reinhold Niebuhr (1892–) has the greater popular reputation; indeed, he is one of the few Americans chosen to deliver a series of Gifford Lectures, his *Nature and Destiny of Man* (2 vols., 1941–1943). Other key writings by Reinhold Niebuhr are *Moral Man and Immoral Society* (1932) and *An Independent Christian Ethics* (1935). Both books challenge the absolutism of traditional ethical standards. What the moral life requires, according to Reinhold Niebuhr, is "the nicely calculated less and more of the relatively good and the relatively evil."[29] This might suggest that rational calculation plays a part in this ethics: it does, but reason cannot be the sole base of virtue in man; "his social impulses are more deeply rooted than his rational life."[30] Reinhold Niebuhr is consequently very critical of natural law ethics, opposing it on three grounds: (1) |human reason is too weak to sustain such a theory, (2) human nature is essentially mutable, and (3) love is ethically much more important than law or justice.[31] Here, again, the principíe of love is given primary place in contemporary ethics. In fact, Reinhold Niebuhr says: "There is no possibility of giving any rational definition of a just relation between man and man, and man and nation, or nation and nation, short of a complete love in which each life affirms the interests of the other."[32]

Less insistent than Reinhold on the social obligations of Christian ethics, was his brother, H. Richard Niebuhr (1894–1962). In "The Grace of Doing Nothing,"[33] Richard argued that the good Christian does not have to be a social activist. In his view, the concerns of Christian ethics rise above the constantly changing tensions of everyday life. Reinhold disagrees and insists that good faith requires action.[34] Richard Niebuhr's general ethical view is developed in *The Kingdom of God in America* (1937).

Of recent years, some writers on Protestant Christian ethics have emphasized what is called "situation ethics," or the "new morality." The name and basic concept goes back to a German book *(Gegenwart: eine kritische Ethik)* written in 1928 by Eberhard Grisebach (1880–1945). He simply claimed that there are no longer any universal rules or judgments in modern ethics, that each moral problem is unique and must be decided individually on its own conditions. This approach was called "Situationsethik."[35] During World War II, the Lutheran thinker Dietrich Bonhoeffer (1906–1945) became concerned about Hitlerism, eventually died in a Nazi prison as a result of his inolvement in an attempt to overthrow Hitler. He left a quantity of fragmentary writings in which he protested against the older concepts of Christianity and its legalistic moral teaching. Bonhoeffer's *Ethics* has become the focal point of interest for a new generation of younger Christian ethicians.[36] The central notion in Bonhoeffer's ethics is that a person may do anything (such as killing a dictator), provided he is motivated by Christian love and concern for his fellow men. Each moral decision is unique and general rules are of little avail, as these lines suggest:

> The question of good is posed and is decided in the midst of each definite, yet unconcluded, unique and transient situation of our lives, in the midst of our living relationships with men, things, institutions and powers, in other words in the midst of our historical existence.[37]

Dietrich Bonhoeffer was not an existentialist philosopher, of course, but a religious-minded man trying to find a point of view from which to handle moral problems of immediate concern. He has become a leading figure in situational ethics.

Anglican Bishop John A. Robinson (1919–) has recently come to the fore as an exponent of situation ethics. His book *Honest to God* (1963) is a contribution to the "God is dead" literature which is closely associated with situationism. Robinson's *Christian Morals Today* (1964) insists that Christ's precepts were not legal rules and have no universal validity. Instead, they illustrate various applications of the principle of love in the period in which Christ lived. Hence, in a radical "ethic of the situation," nothing is required except love.[38] In the United States, a very similar approach to Christian ethics is taken in the work of Joseph Fletcher (1905–).

In continental Europe, the leading Catholic exponent of phenomenological existentialism is Gabriel

Marcel (1889–). He has recently repudiated the name "existentialist" but his thought bears more resemblance to this school than to any other. Certainly, he is not a Thomist. Works like *Being and Having* (1935), *Homo Viator* (1944), *The Mystery of Being* (Gifford Lectures, 1949–1950), and *L'Homme problématique* (1955) show that Marcel has always been more interested in the ontology of man than in ethics. However, Marcel does have a good deal to say about the moral point of view; much of it is found in a newly translated work from his youth, *Philosophical Fragments 1904–1914*.[39]

Being opposed to systematic ethics and favoring a morality of love, Marcel directs his criticism against three kinds of ethics. First of all, the rationalistic ethics of the Enlightenment is no longer of any value, for it simply offered an artificial justification of the norms current in its time and milieu. Second, the theory (Hegelianism) that tried to ground an ethics on some concept of an abstract "Mind" is also useless, according to Marcel. Nor is an ethics based on "what science teaches" any better.[40] In the third place, Marcel attacks the sort of ethics that takes "life" as its supreme value. What life, Marcel asks, yours, mine, or life in general? Under this same heading, he condemns the whole program of American naturalistic ethics: it depersonalizes man, he thinks. Marcel has a tremendous capacity for disliking things. He does not care for Sartre's ethics, either. It is mistaken about the character of freedom (this is a foul blow, for Sartre thinks that he is an authority on freedom), and Sartrean existentialism is wrong about the self-creation of values. Moreover, as a strong-minded theist, Marcel resents Sartre's atheism.[41] Characteristically, he says: "I do not choose my values at all, but I *recognize* them and posit my actions in accordance or in contradiction with these values. . . ."[42]

Marcel's view of human freedom is, first of all, based on a denial of other notions of it. Freedom is not "liberty of indifference," it is not a predicate belonging to the essence of man, and it is not an affair of causality. Freedom, as Marcel sees it, is "something that I decide," without any appeal.[43] The very existence of man is his freedom; and, like other philosophers of existence, Marcel stresses the personal encounter, the existential "We" and intersubjectivity.[44] A strong social emphasis adds a new dimension to Marcel's initially personalistic approach to morality. Obligation and moral responsibility are nothing without a being higher than oneself.[45] For Marcel, this being is God. Perhaps Georges Gusdorf (1912–) is the follower who has done most to write an ethics in the pattern of Marcellian thought. His *Traité de l'existence morale* (1949) stresses the immanence of moral values within the existing man, rather than the fact that they may come originally from a transcendent source.

Two great Spanish writers are sometimes called existentialists because they share some of the attitudes toward life and morality that distinguish that school. Miguel de Unamuno (1864–1936) studied German philosophy and came under the strong influence of Kierkegaard, whose thought he introduced into Spanish literature. Unamuno's great work in this field is the *Tragic Sense of Life* (1914). A giant protest against the pretensions of science and reason, it presents life, immortality, and faith as Unamuno's prime values. He thought that reason kills them. Long before other existentialists began their twentieth-century attack on rationalism, Unamuno was the apostle of irrationalism.

The second of these Spanish thinkers was José Ortega y Gasset (1883–1955), also a student of German philosophy, under the value philosopher Georg Simmel. Nietzsche appealed to Ortega and exerted a considerable influence on his writing. In Ortega's brand of personalistic idealism, "life" is all-important. In spite of his professed respect for traditional ethical values, Ortega held that the political hero (who has some of the attributes of the *Übermensch)* is not subject to the ordinary norms of ethical judgment. It is on this score that he is compared with existentialist moralists, but his chief impact has been on the philosophy of history and politics. In this area he has opposed totalitarianism.

The most formal contribution to phenomenological ethics that has been published in contemporary France is the *Eléments pour une éthique* (1962) by Jean Nabert (1881–1960). Unfortunately, he is little known outside France.[46] A very sincere Protestant, religious values were quite important to Nabert. His "ethics" is not, however, a moralizing treatise but a conscious account of man's effort to realize his will to exist on a human level. Thus, Nabert offers a phenomenological "description" of a person's experience of moral failure *("l'experience de la faute"),* the awareness of being blocked *("l'échec"),* and the profound feeling of solitude.[47] This leads Nabert to a reflection on the meaning of moral consciousness and the development of an awareness of values. A long third section of Nabert's book deals with various aspects of personal existence, its teleological tendencies, its oughtness *("le devoir de l'existence"),* its virtues viewed as spiritual forms, and its sources of religious veneration.[48]

Nabert's suggestive theory of values (in his fifth chapter) is close on many points to the position of Marcel. Both men regard freedom as the stuff of personal existence, and there is no immutability in ethical matters. As Nabert expresses the situation, toward the end of his book:

> The moral and religious categories by which we judge, the values whereby we appreciate, the rules themselves which we obey, in the most impersonal guise that they assume and with all their air of permanence—must be referred to highly contingent starting-points; they are contingent by virtue of the act which

> encompasses them, not by the principle which they produce.[49]

Much the best-known French existentialist, of course, is Jean Paul Sartre (1905–). A powerful writer who has used plays and novels, as well as philosophical writings, to put across his point, Sartre knows the technique of German phenomenology. Moreover, his *Outline of a Theory of the Emotions* (1939) shows his undoubted ability as a descriptive psychologist. *Being and Nothingness* (1943) is the basic work, however, both for the understanding of his ontology of man and for the foundations of his ethical views. *Saint Genet* (1952) is important for certain comments which it offers concerning the possibility of an ethics. Many people looked forward to his *Critique de la raison dialectique* (1960), in the expectation that it might be his long-awaited treatise on ethics. It is not that; at least in its first volume (the only one yet published), it is more concerned with Marxism than with ethics.

Two kinds of being are distinguished by Sartre: *être en-soi,* to be in-itself, is the reality of a static *thing,* the being of anything inanimate, with no openness to be anything else; and *être pour-soi,* which is to be consciously, to be human in the sense that the subject is able to be separated from himself, to be pregnant with dynamic potentiality.[50] It will be evident why "ambiguity" is a constant theme in Sartre: he feels that there are always internal and contrary tensions implicit in the human person.

Yet this radical contingency of human consciousness is its very existence, for Sartre. There is no human nature, or essence of man, to limit the openness of being *pour-soi.* This contingency is, of course, man's freedom.[51] To the extent that there is a Sartrean ethics, it consists in the exigency to actualize one's freedom. Hence, the ground of all moral values is in freedom.[52] The great virtue, according to Sartre, is "authenticity": a kind of honesty and courage. The authentic individual faces things which the in-authentic (and bad) person is afraid to face.[53] Not a mere attitude, Sartre's "authenticity" involves action and the making of free decisions. The worst vice, in Sartre" estimation, is "bad faith." It consists in the individual's negation of his own freedom, a failure to be a man.[54] The notion of intersubjectivity is also stressed by Sartre, as in all versions of phenomenological ethics. In his relations with other persons, a man comes to be a developed person; their awareness of him is a part of his own openness as a person. Some sort of intercommunion with others is implied in the very meaning of consciousness.

Ethics is described in *Saint Genet*[55] as a "synthesis of good and evil," a Hegelian *Aufhebung.* To have a wholly good person, Sartre feels, would involve a separation of evil from the good, and this would result in an "alienation" of man. There is, then, something oddly impossible about a Sartrean ethics; for, an "ethic of praxis" would find the ego defined only by the "complex of its own decisions."[56] Clearly, such an ethics would be unteachable. Every value contains an inner contradiction: first, a tendency toward being incorporated into existence; and second, a need to stand beyond such realization. Here, again, we have an ineradicable ambiguity within value itself. "The moral agent can satisfy this twofold exigency only, so it seems, by giving his life to realize the ethical imperative and by dying as a result of not having achieved his goal." Obviously, it is not easy to be a Sartrean hero.

In *Critique de la raison dialectique* Sartre criticizes contemporary Marxists (notably the French theoretician, Pierre Naville) for their failure to develop the implications of Karl Marx's original teachings—and for their positive distortions of Marxism. Among other things, he accuses them of turning to an extreme materialism, because they have not understood how a dialectic can take place within the domain of consciousness or thought.[57] Sartre obviously thinks that his own view of consciousness is much better, but his accusation of crude materialism has been violently resented by more orthodox Marxists. Yet Sartre keeps on insisting that he is a true Marxist, in his social and political thought. But the French Marxists want nothing to do with him. A large part of the *Critique* is given over to an elaborate discussion of dialectic in history and he promises to finish off this question in a second volume.[58] What is quite evident is that this book does little to advance the ethical position of Sartre.

Some writers consider that Simone de Beauvoir (1908–) has produced the key work in existential ethics of the French school, in her *Ethics of Ambiguity* (1946). That judgment is somewhat exaggerated.[59] We find in her book much the same set of notions that have just been seen in Sartre. Ethics, she says, is "the triumph of freedom over facticity."[60] Here, as in Sartre, "facticity" means the contingency of being for-itself.[61] Admittedly, Simone de Beauvoir makes it very clear how the Sartrean man is forced by this very odd notion of freedom to deny God. An existing God, as she explains, would set limits to man's radical freedom to create his own values. Consequently, she agrees with Sartre's reading of Kant, that any law that is not self-imposed is opposed to man's own dignity.[62]

There can be no definite judgments (and certainly no absolute ones) in Simone de Beauvoir's ethics. She discusses, for instance, the admitted violence practiced against many people under Stalinism in the Soviet Union. This was not necessarily evil, she argues, because what was done helped to alleviate the suffering of other people.[63] However, at other places she vehemently supports the value of respect for other people and their freedom. This has the status of an ethical imperative: "Such a law imposes limits upon action and at the same time immediately gives it a content."[64] For the ethics of ambiguity the great vice is seriousness. "*Le sérieux*" (the eager-beaver) is a man who prizes moral security, will take no chances, tries to do all the "right things." His attitude is the antithesis of conscious freedom.[65]

Two French phenomenologists with impeccable academic reputations have also made a peripheral contribution to ethics. One is Maurice Merleau-Ponty (1907–1961), who was most interested in the psychology and ontology of man. His *Sens et non-sens* contains material on the fringe of ethics and theology; and the book *Humanisme et Terreur* is a series of essays on the philosophy of history and Communism, in which Merleau-Ponty works out a theory of the *conscience engagée* (involved consciousness) that represents an advance beyond Sartre.[66] The other French thinker, Paul Ricoeur (1910–), used the phenomenological method in his *Philosophie de la volonté* (1950–1960) to develop a new approach to the affective side of man's nature. The second volume *(Finitude et culpabilité)* may be the prelude to a not yet developed phenomenological ethics.

Associated with Sartre and Simone de Beauvoir in the editing of a journal but eventually alienated as a result of a disagreement over Sartre's interests in Communism, Albert Camus (1913–1960) had a key role in the popularizing of existentialism. Camus's *Myth of Sisyphus* (1942) and *The Rebel: an Essay on Man in Revolt* (1951) are important parts of the literature of this movement. It is hardly possible to summarize what Camus represented in the field of ethical thinking, because his message is merely suggested in novels and plays. Quite opposed to systematic and rational thinking, Camus shows in his novels the complete absurdity of life. He certainly felt that academic ethics solves no practical problems. Yet Camus had a tremendous concern for people and a certain personal sincerity manifested in every line that he wrote.

In the United States, existentialism has had few adherents. One important book on phenomenological ethics (with no existentialist affiliations) has been published by Maurice Mandelbaum (1908–). His *Phenomenology of Moral Experience* (1955) is a scholarly effort which has a background in the thought of Max Scheler and some of the British ethicians, such as W. D. Ross and Prichard. Starting with a description of four approaches to ethics—the metaphysical, psychological, sociological, and phenomenological—Mandelbaum explains that only the last employs "a direct examination of the data of men's moral consciousness."[67] Hence, his version of the phenomenological method is eductive rather than deductive: the answers to the problems of ethics are to be "educed from, and verified by, a careful and direct examination of individual moral judgments."[68]

Objecting forcefully to the separation of the normative and descriptive disciplines that has developed in much of recent ethics, Mandelbaum endeavors to bridge the gap by insisting on the generic character of moral judgments. In other words, he tried to restore the status of universal meanings in ethics.[69] From the fact that men do make moral judgments Mandelbaum takes his start and distinguishes three levels of such conclusions. First, there are direct judgments of the moral rightness or wrongness of the conduct of an individual person. Second, there are judgments of rightness or wrongness, made at one remove from the concrete. Third, come judgments of moral worth, concerned with specific traits of character or with the total character of a person.[70] A whole later section of Mandelbaum's book treats virtues, vices, and moral character in a fashion similar to what one would find in Max Scheler or Nicolai Hartmann.

One of the more suggestive parts of Mandelbaum's ethics comes with his explanation of what he regards as universally accepted principles of moral judgment. It is here that he, quite obviously, tries to return to the tradition of universal rules, calling his first principle that of the "primacy of the facts." Mandelbaum states it as follows: "To be valid, the predication of a moral quality must arise as a direct response to the apprehension of the nonmoral properties which the object which is praised or blamed actually possesses."[71] This is clearly a move in the direction of naturalism. Mandelbaum's second rule is the "principle of universality." Directed against relativism, it reads: "To be valid, a moral judgment must make an assertion which is not restricted by a reference to the conditions under which the judgment was made."[72] Finally, Mandelbaum's principle of ultimacy states: "Any moral judgment which is believed to be valid is incorrigible, and any incorrigible moral judgment must be acknowledged to be binding upon thought and upon action." In his final pages, Mandelbaum offers an impressive demonstration of the use of these ethical principles in actual practice.[73] This effort of Mandelbaum's represents something of a return to the rational procedures of an earlier age but it is hardly typical of twentieth-century ethics in the sixties.

At the end of this history of ethical theories, in which an attempt has been made to let each type of ethics speak for itself without conscious criticism from the writer, a word of final appraisal may be permitted. Clearly, many of the older and more traditional kinds of ethics have now lost their appeal for the philosophers of our time. Of course, many people are still writing and teaching solid, but unremarkable, versions of the various theories seen in the earlier pages of this survey. These, however, do not represent the spirit of strictly contemporary ethics, in which I see only three distinct approaches: naturalism, linguistic analysis, and existentialism.

Of these three, existentialism really rejects theoretical ethics, and language analysis offers no ethical content other than the moral attitudes of the British gentleman who still remembers the period of Queen Victoria. Neither a distinctive new method nor a new set of ethical judgments is forthcoming from these two schools. This leaves us with naturalism as a possible base for an ethics of the future. I do not mean that extreme position which entirely rejects the supernatural and relies on hard science only. There would seem to be some latent possibilities in a broad theory that ethical judgments might find their justification in the experienced facts of human life.

What is needed now is some spark of genius to provide a revised method of making such a reflective justification, perhaps not an entirely new method but one that will keep us open to empirical data and the dimensions of human personality, without shutting us off from the exercise of reason and the light of intuitive understanding. Some people think that "love" will take care of all of man's problems. I do not share this notion. Love is, indeed, a great virtue, but without intelligent reflection and clear factual information love easily degenerates into a dark morass of brute feeling. And I am not willing to accept that sort of thing as ethics.

Mark Twain once wrote: "To be good is noble, but to show others how to be good is nobler—and no trouble." To my mind, he was at least half right: it is an important undertaking to try to show others how to live well. Sometimes people who work at ethics forget that this is what they are really trying to do. Where Mark Twain was wrong, in my estimation, was in saying that such work is no trouble. On the contrary, ethics involves a great deal of trouble, and perhaps this survey will, at least, establish that point.

Notes

Chapter X

Utilitarian and Subjectivist Ethics in Britain

1. Cf. R. B. Brandt, *Ethical Theory* (Englewood Cliffs, N.J., Prentice-Hall, 1959), 355–56, where various divisions of utilitarianism are discussed.
2. A. C. Garnett, *Ethics* (New York: Ronald Press, 1960), 159.
3. Cf. Mary Warnock, "Introduction" to Mill, *Utilitarianism* (New York: Meridian, 1962), 9.
4. *The Methods of Ethics* (New York: Dover, 1966), 96.
5. Cumberland, *Treatise of the Laws of Nature,* in Rand, *Classical Moralists,* 248.
6. Ibid., I, 4; in Rand, 249.
7. Henry Áiken, *Hume's Moral and Political Philosophy,* 44.
8. *History of Ethics,* 205.
9. Hume, *Treatise on Human Nature*, I, 4, 6; ed. Selby-Bigge, 261.

10. Ibid., III, 1; ed. Selby-Bigge, 563.
11. For a more extended analysis of the argument of the *Treatise,* see Bonar, *Moral Sense,* 121.
12. *Treatise,* II, 1, 11; ed. Selby-Bigge, 320.
13. Ibid., III, 3, 1; ed. Selby-Bigge, 576.
14. Ibid., III, 1, 1; ed. Selby-Bigge, 541.
15. *Enquiry concerning the Principles of Morals* III, 1; in *Hume Selections,* ed. C. W. Hendel (New York: Scribner's, 1927), 203.
16. *Enquiry,* III, 6, 1; in Hendel, 228.
17. Price, *Review,* 3; in Selby-Bigge, *British Moralists,* II, 123.
18. *Review,* 2; in Selby-Bigge, II, 120.
19. See, for instance, W. H. Werkmeister, *Theories of Ethics,* 367–72.
20. Adam Smith, *Theory of Moral Sentiments,* Pt. I; in Selby-Bigge, I, 257–84.
21. *Theory,* III, 1–4; in Selby-Bigge, I, 297–306.
22. Cf. Bonar, *Moral Sense,* 175.
23. Reid, *Inquiry into the Human Mind,* 7, 4; ed. Edinburgh, 1819, 394.
24. *Essays on the Powers of the Human Mind,* ed. Edinburgh, 1819, II, 338.
25. See Reid's essay, "The Moral Faculty and the Principles of Morals," reprinted in Edwards and Pap, *A Modern Introduction to Philosophy* (New York: Free Press, 1965), 288–96.
26. Ferguson, *Philosophy of the Active and Moral Powers,* 2, 5, 1; in *Collected Works* (Edinburgh, 1854), VI, 299.
27. Cf. R. B. Perry, *Philosophy of the Recent Past* (New York: Scribner's, 1926), 17.

28. J. Stanlis, *Edmund Burke and the Natural Law* (Ann Arbor: University of Michigan Press, 1965).
29. Burke, *Philosophical Inquiry,* 2nd. ed. (London, 1757), 25–26.
30. Burke, *An Appeal from the New to the Old Whigs* (London, 1891), 19.
31. Cf. H. E. Cushman, *A Beginner's History of Philosophy* (Boston: Houghton Mifflin, 1920), II, 359.
32. Paley, *Principles,* II, 6.
33. See *Mill on Bentham,* in *Utilitarianism,* ed. Mary Warnock, 81.
34. Stuart Hampshire, "Fallacies in Moral Philosophy," *Mind,* LVIII (1949), 473–75.
35. For this text from Blackstone's *Commentaries,* see A. V. Dicey, *Introduction to the Study of the Law of the Constitution* (London: Macmillan, 1939), 62.
36. Bentham, *Fragment,* 54; in *Utilitarianism,* ed. Mary Warnock, 13.
37. Bentham, *Introduction to the Principles of Morals,* 1, 3; in Selby-Bigge, I, 340.
38. Helvétius, *De l'Esprit* (Paris, 1758); Essay II is on *Probity;* for a trans., see Rand, *Classical Moralists,* 471–75.
39. Helvétius, *De l'Homme* (Paris, 1772); the trans. by William Hooper (1777) is reprinted in part in R. E. Dewey *et al, Problems of Ethics* (New York: Macmillan, 1961), 8.
40. *Mill on Bentham,* in *Utilitarianism,* ed. Warnock, 123.
41. For this footnote, see *Utilitarianism,* ed. Warnock, 33.
42. This is the judgment of Sidgwick, *History of Ethics,* 272.

43. Mary Warnock, "Introduction" to *Utilitarianism,* 22–23.
44. Richard Whateley, *Paley's Moral Philosophy* (London, 1859).
45. Newman, *Grammar of Assent,* 4, 2; in *The Essential Newman,* ed. V. F. Blehl (New York: Mentor, 1963), 290–95.
46. Newman, *Fifteen Sermons*, in *The Essential Newman*, 320–21.
47. *Grammar of Assent,* 9; in *The Essential Newman,* 327. Martineau, *Types of Ethical Theory,* II, 29.
48. Martineao, Study *of Religion,* 2 vols. (Oxford: Clarendon Press, 1888).
49. Mill, *Logic of the Moral Sciences,* ed. H. M. Magid (New York: Bobbs-Merrill, 1965), 27.
50. Ibid., . 37–53.
51. Ibid., 145.
52. Ibid., 147.
53. Austin, *The Province of Jurisprudence Determined,* lect. II; in *Utilitarianism,* ed. Warnock, 325; see also 23.
54. Mill, *Utilitarianism, 1;* ed. Warnock, 252.
55. Ibid., 257.
56. Ibid., 279.
57. Ibid., 307–08.
58. Sidgwick, *The Methods of Ethics* (London: Macmillan, 1874; reprinted,, New York: Dover, 1966); see 83–87.
59. Ibid., 381–82.

Chapter XI

German Idealistic Ethics

1. Fichte, *Vocation of Man,* III; ed. R. M. Chisholm (New York: Liberal Arts Press, 1956), 106.

2. Ibid., 93–95.
3. Fichte, *System der Sittenlehre,* in the Trans. of A. E. Kroeger, in Rand, *Classical Moralists,* 574.
4. Fichte, *The Nature of the Scholar,* lectures delivered in 1805, lect. VII; see J. Collins, *Modem European Philosophy,* 563.
5. Frank Thilly and Ledger Wood, *A History of Philosophy,* 3rd ed. (New York: Holt, 1957), 475.
6. Schleiermacher, *Monologues,* trans. H. L. Friess (Chicago: Open Court, 1928); the second monologue is reprinted in Robinson, *Anthology of Modern Philosophy* (New York: Crowell, 1931), 523–36.
7. Cf. H. A. Reyburn, *The Ethical Theory of Hegel* (Oxford: Clarendon Press, 1921), xiii.
8. See Hegel, *Early Theological Writings,* trans. T. M. Knox (Chicago: University of Chicago Press, 1948), 205–09.
9. Hegel, *Phenomenology of Mind,* trans. J. Baillie (London: Macmillan, 1931), 149–78: here, the dialectic is applied to sense certainty and perception.
10. Cf. Reyburn, op. cit., 76.
11. *Phenomenology of Mind,* trans. Baillie, 625–26.
12. Hegel, *Philosophy of Right,* sec. 44; these section nos. are retained in the Dyde and Knox versions, and also in Sterrett's digest.
13. Ibid., sec. 75.
14. Ibid., sec. 82.
15. See the Baillie trans., 381.
16. *Philosophy of Right,* secs. 142–57.
17. Ibid., sec. 142; trans. S. W. Dyde, reprinted in Rand, *Classical Moralists,* 605.
18. Ibid., sec. 137; see Reyburn's comments, op. cit., 173–74.

19. Eugen Fink, *Sein, Wahrheit, Welt* (The Hague: Nijhoff, 1958), 47, denies such an influence; for the opposed view, see E. Gilson, T. Langan, and A. Maurer, *Recent Philosophy: Hegel to the Present* (New York: Random House, 1966), 679.
20. *Philosophy of Right,* sec. 152; trans. Dyde, in Rand, 608–09.
21. Ibid., sec. 158.
22. Hegel, *Philosophy of History,* trans. J. Sibree (New York: Willey, 1900), 47.
23. Cf. W. T. Stace, *The Philosophy of Hegel* (New York: Dover, 1955), 374–438; and the whole argument in Sidney Hook, *From Hegel to Marx* (New York: Reynal & Hitchcock, 1936; reprinted, New York: Humanities Press, 1950).
24. Herbart, *Textbook in Psychology,* trans. M. K. Smith (New York: Appleton, 1891), III, 1; Robinson, op. cit., 635.
25. Ibid., trans. Smith; in Robinson, 634.
26. See the appraisal in Thilly and Wood, *History of Philosophy,* 495.
27. Beneke, *Grundlinien des natürlichen Systems der praktischen Philosophie* (Berlin, 1837), I 3: partly Trans. in Rand, *Classical Moralists,* 634.
28. Schelling, *Philosophische Untersuchungen über das Wesen der menschlichen Freiheit,* in *Werke* (München: Hueber, 1928), IV, 244.
29. See Bourke, *Will in Western Thought,* 205–08, for an extended analysis of this theory of volition.
30. Schopenhauer, *The World as Will and Idea,* IV, 54.
31. Ibid., sec. 55.
32. Ibid., sec. 58.

33. Ibid., sec. 66.
34. Ibid., sec. 71; trans. R. B. Haldane and J. Kemp (London: Kegan Paul, Trench, 1883–86).
35. Schopenhauer, *Essay on the Freedom of the Will,* trans. K. Kolenda (New York: Liberal Arts Press, 1960), 93.
36. Ibid., 97.
37. Schopenhauer, *On the Basis of Morality,* trans. E. F. J. Payne (New York: Library of Liberal Arts, 1965), 49–115; his discussion of Fichte's ethics is on 115–19.
38. Ibid., in Payne, 144.
39. Ibid., 204.
40. Stirner's views are well outlined in Narcyz Lubnicki, "L'Homme et la valeur," *Memorias del XIII Congreso de Filosofia* VII (Mexico, 1964), 308 ff.
41. Lotze, *Microcosmus,* III, 1; trans. E. Hamilton and E. E. C. Jones (New York: Scribner's, 1887), I, 286–87.
42. Ibid., IX, 4, 2.

Chapter XII

Franco-Latin Spiritistic Ethics

1. See the outline of Brownson's views in Gilson-Langan-Maurer, *Recent Philosophy,* 567–87.
2. For this objectivism in French idealism consult Gilson-Langan, *Modern Philosophy* (New York: Random House, 1963), 99.
3. Malebranche, *A Treatise of Morality,* trans. James Shipton, in Rand, *Classical Moralists,* 286.
4. Ibid., 293.
5. Cf. Gilson-Langan, *Modern Philosophy,* 104–06.
6. These words of Henri Gouhier are quoted in Gilson-Langan-Maurer, *Recent Philosophy,* 182.

7. Maine de Biran, *Fondements de la psychologie;* see the text in H. Gouhier, *Oeuvres choisies de Maine de Biran* (Paris: Aubier, 1942), 87.
8. Maine de Biran, *Nouveaux essays d'anthropologie,* in *Oeuvres,* XIV, 333.
9. Ibid., 275; for more data on this voluntarism, see Bourke, *Will in Western Thought,* 94.
10. *Nouveaux essais;* English version from Gilson-Langan-Maurer, *Recent Philosophy,* 189–90.
11. Ibid., 236.
12. Rosmini, *The Origin of Ideas* (London: Kegan Paul, 1886), pars. 428–33.
13. Gilson-Langan-Maurer, *Recent Philosophy,* 251.
14. Gioberti, *Delia protologia,* ed. G. Balsamo-Crivelli (Torino: Paravia, 1924), 103–07.
15. Gioberti, *Del buono,* 8; in edition of Bruxelles: Méline, 1848, 387–88.
16. For this nationalism, see Gilson-Langan-Maurer, *Recent Philosophy,* 255–61.
17. Renouvier, *Future of Science,* Trans. by A. D. Vandam and C. B. Pitman (London: Chapman and Hall, 1891); this section is reprinted in Marsak, *French Philosophers,* 362.
18. Ibid., in Marsak, 369.
19. For a summary of Taine's critique of Cousin, see Gilson-Langan-Maurer, *Recent Philosophy,* 758.
20. Guyau, *L'Irreligion de l'avenir* (Paris: Alcan, 1887), IX.
21. Ibid., 346.
22. Ibid., 350.
23. This theory is developed throughout Boutroux, *De la contingence des lois de la nature* (Paris: Germer-Baillière, 1874).

24. Boutroux, "La psychologie du Mysticisme," in Jean Baruzi, *Philosophes et savants français* (Paris: Alcan, 1926), I, 60–61.
25. Bergson, *L'Evolution Créatrice* (Paris: Alcan, 1907), 270.
26. Bergson, *Les deux sources de la morale et de la religion* (Paris: Alcan, 1932), 5.
27. Ibid., 25.
28. Ibid., 287–88.
29. Ibid., 243; in the English version by Audra and Brereton, 227–28.
30. This is the judgment of E. Gilson, in *Recent Philosophy,* 316.
31. Brunschvicg, *Philosophie de l'esprit* (Paris: Presses Universitaires, 1949), Leçon 16.
32. Brunschvicg, *La raison et la religion* (Paris: Presses Universitaires, 1939), 74.
33. Cf. Roger Mehl, "Situation de la philosophie religieuse en France," in *L'Activité philosophique,* ed. M. Farber, II, 273–76.
34. Colin Smith, *Contemporary French Philosophy* (London: Methuen, 1964), 107.
35. Le Senne's essay, "On the Philosophy of the Spirit," is available in English in *Philosophic Thought in France and the U.S.,* ed. M. Farber, 103–20.
36. Le Senne, *Le devoir* (Paris: Presses Universitaires, 1930), 84.
37. Ibid., 270.
38. Le Senne. *Traité de morale generate* (Paris: Presses Universitaires, 1942), 685–711.
39. Ibid., 702.
40. Cf. Colin Smith, op. cit., 202.

41. Ibid., 48.
42. See Francisco Romero, "Deustua, Kom, Molina y Vaz Ferreira, en paralelo," *Revista Mexicana de Filosofia*, I (1958), 19–21.
43. Vasconcelos, *Etica* (Madrid: Aguilar, 1932), 20–26.
44. Vasconcelos, "The Aesthetic Development of Creation," *Philosophy and Phenomenological Research,* IX (1949), 463.
45. Vasconcelos, *Raza Cosmica* (Mexico: Espasa, 1948), 38.
46. A portion of Zubiri's *Naturaleza, Historia, Dios* (Madrid: Editorial Nacional, 1944), has been digested in English as "Socrates and Greek Wisdom," *Thomist,* VII (1944), 40–45.
47. *Naturaleza, Historia, Dios,* 369.
48. Ibid., 370.
49. See Ferrater Mora, José, "The Philosophy of Xavier Zubiri," in *European Philosophy Today,* ed. George Kline (Chicago: Quadrangle Books, 1965), 24–25.
50. Sciacca, "La Struttura della libertà nella 'costituzione' ontologica del'uomo," in *Memorias del XIII Congreso Internacional de Filosofia,* I (Mexico, 1963), 26–27, trans. Bourke.

Chapter XIII

Societal Ethics in Europe

1. Vico, *Politics and Morals,* trans. S. J. Castiglione (New York: Philosophical Library, 1945), 65.
2. *De universi juris uno principio,* I, 13.
3. Ibid., axioms 14–16.
4. Deschamps, *Le vrai système* (Paris: Alcan, 1939), 83–84.

5. Deschamps, *La voix de la raison* (Bruxelles, 1770), 11–15.
6. Cf. Crocker., *Nature and Culture,* 117–18.
7. *Histoire de Juliette,* IV, 178–79; the Trans. is from Crocker, ibid., 198.
8. Condorcet, *The Progress of the Human Mind,* see the "Introduction," printed in L. M. Marsak, *French Philosophers,* 266–69.
9. See Marsak, ibid., 279–81.
10. Condorcet's Letter I, m Marsak, 308.
11. Ibid., 322.
12. On the American influence from Fourier, see Gilson *et al., Recent Philosophy,* 266, 751–52.
13. Jacques Maritain, *Moral Philosophy* (New York: Scribner's, 1964), 261–350, provides a very detailed study of Comte's place in the history of ethics.
14. *The Positive Philosophy of Auguste Comte,* trans. H. Martineau (London, 1853), I, 1.
15. Ibid., I, 20–24.
16. Ibid., II, 312.
17. *General View of Positivism,* trans. J. H. Bridges (London: Routledge, 1910), 378–85.
18. This is from the Appendix by Pierre Laffitte to Comte's *Catéchisme positiviste,* 329; cited in English in Maritain, *Moral Philosophy,* 329.
19. Ibid., Appendix, 59.
20. Cf. Jean Wahl, "The Present Situation of French Philosophy," in *Philosophic Thought in France and the United States,* ed. M. Farber (Buffalo, N.Y.: University of Buffalo, 1950), 38.
21. *Capital* (Moscow: Foreign Languages Publishers, 1954), I, 20.

22. See *The Economic and Philosophical Manuscripts,* trans. T. B. Bottomore, in E. Fromm, *Marx's Concept of Man* (New York: Ungar, 1961), Appendix.
23. Ibid., for selected texts on Marxian "alienation," see Mann-Kreyche, *Approaches to Morality,* 253–60.
24. Isaiah Berlin, *Karl Marx—His Life and Environment* (New York: Oxford University Press, 1963), 140.
25. Cf. T. E. Hill, *Contemporary Ethical Theories,* 141–45; and Jacques Maritain, *Moral Philosophy,* 253–60.
26. Engels, *Anti-Dühring,* trans. E. Burns (New York: International Publishers, 1939), 110.
27. See the text in Mann-Kreyche, *Approaches to Morality,* P274–75.
28. Kautsky, *Ethics and the Materialist Conception of History,* trans. J. B. Askew (Chicago: Kerr, 1918).
29. Further analysis of Kautsky's ethics in Hill, *Contemporary Ethical Theories,* 146–48.
30. See the selection "Socialism and Religion," from Lenin's *Selected Works* (New York: International Publishers, 1935–38), Vol. XI, Pt. III, in J. B. Hartmann, *Philosophy of Recent Times* (New York: McGraw-Hill, 1967), II, 123–26.
31. Lenin, *Materialism and Empirio-Criticism,* ed. C. Dutt, in *Collected Works* (Moscow: Foreign Languages Publishers, 1960), Vol. XIV; for selections, see Edie, *Russian Philosophy* (Chicago: Quadrangle Books, 1965), III, 410–36.
32. Cf. G. Wetter, *Dialectical Materialism* (New York: Praeger, 1958), cha10.
33. See L. Labedz, *Revisionism: Essays on the History of Marxist Ideas* (New York: Praeger, 1962), 166–78.
34. G. Kline, *European Philosophy Today* (Chicago: Quadrangle Books, 1965), 136–37.

35. Cf. Viktor Antolin, "Communist Morality," *Philosophy Today,* I (1957), 107–08.
36. Soloviev, *The Justification of the Good,* trans. N. Duddington (London: Constable, 1918), 474.
37. This is the appraisal of Boris De Schloezer, "Un penseur russe: Léon Chestov," *Mercure de France* (Paris, 1922), 82–115.
38. Berdyaev, *The Destiny of Man,* trans. N. Duddington (New York: Harper Torchbook, 1960), 15.
39. Berdyaev, *Dialectique existentielle* (Paris: Janin, 1947), 96–97.
40. *The Destiny of Man,* 40, 126–53.
41. Berdyaev, *Subjectivism and Individualism in Social Philosophy,* trans. G. Kline, in Edie, *Russian Philosophy,* III, 155.
42. This point is well developed in R. Borzaga, *Contemporary Philosophy* (Milwaukee: Bruce, 1966), 245–48.
43. Gilson *et al, Recent Philosophy,* 283.
44. Lévy-Bruhl, *La Morale et la science des moeurs* (Paris: Alcan, 1903); the English is adapted from S. Deploige, *The Conflict between Ethics and Sociology* (St. Louis: Herder, 1938), 187.
45. Hill, *Contemporary Ethical Theories,* 90–91, classifies Lévy-Bruhl's thought as a social approbative ethics.
46. See for this summary of Rauh's view, E. Forti, "La Méthode scientifique en morale et en psychologie suivant l'oeuvre de Frederic Rauh," *Revue de métaphysique et de morale,* XLI (1934), 22.
47. Croce, "The Absolute Spirit," *Proceedings of the Sixth International Congress of Philosophy* (New York: Longmans, Green, 1926), 551–54; trans. R. Piccoli, in Robinson, *Anthology of Recent Philosophy* (New York: Crowell, 1929), 162–65.

48. Croce, *Filosofia della pratica* (Bari: Laterza, 1909), 133; cf. ibid., 245, and *Elementi di politica* (Bari: Laterza, 1925), where Croce speaks of the "amoralità della politica."
49. *Filosofia della pratica,* 139.
50. Croce, *Etica e Politica* (Bari: Laterza, 1931), 291, 324; and see Adriano Bausola, *Etica e Politica net pensiero di Benedetto Croce* (Milano: Vita e Pensiero, 1966), 133.
51. *Etica e Politica,* 327, 347.
52. Croce, *The Conduct of Life,* trans. Arthur Livingston (New York: Harcourt, Brace, 1924), 270.
53. Ibid., 271–73.
54. Gentile, *Introduzione alia filosofia* (Firenze: Sansoni, 1933), 49.
55. Gentile, *Genesi e struttura della società* (Firenze: Sansoni, 1946), 46–67.
56. Ginsberg, "On the Diversity of Morals," in *Essays* (London: Heinemann, 1956), Vol. I; partly reprinted in Jones *et al Approaches to Ethics,* 484–93.
57. Gobineau, *The Inequality of Human Races,* trans. A. Collins (New York: Holt, 1915), 145–46, 207.
58. Ibid., 205.
59. Lagarde, *Deutsche Schriften* (Göttingen, 1878), Bk. I, 72–76, 317.
60. Chamberlain, *The Foundations of the Nineteenth Century,* trans. J. Lees (New York: Lane, 1912), 321.
61. Rosenberg, *Der Mythus des 20 Jahrhunderts* (München: Hoheneichen, 1938), 268.

Chapter XIV

Axiological Ethics

1. Urban, "Metaphysics and Value," *Contemporary American Philosophy,* II (1930), 361, "The term 'axiological'

was coined by me wholly independently"; but on its earlier use, see E. S. Brightman, "Axiology," *Dictionary of Philosophy* (New York: Philosophical Library, 1942), 32–33.

2. Perry, *General Theory of Value* (New York: Longmans, Green, 1926), 115–20.
3. Brentano, *Psychologie yom empirischen Standpunkte* (Leipzig: Meiner, 1874), I, 111.
4. For English passages illustrating Brentano's theory of "objects," see R. Chisholm, *Realism and the Background of Phenomenology* (Glencoe, III: Free Press, 1960), 39–75.
5. Meinong, "The Theory of Objects," Trans. in Chisholm, 76–117.
6. Ibid., 109.
7. See Chisholm's *Introduction,* ibid., 11.
8. Scheler, *The Nature of Sympathy,* trans. Peter Heath (New Haven: Yale University Press, 1954), develops the theory of these feelings; see the analysis in Manfred Frings, *Max Scheler* (Pittsburgh: Duquesne University Press, 1965), 56.
9. Cf. James Collins, "The Moral Philosophy of Max Scheler," *Encyclopedia of Morals* (1956), 517–24.
10. Scheler, *Der Formalismus in der Ethik* (Halle, 1913), I, 267–71.
11. Ibid., 312–19; cf. Frings, op. cit., 67–80.
12. Ibid., 110–17; cf. W. H. Werkmeister, *Theories of Ethics,* 259–60.
13. Ibid., 120–25.
14. Ibid., 49.
15. Ibid., 200–25; cf. Frings, op. cit., 103–32; and Werkmeister, op. cit., 261–67.

16. See, for instance, I. M. Bochenski, *Contemporary European Philosophy* (Berkeley: University of California Press, 1956), 212; and Oliver Johnson, *Ethics: Selections* (New York: Holt, Rinehart, 1965), 380.
17. Hartmann, *Ethics,* trans. Stanton Coit (London: Allen & Unwin, 1932), I, 183–231.
18. On Hartmann's view of values as essences, see the texts in Jones *et al., Approaches to Ethics,* 453–55.
19. Hartmann, *Ethics,* I, 86, 100–02, 179; cf. Werkmeister, op. cit., 267–68.
20. Hartmann, *Ethics,* II, 25.
21. Ibid., 52.
22. This table is condensed from *Ethics,* II, 170–380.
23. *Ethics,* I, 248 and 304; II, 247–50.
24. *Ethics,* III, 135–80.
25. Sorley, "Value and Reality" *Contemporary British Philosophy,* II (1925), 254–55.
26. Sorley, *Moral Values and the Idea of God* (Cambridge, Eng.: University Press, 1918), 238.
27. Urban, *Valuation. Its Nature and Laws* (New York: Macmillan, 1909), 54.
28. Urban, *Fundamentals of Ethics* (New York: Holt, 1930), 16; cf. J. L. Blau, *Men and Movements in American Philosophy* (New York: Prentice-Hall, 1952), 305.
29. *Fundamentals of Ethics,* 353, 399.
30. Ibid., 240.
31. Urban, *Beyond Realism and Idealism* (New York: Macmillan, 1949), 207–08.
32. Urban, *Humanity and Duty* (New York: Macmillan, 1951), 195–96; cf. Blau, op. cit., 302–12, for a good appraisal of Urban's ethics.
33. Schlick, *Problems of Ethics,* trans. D. Rynin (New York:

Prentice-Hall, 1939), 8–28.

34. Ibid., 17.
35. Ibid., 117–18.
36. Ibid., 142–56.
37. For this judgment, see R. B. Brandt, *Ethical Theory* (New York: Prentice-Hall, 1959), 314.
38. Lewis, *An Analysis of Knowledge and Valuation* (La Salle, Ill.: Open Court, 1946), 386–87.
39. Brightman, *Moral Laws* (New York: Abingdon Press, 1933), p89–91, 265.
40. Cf. A. Reck, *Recent American Philosophy* (New York: Pantheon, 1964), 311–36.
41. Parker, *Human Values* (New York: Harper, 1931), 34.
42. For a further estimate, see Hill, *Contemporary Ethical Theories,* 234–35.
43. Werkmeister, *Theories of Ethics* (Lincoln, Neb.: Johnsen, 1961), 430.
44. See Jesse Mann, ed., *The Philosophical Work of Rudolf Allers: A Selection* (Washington, D.C.: Georgetown University Press, 1965), 118.
45. Cf. J. V. Walsh, "Love and Philosophy," in *The Human Person and the World of Values, A Tribute to Dietrich von Hildebrand,* ed. B. V. Schwarz (New York: Fordham University Press, 1960), 36–48.

Chapter XV

Self-Realization and Utilitarian Ethics

1. Martineau, *Types of Ethical Theory* (Oxford: Clarendon Press, 1891), II, 25; the sub-quotations are from F. H. Bradley, *Ethical Studies,* 207–08, and T. H. Green, *Prolegomena to Ethics,* 97.
2. Ibid., II, 270.

3. Ibid., II, 266; for the full table, see W. S. Sahakian, *Systems of Ethics* (Paterson, N.J.: Littlefield, Adams, 1964), 93–94.
4. Green, *Prolegomena to Ethics* (Oxford, 1890), 191.
5. Ibid., 210–63.
6. Bradley's Essay II is reprinted in Melden, *Ethical Theories,* 345–59.
7. Ibid., 357.
8. Bradley's *Essay* "Duty for Duty's Sake" is reprinted in Jones, *Approaches to Ethics,* 369–70; for fuller analysis, consult A. J. M. Milne, *The Social Philosophy of English Idealism* (London: Allen & Unwin, 1962), 56–86.
9. These articles by Bosanquet run from Vol. 4 (1894) to Vol. 20 (1910) in the journal now entitled *Ethics.*
10. Bosanquet, "Life and Philosophy," *Contemporary British Philosophy,* I (1924), 58.
11. Rashdall, *The Theory of Good and Evil* (Oxford: Clarendon Press, 1907), Bk. II, ch.3.
12. See the selection from Rashdall, op. cit., in R. E. Dewey, *Problems of Ethics* (New York: Macmillan, 1961), 257–60.
13. Ross, *The Right and the Good* (Oxford: Clarendon Press, 1930), 3–42.
14. Ibid., 140.
15. Ross, *Foundations of Ethics* (Oxford: Clarendon Press, 1939), p10–11.
16. Ibid., 54–56.
17. Ibid., 148, 186.
18. Prichard, "Does Moral Philosophy Rest on a Mistake?" *Mind,* XXI (1912), 487–99; this article is frequently reprinted in books of readings in ethics.

19. Royce, *The Religions Aspect of Philosophy* (Boston, 1885), 425–30.
20. Royce, *The Conception of God* (New York: Macmillan, 1898), 43.
21. Royce, *The World and the Individual* (New York: Macmillan, 1900), I, 341–42.
22. *The Religious Aspect of Philosophy,* 27.
23. Ibid., 149.
24. Royce, *The Philosophy of Loyalty* (New York: Macmillan, 1908), lect. III, sect. 7, 183–89.
25. Royce, *The Problem of Christianity* (New York: Macmillan, 1913), II, 425.
26. This is the view of R. Le Senne, *Traité de morale générale,* (Paris: Presses Universitaires, 1942), 534–35.
27. Santayana, *Realms of Being* (New York: Scribner's, 1942), 474.
28. Santayana, *The Life of Reason, Reason in Common Sense* (New York: Scribner's, 1906), 236.
29. Santayana, "Brief History of My Opinions," *Contemporary American Philosophy,* II (1930), 249.
30. Santayana, *Skepticism and Animal Faith* (New York: Scribner's, 1923), 77.
31. Ibid., 129; cf. Hill, *Contemporary Ethical Theories,* 209.
32. Santayana, *Realms of Being,* 473.
33. See the excellent study of Jordan, in Reck, *Recent American Philosophy,* (New York: Pantheon, 1964), 276–310.
34. Cf. H. C. McElroy, *Modern Philosophers: Western Thought Since Kant* (New York: Moore, 1950), 234.
35. Schweitzer, *Civilization and Ethics,* trans. John Naish (New York: Macmillan, 1923), xvi.

36. See A. C. Gamett, *Ethics* (New York: Ronald Press, 1960), 403–06, for two representative selections.
37. Wright, *Self-Realization. An Outline of Ethics* (New York: Holt, 1924), chaps. 5 and 6.
38. Stace, *Religion and the Modern Mind* (New York: Lippincott, 1952), cha11.
39. Blanshard, *Reason and Goodness* (New York: Macmillan, 1961), 55–69, for the ethics of feeling in St. Francis.
40. Ibid., 409.
41. Ibid., 397.
42. See Hare, *Freedom and Reason* (Oxford: Clarendon Press, 1963), 112.
43. Braithwaite, *Theory of Games as a Tool for the Moral Philosopher* (Cambridge: University Press, 1963), 9.
44. See W. E. Frankena, *Ethics* (New York: Prentice-Hall, 1963), 30–35; and R. B. Brandt, *Ethical Theory* (New York: Prentice-Hall, 1959), 396–400.
45. Smart, *An Outline of a System of Utilitarian Ethics* (Melbourne: Melbourne University Press, 1961), 6–7.
46. Ibid., 20–26.
47. Ibid., 29–32.
48. Ibid., 14.
49. Singer, *Generalization in Ethics* (New York: Knopf, 1961), 193–204.
50. Ibid., 4, 67–68.
51. Ibid., 5, 17–20.
52. Ibid., 217–37.

Chapter XVI

Naturalistic Ethics

1. Moore, *Principia Ethica,* cha1, secs. 10–14.
2. Cf. C. D. Broad, "Some of the Main Problems of Ethics," *Philosophy,* XXI (1946), 99; George Nakhnikian, "Contemporary Ethical Theories and Jurisprudence," *Natural Law Forum,* II (1957), 8.
3. See Vergilius Ferm, "Varieties of Naturalism," in *History of Philosophical Systems* (New York: Philosophical Library, 1950), 429–40.
4. This point is stressed in McGlynn-Toner, *Modern Ethical Theories* (Milwaukee: Bruce, 1962), 63–64.
5. Cf. Nakhnikian, *art. cit.,* 7–8.
6. Darwin, *Descent of Man* (New York: Appleton, 1876), 612.
7. Spencer, *Principles of Ethics,* Pt. I, cha2, n. 4; reprinted in Rand, *Classical Moralists,* 682–88.
8. Ibid., nn. 105–06; in Rand, 698–702.
9. T. H. Huxley, *Evolution and Ethics* (London, 1893); cited in Blanshard, *Reason and Goodness* (London: Allen & Unwin, 1961), 381.
10. Kropotkin, *Etika,* ed. N. K. Lebedev (Moskva, 1923); Trans. as *Ethics: Origin and Development,* by L. S. Friedland and J. R. Piroshnikofi (New York: Deal Press, 1924).
11. Cf. Hill, *Contemporary Ethical Theory,* 126–27.
12. Stapledon, A *Modern Theory of Ethics* (London: Methuen, 1929), 251.
13. For Freud's ethical view, see McGlynn-Toner, *Modern Ethical Theories,* 115–38; and Hill, *Contemporary Ethical Theories,* 36–44.
14. He is so classified in Hill, ibid., 37.

15. Cf. Philip Riefi, *Freud: The Mind of the Moralist* (Garden City, N.Y.: Doubleday, 1961), 161.
16. Freud, *Beyond the Pleasure Principle,* trans. J. Strachey (New York: Liveright, 1922), cha4.
17. Freud, *General Introduction to Psychoanalysis,* trans. Joan Riviere (New York: Garden City, 1943), 296.
18. Freud, *The Ego and the Id* (London: Hogarth, 1923), 30; for a fuller secondary account, consult Rieff, op. cit., 29–69.
19. This is Rieff's interpretation, ibid., 329–60.
20. Cf. J. Dougherty, "Introduction," in Mann-Kreyche, *Approaches to Morality,* 292.
21. James, *The Moral Philosopher and the Moral Life,* in *Essays on Faith and Morals* (New York: Meridian, 1962), 185.
22. Ibid., 185–205; the quotation is from 205.
23. Dewey, *Theory of the Moral Life* (New York: Holt, Rinehart & Winston, 1960), 5; in the original *Ethics* (New York: Holt, 1908), 173.
24. *Theory of the Moral Life,* 59–60.
25. Dewey, *Reconstruction in Philosophy* (New York: Mentor, 1953), 132–33.
26. Dewey, *Human Nature and Conduct* (New York: Holt, 1922), 87–88.
27. On this point, see Rieff, op. cit., 31.
28. *Human Nature and Conduct,* 227.
29. *The Quest for Certainty* (New York: Minton, Balch, 1929), 260–75.
30. Dewey, *Theory of Valuation* (Chicago: University of Chicago Press, 1939), 33–34.
31. Ibid., 28–35.
32. See L. Saxe Eby, *The Quest for Moral Law* (New York:

Columbia University Press, 1944), 186.

33. Whitehead, *Science and the Modern World* (New York: Mentor, 1956), 173–80.
34. Perry, *General Theory of Value* (Cambridge: Harvard University Press, 1926), 115–24; see also Sahakian, *Systems of Ethics,* 381–85.
35. Perry, *The Moral Economy* (New York: Scribner's, 1909), 11–15.
36. *General Theory of Value,* 630–36.
37. Ibid., 682.
38. Cf. Hill, *Contemporary Ethical Theories,* 129–31.
39. Teilhard de Chardin, *The Divine Milieu* (New York: Harper Torchbook, 1965), 121–44.
40. Ibid., 114.
41. Cf. James Collins, *Three Paths in Philosophy,* 186–87.
42. Wilfrid Desan, "Introduction," in Mann-Kreyche, *Approaches to Morality,* 579–80.
43. Macbeath, *Experiments in Living* (London: Macmillan, 1952), lecture 13; partly reprinted in R. E. Dewey, *Problems of Ethics,* 375–80.
44. Cf. Margaret Mead, "Some Anthropological Considerations concerning Natural Law," *Natural Law Forum,* VI (1961), 51–64.
45. Pepper, *Ethics* (New York: Appleton-Century-Crofts, 1960), 314–15.
46. Ibid., 326–35.
47. Maritain, *Science and Wisdom* (New York: Scribner's, 1940), 81.
48. Leclercq, "Natural Law the Unknown," *Natural Law Forum,* VII (1962), 15.
49. Leclercq, *Du droit naturel à la sociologie* (Paris: Spes, 1960), II, 102; three paragraphs from this passage are

translated in my *Ethics in Crisis,* 113.

50. Fromm, *Escape from Freedom* (New York: Rinehart, 1941), 24–26.
51. Ibid., 105.
52. Fromm, *Man for Himself* (New York: Rinehart, 1947), 8–12.
53. Ibid., 133–34.
54. Ibid., 16–20.
55. Fromm, *The Sane Society* (New York: Rinehart, 1955), 7–69.
56. Ibid., 29–30.
57. Olson, *The Morality of Self-interest* (New York: Harcourt, Brace, 1965), v, 157–74.
58. Russell, *Mysticism and Logic,* 46–57.
59. *Morality of Self-interest,* 176–77.
60. Lamont, *Humanism as a Philosophy* (New York: Philosophical Library, 1949), p273–97.
61. Vivas, *The Moral Life and the Ethical Life* (Chicago: University of Chicago Press, 1950), 177–80.
62. Ibid., 326–46.
63. Rice, *On the Knowledge of Good and Evil* (New York: Random House, 1955), 109.
64. Ibid., 122.
65. Ibid., 194, 255.
66. Edel, "Some Trends in American Naturalistic Ethics," in *Philosophic Thought in France and the U.S.* (Buffalo: Publications of the University of Buffalo, 1950), 610.
67. Romanell, *Toward a Critical Naturalism* (New York: Macmillan, 1958), 41–42, 44.
68. Foot, "Moral Arguments," *Mind,* LXVII (1958), 502–13; reprinted in Margolis, *Contemporary Ethical Theory* (New York: Random House, 1966), 176–90.

69. Edwards, *The Logic of Moral Discourse* (Glencoe, Ill.: Free Press, 1955), 179–82.
70. E. M. Adams, *Ethical Naturalism and the Modern World- View* (Chapel Hill, N.C.: University of North Carolina Press, 1960), offers a strongly critical view of the whole movement.

Chapter XVII

Analytic Ethics

1. Hume, *Treatise of Human Nature,* ed. L. A. Selby-Bigge (1888), 468–69.
2. Maritain, *Neuf leçons sur les notions premières de la philosophie morale,* 42.
3. This division has become standard; Cf. W. K. Frankena, *Ethics,* (Englewood Cliffs, N.T.: Prentice-Hall, 1963), 1–10.
4. Moore, *Principia Ethica* (Cambridge, Eng.: University Press, 1903), chap. 5, nn. 88–89.
5. Cf. Mary Warnock, *Ethics Since* 1900 (London: Oxford University Press, 1960), 48–51.
6. Moore, *Ethics* (London: Oxford University Press, 1965), 55.
7. Ibid., 83; italics in the original.
8. Ibid., 47.
9. Ibid., 31.
10. Moore, "Reply to My Critics," in *The Philosophy of G. E. Moore,* ed. A. Schilpp (Evanston, Ill.: Northwestern University Press, 1942), 554.
11. Ibid., 591.
12. Printed as a footnote to Bertrand Russell's "The Elements of Ethics," in Sellars-Hospers, *Readings in Ethical Theory,* (New York: Appleton-Century-Crofts, 1952), 1.

13. Russell, *Mysticism and Logic* (New York: Norton, 1929), p49–55.
14. See the section of *Religion and Science* reprinted in Edwards-Pap, *A Modern Introduction to Philosophy*, 297–302.
15. Ibid., 298.
16. T. E. Hill, *Contemporary Ethical Theories,* 13–15, notes that Russell has been associated with "three or four" different ethical positions.
17. See, for example, Wittgenstein's discussion of pain, in *Philosophical Investigations* (Oxford: Blackwell, 1953), 88e-l04e; reprinted in Weitz, *20th-century Philosophy: The Analytic Tradition* (New York: Free Press, 1966), 312–26.
18. Wittgenstein, *Tractatus Logico-Philosophicus* (London: Routledge, Kegan Paul, 1922), 6.42; see the digest by Rush Rhees, "Some Developments in Wittgenstein's Views of Ethics," *Philosophical Review,* LXXIV (1965), 17–26.
19. *Tractatus,* 6.422.
20. Rhees, *art. cit.,* 23–24.
21. Wittgenstein, "Lecture on Ethics," *Philosophical Review,* LXXIV (1954), 4.
22. Ibid., 5.
23. Ibid., 6.
24. Ibid., 7.
25. Ibid., 12.
26. Waismann, "Notes on Talks with Wittgenstein," *Philosophical Review,* LXXIV (1965), 12–16.
27. Ibid., German, 13; English, 15.
28. Carnap, *Philosophy and Logical Syntax* (London: Routledge, Kegan Paul, 1936), cha1, sec. 4; reprinted

in Morton White, *Age of Analysis* (New York: Mentor, 1955), 216–18.

29. Ewing, *The Definition of Good* (New York: Macmillan, 1947), 112–15, 166.
30. Ibid., 106.
31. Ibid., 109; cf. Hill, *Contemporary Ethical Theories*, 312–14.
32. Ewing, "Ethical Judgments: Attempted Synthesis of Three Rival Views," *Atti del* XII *Congresso Internazionale di Filosofia* VII (Firenze, 1961), 155–60.
33. *Art. cit.*, 157.
34. See Blanshard, *Reason and Goodness,* 288–89.
35. Urmson, "On Grading," *Mind,* LIX (1950), 145–69; reprinted in Paul Taylor, *The Moral Judgment* (New York: Free Press, 1966), 211–37.
36. Taylor, 223.
37. Stevenson, "The Emotive Meaning of Ethical Terms," *Mind,* XLVI (1937), 10–31; in the reprint in R. E. Dewey, *Problems of Ethics* (1961), see 413.
38. This book is *The Meaning of Meaning* (London: Kegan Paul, 1938); for emotive meaning, see 124–25.
39. Stevenson, *Ethics and Language* (New Haven: Yale University Press, 1944), 267.
40. Ibid., 136.
41. Stevenson, *Facts and Values* (New Haven: Yale University Press, 1963), 97.
42. Ibid., ix.
43. Ayer, *Language, Truth, and Logic* (London: Gollancz, 1936), 103.
44. Ibid., 112–13.
45. Joad, *Critique of Logical Positivism* (London: Gollancz, 1950), 146.

46. Mary Warnock, *Ethics Since* 1900, 91.
47. *Language, Truth, and Logic,* 2nd ed. (New York: Dover, 1952), 21.
48. See Harald Ofstad, "Objectivity of Norms and Value-Judgments according to Recent Scandinavian Philosophy," *Philosophy and Phenomenological Research,* XII (1951–52), 48.
49. Hägerström, *Inquiries into the Nature of Laws and Morals* (Stockholm: Almqvist & Wiksell, 1938), 138.
50. Ibid., 154.
51. On Alf Ross, see Ofstad, *art. cit.,* 53–54.
52. Ross, *On Law and Justice* (Berkeley-Los Angeles: University of California Press, 1959), 274.
53. Nowell-Smith, *Ethics* (Baltimore: Penguin, 1954), 25.
54– Ibid., 30.
55. Ibid., 52.
56. Ibid., 72–73.
57. Ibid., 81–83.
58. This section in chapter 8 is in ibid., 105–21.
59. Ibid., 125.
60. Ibid., 102.
61. Ibid., 182.
62. Aristotle, *On the Motion of Animals,* 700b1–701b1; part of this ancient text on the practical syllogism is printed as an introduction to "good reasons" ethics, in R. E. Dewey, *Problems of Ethics,* 434–35.
63. Hampshire, "Fallacies in Moral Philosophy," *Mind,* LVIII (1949), 466–82.
64. Ibid.; see the reprint in R. E. Dewey, op. cit., 438.
65. Ibid., in Dewey, 442.
66. See Weitz, *20th-Century Philosophy,* 379, for a portion of Baier's talk on "The Meaning of Life," (1957).

67. Baier, *The Moral Point of View* (Ithaca, NX: Cornell University Press, 1958), cha1.
68. Hare, *The Language of Morals* (Oxford: Clarendon Press, 1952), 169.
69. Hare, *Freedom and Reason* (Oxford: Clarendon Press, 1963), 4.
70. Ibid., 86–185; see G. C. Kerner's exposition of Hare's views, in *The Revolution in Ethical Theory* (New York: Oxford University Press, 1966), 138–96. Kerner is not sympathetic with this approach.
71. Toulmin, *An Examination of the Place of Reason in Ethics* (London: Cambridge University Press, 1950), 148, 224.
72. Cf. Kerner, op. cit., 127–37, where again the criticism may be too severe.

Chapter XVIII

Existential and Phenomenological Ethics

1. See William Barrett, *Irrational Man. A Study in Existential Philosophy* (Garden City, N.Y.: Doubleday, 1958), 21.
2. Husserl, *Ideen zu einer reinen Phänomenologie und phänomenologischen Philosophie,* ed. Willy Biemel (Ten Haag; Nijhoff, 1950), I, 154; cf. Quentin Lauer, *The Triumph of Subjectivity* (New York: Fordham University Press, 1958), 1–19.
3. Thus Werkmeister, *Theories of Ethics* (1961), cha7, treats Moore together with Scheler and Hartmann.
4. Kierkegaard, *Either/Or,* trans. W. Lowrie (Princeton, N.J.: Princeton University Press, 1944), II, 163–64; on the same point, see Lowrie, *A Short Life of Kierkegaard* (Princeton, N.J.: Princeton University Press, 1942), 125.

5. *Either/Or,* II, 234–35.
6. Kierkegaard, *Journals,* 1847 entry, cited in Sahakian, *Systems of Ethics* (1964), 307.
7. Cf. Kurt Reinhardt, *The Existentialist Revolt* (Milwaukee: Bruce, 1952), 56.
8. This is the conclusion of Harald Höffding, *History of Modern Philosophy* (New York: Macmillan, 1924), II, 288.
9. For the "immoralist" interpretation, see A. W. Benn, "The Morals of an Immoralist—Friedrich Nietzsche," *Ethics,* XIX (1909), 1–13, 192–203; and for the contrary view, see A. C. Pigou, "The Ethics of Nietzsche," *Ethics,* XVIII (1908), 343–55.
10. See G. A. Morgan, *What Nietzsche Means* (Cambridge: Harvard University Press, 1941), for more information on the fabrication of *The Will to Power.*
11. Nietzsche, *Thus Spake Zarathustra,* in *The Philosophy of Nietzsche* (New York: Random House, 1954), "Prologue," n. 2.
12. See, for instance, *The Gay Science,* in *The Portable Nietzsche,* ed. W. Kaufmann (New York: Viking Press, 1954), 95–96.
13. Nietzsche., *Genealogy of Morals,* in *The Philosophy of Nietzsche,* 7.
14. Nietzsche, *Beyond Good and Evil,* trans. M. Cowan (Chicago: Regnery, 1955), 260.
15. See two illustrative passages from *The Genealogy of Morals,* in Mann-Kreyche, *Approaches to Morality,* 616–26.
16. Part I of *Notes from the Underground* is printed in W. Kaufmann, *Existentialism from Dostoevsky to Sartre* (New York: Meridian, 1957), 53–82.

17. Ibid., in Kaufmann, 56.
18. This is Kaufmann's comment, ibid., 14.
19. Cf. Borzaga, *Contemporary Philosophy,* 238–39.
20. Cf. Lauer, op. cit., 100–17.
21. Buber, *I and Thou,* trans. R. G. Smith (New York: Scribner's, 1958), 34.
22. Tillich, *Systematic Theology* (Chicago: University of Chicago Press, 1963), III, 266–67.
23. Tillich, *Love, Power, and Justice* (New York: Oxford University Press, 1960), 72.
24. *Systematic Theology,* III, 159.
25. Tillich, *Courage to Be* (New Haven: Yale University Press, 1952), 133.
26. Tillich, *The Protestant Era* (Chicago: Phoenix, 1957), 151–54.
27. *Systematic Theology,* III, 45.
28. Ibid., 95, 273–75.
29. Reinhold Niebuhr, *Christian Ethics* (New York: Meridian, 1960), 97.
30. *Moral Man and Immoral Society* (New York: Scribner's, 1949), 41.
31. See *Love and Justice: Selections from the Shorter Writings of Reinhold Niebuhr,* ed. D. B. Robertson (Philadelphia: Westminster Press, 1957), 46.
32. Ibid., 53; see also Niebuhr, *Christian Realism and Political Problems* (New York: Scribner's, 1953), 173.
33. H. Richard Niebuhr, in *The Christian Century,* March 23, 1932, 378–80; reprinted in *Contemporary Moral Issues,* ed. H. K. Girvetz (Belmont, Calif.: Wadsworth, 1963), 321–25.
34. Reinhold Niebuhr, in *The Christian Century,* March 30, 1932, 415–17; see Girvetz, 326–30.

35. For a full exposition in English of the ethics of Grisebach, see G. A. Rauche, *The Philosophy of Actuality* (Fort Hare, Republic of South Africa: Fort Hare University Press, 1964).
36. Bonhoeffer's *Ethics* was completed and edited by his friend, Pastor Eberhard Bethge, translated by Neville Smith (New York: Macmillan, 1965).
37. Ibid., 214.
38. Robinson, *Christian Morals Today* (Philadelphia: Westminster Press, 1964), 39.
39. Marcel, *Philosophical Fragments,* 1904–1914 (Notre Dame, Ind.: University of Notre Dame Press, 1965).
40. Ibid., 112, 181.
41. Marcel, *The Philosophy of Existentialism* (New York: Citadel Press, 1965), 69–87.
42. Ibid., 88–89.
43. Marcel, *The Mystery of Being* (Chicago: Regnery, 1951), II, 113–17.
44. *Philosophical Fragments,* 1904–1914, 10; and *Homo Viator,* trans. E. Craufurd (Chicago: Regnery, 1951), 26.
45. Marcel, *Being and Haying,* trans. K. Farrer (Boston: Beacon Press, 1951), 15; *Homo Viator,* 7–8.
46. The whole issue of *Etudes Philosophiques,* Vol. III, 1962, is devoted to Nabert.
47. Nabert, *Elements pour une éthique* (Paris: Presses Universitaires, 1943), 19–58.
48. Ibid., 105–221.
49. Ibid., 218–19, trans. Bourke.
50. Sartre, *Being and Nothingness,* trans. Hazel Barnes (New York: Philosophical Library, 1956), 74–90.
51. Ibid., 484–85.

52. Sartre, *Existentialism,* trans. B. Frechtman (New York: Philosophical Library, 1947), 21.
53. *Being and Nothingness,* 566.
54. Ibid., 34–35.
55. Sartre, *Saint Genet,* trans. B. Frechtman (London: Allen & Unwin, 1964), 186.
56. Ibid., , 187, 190.
57. *Critique de la raison dialectique* (Paris: Gallimard, 1960), 123.
58. Ibid., 755.
59. Cf. Ria Stavrides, "French Existentialism and Moral Philosophy," in *Encyclopedia of Morals,* by V. Ferm (New York: Philosophical Library, 1956), 167, places a high value on the ethics of Madame de Beauvoir.
60. Beauvoir, *Ethics of Ambiguity,* trans. B. Frechtman (New York: Philosophical Library, 1948), 44.
61. On "facticity" see Colin Smith, *Contemporary French Philosophy,* 28.
62. See James Collins, "Freedom as Atheistic Heroism," *Giornale di Metafisica,* IV (1949), 578.
63. *Ethics of Ambiguity,* 146.
64. Ibid., 60.
65. Cf. Colin Smith, op. cit., 212.
66. Merleau-Ponty, *Humanisme et Terreur* (Paris: Gallimard, 1947).
67. Mandelbaum, *The Phenomenology of Moral Experience* (Glencoe, Ill.: Free Press, 1955), 16–30.
68. Ibid., 30–31.
69. Ibid., 32–39.
70. Ibid., 45; for the theory of the virtues, see 134–81.
71. Ibid., 245.

72. Ibid., 277.
73. Ibid., 291–309.

Bibliography

Note

THE LAST FULL-SCALE history of ethics in English is almost one hundred years old. Henry Sidgwick's *Outlines of the History of Ethics* was written before 1886. In the sixth edition (1931), Alban G. Widgery added a chapter on ethics in the first quarter of the twentieth century. Despite its obvious lacunae, Sidgwick's work has remained a standard source of information in this field. It is very weak on the ethics of the Middle Ages and on non-British modern and contemporary ethics. Of course, a great deal has happened in twentieth-century ethics since the last revision of Sidgwick. The *Short History of Ethics* written by R. A. P. Rogers in 1911 is briefer and less informative than Sidgwick. After most of the research and writing on the present book was completed, Alasdair MacIntyre's *A Short History of Ethics* (1966) was published. He has chosen to concentrate on the ethical views of about thirty main thinkers, from the Sophists to Sartre, and to ignore lesser figures in the field. My effort has been to treat a much larger number of ethicians.

Of histories of ethics in other languages, Ottmar Dittrich's four-volume *Geschkhte der Ethik* (1923–1932) is the most complete work. However, it includes a great deal of material that is not central to ethics, and it does not cover recent ethics, of course. The most helpful French history of the subject is found in René Le Senne's *Traité de morale générale* (1942), but it is not (and was not intended to be) a complete history of ethics. Excellent surveys of the history of ethical thinking are now available for most of the distinct periods of philosophy. The only era that is not well covered by such special studies is the medieval; we are just beginning to learn the history of medieval philosophy. Alois Dempf's work *Die Ethik des Mittelalters* (1927) is extremely brief and its coverage is inadequate. There is much more information on the ethics of the Middle Ages in a general work such as F. C. Copleston's *History of Philosophy.* Most general histories of philosophy, however, give little space to ethical theory.

The bibliographical lists offered herein are more complete than in most other histories. Data on original writings in ethics, chief translations and collections of texts, plus the most helpful secondary studies make up the bibliographies appended to each chapter. In the case of Greek, Arabic, and Russian works, the original titles and terms have been transliterated or given in translation. The difficulties of printing in non-Roman alphabets probably outweigh the value of having these data in the original. It is hoped that the information included on the literature of ethics will help to make up for the brevity and defects of the doctrinal expositions in this history.

General Works

Brinton, Crane. *A History of Western Morals.* New York: Harcourt, Brace, 1959.

Brunschivicq, Léon. *Le progrès de la conscience dans la philosophie occidentals* 2 vols. Paris: Alcan, 1927.

Copleston, F. C. *A History of Philosophy.* 8 vols. Westminster, Md.: Newman Press, 1946–66; reprinted New York: Doubleday Image Books, 1962–65.

Dittrich, Ottmar. *Geschichte der Ethik.* 4 Bde. Leipzig: Meiner, 1923–32.

Ferm, Vergilius (ed.). *Encyclopedia of Morals.* New York: Philosophical Library, 1956.

Hastings, James (ed.). *Encyclopaedia of Religion and Ethics.* 12 vols. Edinburgh: Clark, 1908–21. 7 vols. New York: Scribner's, 1924–27.

Hobhouse, L. T. *Morals in Evolution. A Study in Comparative Ethics.* London: Chapman & Hall, 1906; New York: Macmillan, 1951.

Janet, Paul. *Histoire de la philosophie morale et politique dans l'antiquité et les temps modernes.* 2 vols. Paris: Delagrave, 1852.

Jodl, Friedrich. *Geschichte der Ethik als philosophischer Wissenschaft.* 2 Bde. Stuttgart: Cotta, 1906, 1912.

Kropotkin, P. A. *Ethics, Origin and Development.* Trans. L. S. Friedland and J. R. Piroshnikoff. New York: Dial Press, 1924; reprinted 1947.

Lecky, W. E. H. *History of European Morals from Augustus to Charlemagne.* 2 vols. New York: Appleton, 1869; reprinted in 1 vol., New York: Braziller, 1955.

Leclercq, Jacques. *Les grandes lignes de la philosophic morale.* Louvain-Paris: Vrin, 1946; 2me éd., 1964.

Le Senne, René. *Traité de morale générate,* Paris: Presses Universitaires, 1942.

MacIntyre, Alasdair. *A Short History of Ethics.* New York: Macmillan, 1966.

Maritain, Jacques. *Moral Philosophy.* Trans. Marshall Suther *et al.* New York: Scribner's, 1964.

Martineau, James. *Types of Ethical Theory.* 2 vols. Oxford: Clarendon, 1866; New York: Macmillan, 1886.

Meyer, Hans. *Abendländische Weltanschauung.* 5 Bde. Paderborn: Schöningh, 1949–53.

Rogers, R. A. P. *A Short History of Ethics, Greek and Modern.* London: Macmillan, 1911; reprinted 1964.

Schweitzer, Albert. *Civilization and Ethics.* New York: Macmillan 1923.

Sidgwick, Henry. *Outlines of the History of Ethics.* London: Macmillan, 1886; revised ed. of 1931, reprinted Boston: Beacon, 1964.

Wentscher, M. *Geschichte der Ethik.* Berlin: De Gruyter, 1931.

Werkmeister, W. H. *Theories of Ethics.* Lincoln, Neb.: Johnsen, 1961.

Westermarck, E. A. *The Origin and Development of Moral Ideas.* London: Macmillan, 1926.

Chapter X

Albee, Ernest. *A History of English Utilitarianism.* London: Swan Sonnenschein, 1902. Reprinted, New York: Macmillan, 1962.

Albonico, C. G. *La teoria dei sentimenti morali di Adam Smith.* Mantova: Mondivi, 1920.

Anschutz, R. P,. *The Philosophy of J. S. Mill* Oxford: Clarendon Press, 1953.

Aqvist, Lennart. *The Moral Philosophy of Richard Price.* Copenhagen: Munksgaard, 1960.

Austin, John. *The Province of Jurisprudence Determined.* London, 1832. Ed. H. L. A. Hart. London: Weidenfeld & Nicolson, 1954.

Bagolini, L. *La simpatia nella morale e nel diritto: aspetti del pensiero di Adamo Smith.* Bologna: Zuffi, 1952.

Bain, Alexander. *Mental and Moral Science.* London: Longmans, 1868.

———. *The Emotions and the Will.* New York: Appleton, 1888.

Barnes, W. H. F. "Richard Prince: A Neglected Eighteenth-Century Moralist," *Philosophy,* XVII (1942), 159–73.

Baumgardt, David. *Bentham and the Ethics of Today.* Princeton, N.J.: Princeton University Press, 1952.

Beattie, James. *Dissertations Moral and Critical.* London, 1783.

———. *Elements of Moral Science.* 2 vols. Edinburgh, 1790–93.

Beck, L. W. (ed.). *18th-Century Philosophy.* New York: Free Press, 1966.

Bentham, Jeremy. *Works,* ed. John Bowring. 11 vols. Edinburgh: Tait, 1838–43. Reprinted, New York: Russell & Russell, 1964.

———. *An Introduction to the Principles of Morals and Legislation,* London, 1780. Ed. by W. Harrison. Oxford: Blackwell, 1948.

———. *Deontology: Or, the Science of Morality.* Arranged and edited from the MS of J. Bentham by John Bowring. London: Longmans, 1834.

Bentham, Jeremy, and Mill, J. S. *Utilitarians.* Garden City, N.Y.: Doubleday, 1961.

Broiles, R. D. *The Moral Philosophy of David Hume.* The Hague: Nijhoff, 1964.

Brown, Thomas. *Lectures on the Philosophy of the Human Mind.* 4 vols. Edinburgh, 1820.

———. *Lectures on Ethics.* London, 1856.

Burke, Edmund. *Works.* 6 vols. London: Oxford University Press, 1925.

———. *A Philosophical Inquiry into the Origin of Our Ideas on the Sublime and Beautiful.* London, 1756. Ed. J. T. Boulton. New York: Columbia University Press, 1958.

———. *Philosophy of Edmund Burke,* ed. L. I. Bredvold and R. G. Ross. Ann Arbor: University of Michigan Press, 1961. Castell, Alburey. *Mill's Logic of the Moral Sciences. A Study of the Impact of Newtonism.* Chicago: University of Chicago Dissertation, 1936.

Coleridge, Samuel Taylor. *Philosophical Lectures.* London, 1818. Ed. Kathleen Coburn. New York: Philosophical Library, 1949.

———. *Aids to Reflection.* London: Bohn, 1825.

Cua, A. S. *Reason and Virtue: A Study in the Ethics of Richard Price.* Athens, Ohio: Ohio University Press, 1966.

Douglas, Charles. *The Ethics of J. S. Mill.* London: Blackwood, 1897.

Ferguson, Adam. *Institutes of Moral Philosophy.* Edinburgh, 1772.

———. *Principles of Moral and Political Science.* Edinburgh, 1792.

Fulton, R. B. *Adam Smith Speaks to Our Times: A Study of His Ethical Ideas.* Boston: Christopher Publishing House, 1963. Gizycki, Georg von. *Die Ethik David Humes in ihrer geschichtlichen Stellung.* Breslau: Koehler, 1878.

Glathe, A. B. *Hume's Theory of the Passions and of Morals.* Berkeley, Calif.: University of California Press, 1950.

Godwin, William. *Inquiry concerning Political Justice and Its Influence on Morals and Happiness.* London, 1793.

Guyau, J. M. *La morale anglaise contemporaine.* Paris: Alcan, 1900.

Halévy, Elie. *The Growth of Philosophical Radicalism.* Trans. M. Morris. London: Faber & Faber, 1928.

Hamilton, Sir William. *Discussions on Philosophy and Literature.* London-Edinburgh, 1852. (Includes the *Essay on Moral Philosophy.*)

Havard, W. C. *Henry Sidgwick and Later Utilitarian Political Philosophy.* Gainesville, Fla.: University of Florida Press, 1959. Hedenius, Ingemor. *Studies in Hume's Ethics.* Uppsala: Almqvist & Wiksell, 1937.

Hume, David. *Philosophical Works,* ed. T. H. Green and T. H. Grose. 4 vols. London: Longmans, Green, 1874–75.

———. *A Treatise of Human Nature,* London, 1739. Ed. L. A. Selby-Bigge, Oxford: Clarendon Press, 1888, 1951.

———. *An Enquiry concerning Human Understanding.* London, 1748. Ed. (with the *Principles of Morals)* L. A. Selby-Bigge. Oxford: Clarendon Press, 1902, 1951.

———. *An Enquiry concerning the Principles of Morals.* London, 1751. Ed. C. W. Hendel. New York: Library of Liberal Arts, 1957.

———. *Hume's Ethical Writings,* ed. Alasdair Maclntyre. New York: Macmiïlan, 1965.

———. *Hume's Moral and Political Philosophy,* ed. Henry Aiken. New York: Hafner, 1948.

———. *Hume Selections,* ed. C. W. Hendel. New York: Scribner's, 1927.

Kydd, Rachel M. *Reason and Conduct in Hume's Treatise.* London: G. Cumberlege, 1946.

Limentani, G. *La Morale della simpatia, saggio sopra l'etica di Adamo Smith.* Genova: Formiggini, 1914.

McCosh, James. *The Scottish Philosophy, Biographical, Expository, Critical.* London, 1875.

MacCunn, John. *Six Radical Thinkers: Bentham, J. S. Mill, Cobden, Carlyle, Mazzini, Green.* London, 1907. Reprinted, New York: Russell & Russell, 1964.

MacNabb, D. G. *David Hume: His Theory of Knowledge and Morality.* London: Hutchinson, 1951.

Mill, James. *Analysis of the Human Mind.* London, 1820.

Mill, John Stuart. *Collected Works.* Toronto: University of Toronto Press, 1965 ff. (3 vols. published by 1966).

———. *System of Logic,* London, 1843; of which Bk. VI is *On the Logic of the Moral Sciences,* ed. H. M. Magid. New York: Bobbs-Merrill, 1965.

———. *Utilitarianism,* London, 1863. Ed. O. Piest. Indianapolis: Library of Liberal Arts, 1957. Ed. Mary Warnock, New York: Meridian, 1962.

Monro, D. H. *Godwin's Moral Philosophy, an Interpretation.* London: Allen & Unwin, 1953.

Newman, John Henry. *Works.* 40 vols. London: Longmans, Green, 1874–1921. Some reprinted, Longmans, 1945 ff.

———. *An Essay in Aid of a Grammar of Assent,* ed. C. F. Harrold. London: Longmans, 1947; New York: Doubleday Image, 1955.

———. *Philosophical Readings in Cardinal Newman.* Chicago: Regnery, 1961.

———. *The Essential Newman,* ed. V. F. Blehl. New York: Mentor, 1963.

Paley, William. *Works.* 8 vols. London, 1805–08.

———. *The Principles of Moral and Political Philosophy.* London, 1785.

———. *Natural Theology: Selections,* ed. F. Ferré. New York: Library of Liberal Arts, 1960.

Parkin, Charles. *The Moral Basis of Burke's Political Thought.* New York: Cambridge University Press, 1957.

Passmore, J. A. *A Hundred Years of British Philosophy.* London: Duckworth, 1957.

Plamenatz, John. *The English Utilitarians.* Oxford: Blackwell, 1944.

———. *Mill's Utilitarianism Reprinted with a Study of the English Utilitarians.* Oxford: Blackwell, 1949.

Price, Richard. *A Review of the Principal Questions in Morals.* London, 1758. Ed. D. D. Raphael. Oxford: Clarendon Press, 1948.

Reid, Thomas. *An Essay on Quantity . . . Applied to Virtue and Merit.* Edinburgh: Philosophical Transactions, 1948.

———. *An Inquiry into the Human Mind on the Principles of Common Sense.* Edinburgh, 1764.

———. *Essays on the Active Powers of Man.* Edinburgh, 1788.

Schneewind, J. B. "First Principles and Common Sense Morality in Sidgwick's Ethics," *Archiv für Geschichte der Philosophie,* XLV (1963), 137–56.

Schneider, H. W. *Smith's Moral and Political Philosophy.* New York: Hafner, 1948.

Sidgwick, Henry. *The Methods of Ethics.* London: Macmillan, 1874. Reprinted, New York: Dover, 1966.

———. *Practical Ethics.* London: Macmillan, 1898.

Smith, Adam. *Collected Works.* 5 vols. Edinburgh, 1811–12.

———. *Theory of Moral Sentiments.* Edinburgh, 1759.

———. *The Wealth of Nations.* Edinburgh, 1776. 2 vols. New York: Dutton, 1924.

Stanlis, P. J. *Edmund Burke and the Natural Law.* Ann Arbor: University of Michigan Press, 1958, 1965.

Stephen, Leslie. *History of English Thought in the Eighteenth Century.* London: Duckworth, 1876. Reprinted, New York: Harcourt, 1902.

———. *The English Utilitarians.* 3 vols. London: Duckworth, 1900. Reprinted, London: London School of Economics, 1950.

Stewart, Dugald. *Outlines of Moral Philosophy.* Edinburgh, 1793. With notes by J. McCosh. London, 1863.

———. *Dissertation Exhibiting the Progress of Metaphysical, Ethical and Political Philosophy.* London: Supplement to *Encyclopaedia Britannica,* in Two Parts, 1815 and 1821.

———. *Philosophy of the Active and Moral Powers of Man.* 2 vols.

Edinburgh-Boston, 1828.

Swabey, W. C. (ed.). *Ethical Theory from Hobbes to Kant.* New York: Philosophical Library, 1961.

Taylor, W. L. *Francis Hutcheson and David Hume as Predecessors of Adam Smith.* Durham, N.C.: Duke University Press, 1965.

Ward, James. "John Stuart Mill's Science of Ethology," *Ethics,* I (1890), 446–59.

Whateley, Richard. *Paley's Moral Philosophy: With Annotations.* London: Parker, 1859.

Willey, Basil. *The Eighteenth Century Background.* New York: Norton, 1940.

———. *Nineteenth Century Studies.* New York: Columbia University Press, 1949.

Chapter XI

Aiken, H. D. (ed.). *The Age of Ideology.* New York: Mentor, 1956.

Barth, Karl, *Protestant Thought from Rousseau to Ritschl.* New York: Harper & Row, 1959.

Basch, Victor. *L'Individualisme anarchiste: Max Stirner.* Paris: Alcan, 1904.

Beneke, Friedrich E. *Grundlinien des natürlichen Systems der praktischen Philosophie.* Berlin, 1837. Chap. 3 Trans. by B. Rand as "The Natural System of Morals" in *Classical Moralists,* pp. 626–46.

Benz, R. E. *Die deutsche Romantik.* Leipzig: Reclam, 1937.

Birkner, H. J. *Schleiermachers christliche Sittenlehre.* Berlin: De Grayter, 1964.

Bréhier, Emile. *Histoire de la philosophie allemande.* Paris: Michel, 1933.

Cohen, H. *Ethik des reinen Willens.* Aufl. 2. Berlin: Cassirer, **1921.**

Copleston, F. *Arthur Schopenhauer: Philosopher of Pessimism.* London: Burns, Oates, 1946.

Eucken, R. *The Value and Meaning of Life.* Trans. W. R. B. Gibson. London: Black, 1909.

Fichte, Johann Gottlieb. *Grundlage des Naturrechts.* Jena, 1796. Trans. by A. E. Kroeger, as *The Science of Rights.* Philadelphia: Lippincott, 1869.

———. *Die Bestimmung des Menschen.* Berlin, 1800. Trans. by W. Smith as *The Vocation of Man* in *Popular Works of J. G. Fichte.* London: Trübner, 1889. Ed. with Introduction by R. M. Chisholm. New York: Liberal Arts Press, 1956.

———. *Reden an die deutsche Nation.* Berlin, 1807–08. Trans. by R. F. Jones and G. H. Turnbull as *Addresses to the German Nation.* Chicago: Open Court, 1922.

Friedrich, Carl J. *The Philosophy of Hegel.* New York: Scribner's, 1954.

Fries, Jakob F. *Rechtslehre.* Berlin, 1804.

———. *Ethik.* Berlin, 1818.

———. *Psychischen Anthropologie.* Berlin, 1821.

Gardiner, P. *Schopenhauer.* Baltimore: Penguin, 1963.

Gurvitch, Georges. *Fichtes System der konkreten Ethik.* Tübingen: Mohr, 1924.

Hartmann, J. B. (ed.). *Philosophy of Recent Times. I: Readings in Nineteenth-Century Philosophy.* New York: McGraw-Hill, 1967.

Hartmann, Nicolai. *Die Philosophie des deutschen Idealismus.* 2 vols. Berlin-Leipzig: De Gruyter, 1923–29.

Hegel, Georg W. F. *Sämmtliche Werke* (kritische Ausgabe), hrsg. G. Lasson u. J. Hoffmeister. Leipzig-Hamburg: Meiner, 1905 if.

———. *Hegels theologische Jugendschriften*, hrsg. H. Nohl. Tübingen: Mohr, 1907. Partly Trans. by T. M. Knox as *Early Theological Writings.* Chicago: University of Chicago Press, 1948.

———. *Die Phänomenologie des Geistes.* Berlin, 1807. Trans. by Baillie as *The Phenomenology of Mind.* London: Macmillan, 1931.

———. *Grundlinien der Philosophie des Rechts.* Berlin, 1821. Trans. by J. M. Sterrett as *The Ethics of Hegel: Selections from the Philosophy of Right.* Boston: Ginn, 1893. Trans. by T. M. Knox as *The Philosophy of Right.* Oxford: Clarendon Press, 1942, 1953. Also Trans. by S. W. Dyde. London: Bell, 1896.

———. *System der Sittlichkeit.* Berlin, 1893.

———. *Ueber die Differenz des Fichteschen und Schellingschen Systems.* Jena, 1801.

Herbart, Johann Friedrich. *Sämmtliche Werke,* ed. G. Hartenstein. 12 vols. Leipzig, 1850–52.

———. *Allgemeine praktische Philosophie.* Jena, 1808.

———. *Lehrbuch zur Psychologic* Berlin, 1816. Trans. by Margaret K. Smith as *A Textbook in Psychology.* New York: Appleton, 1891.

Jankélévitch, Vladimir. *L'Odysée de la conscience dans la dernière philosophie de Schelling.* Paris: Alcan, 1933.

Jodl, Friedrich. *Geschichte der Ethik in der neueren Philosophie.* Stuttgart-Berlin: Frommann, 1912.

Jones, W. T. *Contemporary German Thought.* 2 vols. New York: Macmillan, 1931.

Kelley, M. *Kant's Ethics and Schopenhauer's Criticism.* London: Swan-Sonnenschein, 1910.

Kojève, Alexandre. *Introduction à la. lecture de Hegel.* Paris: Gallimard, 1947.

Kropotkin, Peter. *Ethics: Origin and Development.* Trans. L. S. Friedland and J. R. Piroshnikofí. New York: Dial Press, 1924, 1936.

Lévy-Bruhl, Lucien. *L'Allemagne depuis Leibniz. Essai sur le développement de la conscience nationale en Allemagne, 1700–1848.* Paris: Hachette, 1890.

Lotze, Rudolf Hermann. *Mikrokosmos.* 2 vols. Leipzig, 1856–64. Trans. by E. Hamilton and E. E. C. Jones, as *Microcosmus.* 2 vols. New York: Scribner's, 1887.

MacInryre, Alasdair (ed.). *Nineteenth-Century Philosophy: Hegel to Nietzsche.* New York: Free Press, 1967.

Mazzei, V. *Il pensiero etico-politica di Friedrich Schelling.* Roma: Sestante, 1938.

Moore, V. F. *Ethical Aspects of Lotze's Metaphysics.* Ithaca, N.Y.: Cornell University Press, 1901.

Nelson, Leonard. *System of Ethics.* Trans. Norbert Guterman. New Haven: Yale University Press, 1956.

Peperzak, A. T. *Le jeune Hegel et la vision morale du monde.* Ten Haag: Nijhoff, 1960.

Pringle-Pattison, A. Seth. *The Development from Kant to Hegel.* 2nd ed. New York: Stechert, 1924.

Raich, M. *Fichte, seine Ethik und seine Stellung zum Problem des Individualismus.* Tübingen: Mohr, 1905.

Reyburn, H. A. *The Ethical Theory of Hegel: A Study of the Philosophy of Right.* Oxford: Clarendon Press, 1921.

Schelling, Friedrich W. J. *Philosophische Untersuchungen über das Wesen der menschlichen Freiheit.* Tübingen, 1809. Trans. by J. Gutman as *Of Human Freedom.* Chicago: Open Court, 1936.

———. *Methode des akademischen Studiums.* Tübingen, 1803.

Trans. by E. S. Morgan as *On University Studies.* Athens, Ohio: Ohio University Press, 1966.

———. *Die Zeitalter.* München, 1811. Trans. by F. de W. Bolman as *The Ages of the World.* New York: Columbia University Press, 1942.

Schleiermacher, Friedrich D. E. *Grundlinien einer Kritik der bisherigen Sittenlehre.* Berlin, 1803.

Schopenhauer, Arthur. *Sämmtliche Werke,* hrsg. P. Deussen. 13 vols. München: Piper, 1911–42.

———. *Die Welt als Willie und Vorstellung.* Dresden, 1819. Trans. by R. B. Haldane and J. Kemp as *The World as Will and Idea.* 2 vols. London: Kegan Paul, Trench, 1883–86. Reprinted, New York: Doubleday, 1961.

———. *Die beiden Grundprobleme der Ethik.* Frankfurt, 1841; Leipzig, 1881. Essay I Trans. by K. Kolenda as *Essay on the Freedom of the Will* New York: Liberal Arts Press, 1960. Essay II Trans. by A. B. Bullock as *The Basis of Morality.* New York: Macmillan, 1903. Also Trans. by E. F. J. Payne. New York: Library of Liberal Arts, 1965.

Sterrett, J. M. "The Ethics of Hegel," *Ethics,* II (1892), 176–201.

Stirner, Max. *Der Einzige und sein Eigentum.* Berlin, 1845.

Wahl, Jean. *La conscience malheureuse dans la philosophie de Hegel.* Paris: Aubier, 1951.

Werkmeister, W. H. *Theories of Ethics.* Lincoln, Neb.: Johnsen, 1961.

Wundt, Wilhelm M. *Ethik.* Leipzig, 1886. Trans. by E. B. Titchener *et al.* as *Ethics.* 3 vols. New York: Macmillan, 1897–1901.

Zimmern, Helen. *Arthur Schopenhauer, His Life and His Philosophy.* London: Allen & Unwin, 1876; New York: Scribner's, 1932 (chap. 12).

Chapter XII

Alcorta, J. I. "La filosofia etica esencialista-existencialista de Lavelle y Le Senne," *Espiritu,* III (1959), 35–40; V (1961), 20–27.

Baruzzi, Jean (ed.). *Philosophes et savants français du XXe siècle.* Tome III: "Le problème moral." Paris: Alcan, 1926.

Benrubi, Isaak. *Contemporary Thought of France.* Trans. E. B. Dicker. New York: Knopf, 1926.

Bergson, Henri. *Oeuvres,* texts annotés par André Robinet. Paris: Presses Universitaires, 1959 ff.

———. *Extraits e Lucrèce.* Paris: Alcan, 1884.

———. *Essai sur les données immédiates de la conscience.* Paris: Alcan, 1889. Trans. by F. L. Pogson as *Time and Free Will: An Essay on the Immediate Data of Consciousness.* New York: Macmillan, 1950.

———. *Les deux sources de la morale et de la religion.* Paris: Alcan, 1932. Trans. by R. A. Audra and C. Brereton as *The Two Sources of Morality and Religion.* New York: Holt, 1935. Reprinted, New York: Doubleday Anchor, 1954.

———. *Bergson: Choix de textes,* éd. par R. Gillouin. Paris: Alcan, 1928.

———. *Selections from Bergson,* ed. H. A. Larrabee. New York: Appleton-Century-Crofts, 1949.

Bochenski, I. M. *Contemporary European Philosophy.* Trans. D. Nicholl and K. Aschenbrenner. Berkeley-Los Angeles: University of California Press, 1965.

Boutroux, Émile. "The Individual Conscience and the Law," *Ethics,* XXVII (1917), 317–31.

———. "Liberty of Conscience," *Ethics,* XXVIII (1918), 59–72.

———. *Morale et religion.* Paris: Flammarion, 1925.

Bruno, J. F. *Rosmini's Contribution to Ethical Philosophy.* New York: Science Press, 1916.

Brunschvicg, Léon. *Introduction à la vie de l'esprit.* Paris: Alcan, 1900.

———. *La connaissance de soi.* Paris: Alcan, 1931.

———. *La philosophie de l'esprit.* Paris: Presses Universitaires, 1949.

Burnier, André, *La pensée de Charles Secrétan et le problème du fondement métaphysique des jugements de valeur moraux.* Neuchâtel: La Baconnière, 1934.

Carrel, F. "The Morals of Guyau," *Ethics,* XV (1905), 457–69.

Caturelli, Alberto. *La filosofia en Argentina actual.* Cordoba, Argentina: Universidad Nacional de Cordoba, 1962.

Copleston, F. *Bergson on Morality.* New York: Oxford University Press, 1957.

Cousin, Victor. *Oeuvres complètes.* 22 vols. Paris: Ladrange, 1846–47.

———. *Du vrai, du beau, et du bien.* Paris, 1837. Trans. by O. W. Wight as *The True, the Beautiful, and the Good.* New York: Appleton, 1854.

———. *Cours d'histoire de la philosophie morale au XVIIIe siècle.* Paris: Hachette, 1839–40.

Darlu, A. "La morale de Renouvier," *Revue de Métaphysique et de la Morale,* XII (1904), 1–18.

Dehove, J. *La théorie bergsonienne de la morale et de la religion.* Lille: Editions de l'Université, 1933.

Farber, Marvin (ed.). L'*Activité philosophique en France et aux Etats-Unis.* 2 vols. Paris: Presses Universitaires, 1950.

Also in English: *Philosophic Thought in France and the United States.* Buffalo, N.Y.: University of Buffalo, 1950.

Ferrater Mora, José. "The Philosophy of Xavier Zubiri," in *European Philosophy Today,* ed. George Kline. Chicago: Quadrangle Books, 1965. Pp. 15–29.

Foucher, Louis. *La Philosophie catholique en France.* Paris: Vrin, 1955.

Fouillée, Alfred. *Critique des systèmes de morale contemporaines.* Paris: Baillière, 1899.

———. *La morale, l'art et la religion d'après Guyau.* Paris: Alcan, 1897, 1923.

———. "The Ethics of Nietzsche and Guyau," *Ethics,* XIII (1903), 13–27.

Franquiz, J. A. "Personalism in Latin-American Philosophy," *Memorias del* XIII *Congreso Internacional de Filosofia,* IX (Mexico City, 1964), 571–83.

Gioberti, Vicenzo. *Del buono.* Bruxelles: Méline, 1848. Ediz. 2ª, Firenze: Le Monnier, 1853.

———. *Delia protologia.* 2 vols. Torino-Paris, 1857. Ed. G. Balsamo-Crivelli. Torino: Paravia, 1924.

———. *Cours de Philosophie,* ed. M. Battistini e Giovanni Calo. Milano: Fratelli Bocca, 1947.

———. *Gioberti (Antologia),* ed. G. Saitta. Milano: Garzanti, 1952.

Guy, Alain. *Les philosophes espagnols d'hier et d'aujourd'hui.* Toulouse-Paris: Editions Privats, 1956.

Guyau, Jean-Marie. *Esquisse d'une morale sans obligation ni sanction.* Paris: Alcan, 1885. Trans. by Gertrude Kapteyn as *Sketch of Morality Independent of Obligation or Sanction.* London, 1898.

———. *L'Irreligion d'avenir.* Paris: Alcan, 1887. Trans. as *The Non-Religion of the Future.* New York: Holt, 1897.

———. *La morale anglaise contemporaine.* Paris: Alcan, 1900.

Hallie, Philip. *Maine de Biran: Reformer of Empiricism.* Cambridge: Harvard University Press, 1959.

Homenaje a Xavier Zubiri. Madrid: Editorial National, 1953. Jankélévitch, Vladimir. *La mauvaise conscience.* Paris: Alcan, 1933.

———. *Le mal.* Paris: Arthaud, 1947.

———. *Traité des vertus.* Paris: Bordas, 1949.

———. *Le pur et l'impur.* Paris: Flammarion, 1960.

Jouffroy, Théodore. *Mélanges philosophiques.* Paris: Joubert, 1842. "De l'éclecticisme en morale," pp. 273–79.

———. *Cours de droit naturel.* Paris, 1834–35.

Korn, Alejandro. *La Libertad Creadora.* La Plata, Argentina: Troquel, 1922.

———. *Axiologia.* La Plata, Argentina: Troquel, 1930.

Lavelle, Louis. *La conscience de soi.* Paris: Grasset, 1933.

———. *L'Erreur de Narcisse,* Paris: Grasset, 1939.

———. *La philosophie française entre les deux guerres.* Paris: Aubier, 1942.

———. *Quatre Saints.* Paris: Michel, 1951. Trans. by D. O'Sullivan as *The Meaning of Holiness.* London: Downside, 1954.

———. *Conduite à l'égard d'autrui.* Paris: Michel, 1957.

Le Senne, René. *Le devoir.* Paris: Presses Universitaires, 1930.

———. *Obstacle et valeur.* Paris: Aubier, 1934.

———. *Traité de morale générale.* Paris: Presses Universitaires, 1942, 1961.

———. *Traité de caractérologie.* Paris: Presses Universitaires, 1945.

———. "De la 'Philosophie de l'esprit,'" in *L'Activité philosophique,* ed,. M. Farber. II, 113–31.

Lowde, James. *Moral Essays: wherein Some of Mr. Lock's and Mons. Malebranch's Opinions Are Briefly Examined.* London, 1699.

Maine de Biran, Marie Francois Pierre Gonthier. *Oeuvres,* ed. Pierre Tisserand. 14 vols. Paris: Alcan et Presses Universitaires, 1920–49.

———. *Les rapports du physique et du moral de l'homme* (written in 1820). Paris, 1834. In *Oeuvres,* Tome XIII.

———. *Oeuvres choisies de Maine de Biran,* éd. par Henri Gouhier. Paris: Aubier, 1942.

Malebranche, Nicolas. *Oeuvres complètes.* 20 vols. dir. par A. Robinet. Paris: Vrin, 1950 ff.

———. *Traité de morale.* Cologne, 1683. Ed. Henri Joly. Paris, 1882. 3me éd. Paris: Vrin, 1953. Trans. by James Shipton as *A Treatise of Morality.* 1699. Chap. 1 reprinted in Rand, *Classical Moralists.* Pp. 286–93.

———. *Dialogues on Metaphysics and Religion.* Trans. Morris Ginsberg. New York: Macmillan, 1923.

Maritain, J. "Sur l'éthique bergsonienne," *Revue de métaphysique et de la. morale,* LXIV (1959), 141–60. In English in *Moral Philosophy.* Pp. 418–47.

Marquinez, A. German. *En torno a Zubiri.* Madrid: Studium, 1965.

Piersol, Wesley. *La Valeur dans la philosophie de Louis Lavelle.* Paris: Vitte, 1959.

Renan, J. Ernest. *L'Avenir de la science.* Paris, 1890. Trans. by A. D. Vandam and C. B. Pitman as *The Future of Science* London: Chapman and Hall, 1891.

———. *La Réforme intellectuelle et morale,* ed. P. E. Charvet. Cambridge, Eng.: University Press, 1950.

———. *Philosophical Dialogues and Fragments.* Trans. Râs Bihârî Mukhargî. London: Trubner, 1883.

Renouvier, Charles Bernard. *Science de la. morale.* 2 vols. Paris: Alcan, 1869, 1908.

———. *Le Personnalisme.* Paris: Alcan, 1903.

Revue Internationale de Philosophie (Bruxelles). Numéro consacré à la 'Philosophic de l'Esprit,' n. 5 (15 oct. 1939). Rolland, E. *La finalité morale dans le bergsonisme.* Paris: Beauchesne, 1937.

Rome, Beatrice. *The Philosophy of Malebranche.* Chicago: Regnery, 1964.

Romero, Francisco. *Filosofia de la. Persona.* Buenos Aires: Losada, 1938.

———. *Theory of Man.* Trans. W. F. Cooper. Berkeley, Calif.: University of California Press, 1964.

Rosmini, Antonio Serbati. *Opere complete.* 28 vols. Milano: Fratelli Bocca, 1934 ff.

———. *Príncipi della scienza morale.* Milano: Pogliani, 1831. In *Opere complete,* Vols. XXII–XXIII.

———. *Trattato della conscienza morale.* Milano: Pogliani, 1839.

———. *Antonio Rosmini: Anthologie philosophique,* éd. par G. Pusineri *et al.* Lyon: Vitte, 1954.

Sait, U. M. *The Ethical Implications of Bergson's Philosophy.* New York: Columbia University Press, 1914.

Sanabria, José. *El ser y el valor en la filosofía de Louis Lavelle.* Mexico: Universidad Nacional, 1963.

Sanchez Reulet, Anibal. *Contemporary Latin-American Philosophy.* Trans. W. R. Trask. Albuquerque, N.M.: University of New Mexico Press, 1954.

Sciacca, M. F. *La filosofia morale di Antonio Rosmini.* Roma: Perrella, 1938.

———. *Il secolo* XX: *Storia della. filosofia italiana.* 2 vols. Milano: Fratelli Bocca, 1947.

———. *Philosophical Trends in the Contemporary World.* Notre Dame, Ind.: University of Notre Dame Press, 1965.

———. *Etica e Moral.* São Paulo, Brazil: Instituto Brasilerio de Filosofía, 1952.

———. *Ragione etica e intelligenza morale.* Córdoba, Argentina: Universidad Nacional, l953.

Secrétan, Charles. *La philosophie de la liberté.* 2 vols. Paris: Hachette, 1849, 1879.

———. *Le principe de la morale.* Paris: Hachette, 1884.

Smith, Colin. *Contemporary French Philosophy.* London: Methuen, 1964.

Taine, Hippolyte. *L'Intelligence.* 2 vols. Paris, 1870, 1906. Trans. by T. D. Haye as *On Intelligence.* New York: Holt & Williams, 1872.

———. *Philosophie de l'art.* Paris, 1882. Published as *Philosophy of Art.* London: Baillière, 1865.

Truman, N. E. *Maine de Biran's Philosophy of Will.* Ithaca, N.Y.: Cornell University Press, 1964.

Vasconcelos, José. *Ethi*ca. Madrid: Aguilar, 1932.

———. *Historia. del pensamiento filosófico.* Mexico, D.F.: Universidad Nacional, 1937.

Verga, Leonardo. *La filosofia morale de Malebranche.* Milano: Vita e Pensiero, 1964.

Vidari, Giovanni. *Rosmini e Spencer: studio espositivo-critico di filosofia morale.* Milano: Hoepli, 1899.

Yoles, Francisca, *et al. El pensamiento de M. F. Sciacca: Homenaje (1908–1958).* Buenos Aires, Argentina: Troquel, 1959.

Zubiri, Xavier. *Naturaleza, Historia, Dios.* Madrid: Editorial Nacional, 1944.

———. "Socrates and Greek Wisdom," *Thomist,* VII (1944), 40–45.

———. "El hombre, realidad personal," *Revista de Occidente,* I (1963), 5–29.

———. *Sobre la esencia.* Madrid: Editorial Nacional, 1962.

Chapter XIII

Aiken, H. D. (ed.). *The Age of Ideology.* New York: Mentor, 1956.

Antolin, Viktor. "La Moral Communista," *Revista de Filosofia,* LV (1955), 565–74. English digest in *Philosophy Today,* I (1957), 106–8.

Ash, William. *Marxism and Moral Concepts.* New York: Monthly Review Press, 1964.

Banchetti, S. *Il significato morale dell'estetica vichiana.* Milano: Marzorati, 1957.

Bausola, Adriano. *Etica e Política net pensiero di Benedetto Croce.* Milano: Vita e Pensiero, 1966.

Bax, E. B. *The Ethics of Socialism.* London: Swann, Sonnenschein, 1902.

Bazard and Enfantin. *The Doctrine of Saint-Simon, an Exposition.* Trans. George C. Iggers. Boston: Beacon Press, 1958.

Berdyaev, Nikolai. *Smisl Istorii.* Berlin: Obelisk, 1923. Trans. by George Reavey as *The Meaning of History.* New York: Scribner's, 1936.

———. *Freedom and the Spirit.* Trans. O. F. Clarke. London: Bles, 1935.

———. *Solitude and Society.* Trans. G. Reavey. New York: Scribner's, 1939.

———. *The Destiny of Man.* Trans. N. Duddington. London: Bles, 1948. Reprinted New York: Harper Torchbooks, 1960.

———. *Dialectique existentielle du divin et de l'humain.* Paris: Janin, 1947.

———. *Christian Existentialism: a Berdyaev Synthesis,* ed. D. A. Lowrie. New York: Harper Torchbooks, 1962.

Berlin, Isaiah. *Historical Inevitability.* New York: Oxford University Press, 1955.

Blakeley, T. J. *Soviet Philosophy.* Dordrecht: Reidel, 1964.

Bloch, Ernst. *Das Prinzip Hoffnung.* 2 vols. Frankfurt-am-Main, 1959.

———. "Man and Citizen according to Marx," in *Socialist Humanism,* ed. Erich Fromrn. New York: Doubleday, 1965. Pp. 200–06.

Bochenski, I. M. *Contemporary European Philosophy.* Berkeley: University of California Press, 1965.

Bourgin, Hubert. *Fourier, Contribution à l'étude du socialisme français.* Paris: Bellais, 1905.

Bourke, V. J. "The Philosophical Antecedents of German National Socialism," *Thought,* XIV (1939), 225–42.

Calian, C. S. *The Significance of Eschatology in the Thoughts of Nicolas Berdyaev.* Leiden: Brill, 1965.

Caponigri, A. R. *Time and Idea. The Theory of History in J. B. Vico.* London: Routledge, Kegan Paul, 1953.

Chamberlain, Houston Stewart. *Die Grundlagen des neunzehnten Jahrhunderts.* 2 Bde. München, 1899. Trans. by J. Lees as *The Foundations of the Nineteenth Century.* New York: Lane, 1912, 1914.

Collingwood, Robin George. *The Idea of History.* Oxford: Clarendon Press, 1946.

———. *Autobiography.* Oxford: Clarendon Press, 1939.

Comte, Auguste. *Cours de philosophic positive.* 6 vols. Paris: Société Positiviste, 1830–42. Abridged Trans. by Harriet Martineau. *The Positive Philosophy of Auguste Comte.* 3 vols. London: Bohn, 1853.

———. *Discours sur l'ensemble du posítivisme.* Paris: Mathias, 1848. Trans. by J. H. Bridges as *A General View of Positivism.* London: Routledge, 1910; Stanford: Academic Reprints, 1953.

———. *Catéchisme positiviste.* Paris, n.d. Reprinted Paris: Gamier, 1909. Trans. by R. Congreve as *The Cathechism of Positive Religion.* London, 1858.

———. *Oeuvres choisies d'Auguste Comte,* éd. par Henri Gouhier. Paris: Aubier, 1943.

Condorcet, Antoine-Nicolas de. *Oeuvres,* éd. par F. Arago. 12 vols. Paris, 1847–49.

———. *Esquisse d'un tableau historique des progrès de l'esprit humain.* Paris, 1794. Trans. by June Barraclough as *The Progress of the Human Mind.* New York: Noonday Press, 1955. Cornu, Auguste. *The Origins of Marxian Thought.* Springfield, Ill.: Thomas, 1957.

Croce, Benedetto. *Filosofia delta pratica: Economica ed Eti*ca. Bari: Laterza, 1909. Trans. by Douglas Ainslie as *Philosophy of the Practical: Economic and Ethic.* New York: Macmillan, 1913.

———. *Cultura e vita morale.* Bari: Laterza, 1914.

———. *Frammenti di eti*ca. Bari: Laterza, 1922. Trans. by Arthur Livingston as *The Conduct of Life.* New York: Harcourt, Brace, 1924.

———. *Etica e Politica,* Bari: Laterza, 1931. Trans. by S. J. Castiglione as *Politics and Morals.* New York: Philosophical Library, 1945.

———. My *Philosophy, and Other Essays on the Moral and Political Problems of Our Time.* Selected by Raymond Klibansky and Trans. by E. F. Carritt. London: Allen & Unwin, 1951.

Czerna, R. C. *Filosofia juridica de Benedetto Croce.* São Paulo, Brasil: Instituto Brasileiro de Filosofia, 1956.

Deploige, Simon. *The Conflict Between Ethics and Sociology.* Trans. C. C. Miltner. St. Louis: Herder, 1938.

Deschamps, Léger-Marie. *La voix de la raison.* Bruxelles, 1770.

———. *Le vrai système, ou le mot de l'énigme métaphysique et moral,* ed. Jean Thomas et Franco Venturi. Paris: Alcan, 1939.

Dupré, Louis. *The Philosophical Foundations of Marxism.* New York: Harcourt, Brace & World, 1966.

Durkheim, Emíle. *Sociologie et philosophie.* Paris: Alcan, 1924. Trans. by D. F. Pocock as *Sociology and Philosophy.* Glencoe, Ill.: Free Press, 1953.

———. *L'Education morale.* Paris: Alcan, 1925.

———. *Emile Durkheim: Selections from His Work,* ed. by George Simpson. New York: Crowell, 1963.

Edie, J. M., *et al. Russian Philosophy.* 3 vols. Chicago: Quadrangle Books, 1965.

Engels, Friedrich. *Anti-Dühring.* Berlin, 1878. Trans. by Emile Burns as *Herr Eugen Dühring's Revolution in Science.* New York: International Publishers, 1934, 1939.

Evans, Valmai B. "The Ethics of Giovanni Gentile," *Ethics,* XXXIX (1929), 205–17.

———. "The Ethics of Croce," *Ethics,* XLIV (1934), 54–64.

Forti, Edgar. "La Méthode scientifique en morale et en psychologie suivant l'oeuvre de Frédéric Rauh," *Revue de métaphysique et de morale,* XLI (1934), 13–24.

Fourier, Francois M. C. *Théorie des quatre mouvements.* 2 vols. Leipzig-Lyon: Pelzin, 1808.

———. *Le nouveau monde industriel et sociétaire.* 2 vols. Paris: Bossange, 1829–30.

Fromm, Erich. Marx's *Concept of Man.* New York: Ungar, 1961.

Garaudy, Roger. *Le communisme et la. morale.* Paris: Editions Sociales, 1945.

Gentile, Giovanni. *Opere complete.* Firenze: Sansoni, 1938 ff.

———. *L'Atto del pensare come atto puro.* Bari: Laterza, 1912. Trans. by H. W. Carr as *The Theory of the Mind as Pure Act.* New York: Macmillan, 1922.

———. *Discorsi di religíone. III: Il problema morale.* Ed. 4. Firenze: Sansoni, 1957.

Ginsberg, Morris. "Ethical Relativity and Political Theory," *British Journal of Sociology,* II (1951), 1–17.

———. *Essays in Sociology and Social Philosophy,* Vol. I: *On the Diversity of Morals,* 1956; Vol. II, *Reason and Unreason in Society, 1960.* London: Heinemann.

———. *On Justice in Society.* Ithaca, N.Y.: Cornell University Press, 1965.

Gobineau, Arthur de. *Essai sur l'inégalité des races humaines.* 4 vols. Paris, 1853–55. Book I Trans. by A. Collins as *The Inequality of Human Races.* New York: Holt, 1915.

Gumplowicz, Ludwig. *Der Rassenkampf.* Innsbruck: Wagner, 1905; Aufl. 2, 1927.

———. *Geschichte der Staatstheorien.* Innsbruck: Wagner, 1883.

Harris, H. S. *The Social Philosophy of Giovanni Gentile.* Champaign, Ill.: University of Illinois Press, 1960.

Hook, Sidney, *From Hegel to Marx.* New York: Reynal & Hitchcock, 1936.

Kamenenka, Eugen. *The Ethical Foundations of Marxism.* London: Routledge, Kegan Paul, 1962.

Kautsky, Karl. *Ethics and the Materialist Conception of History.* Trans. J. B. Askew. Chicago: Kerr, 1906, 1918.

Kline, G. L. (ed.). *European Philosophy Today.* Chicago: Quadrangle Books, 1965.

———. "Socialist Legality and Communist Ethics," *Natural Law Forum,* VIII (1963), 21–34.

Lagarde, Paul Anton de. *Deutsche Schriften.* 2 Bde. Göttingen, 1878–81.

Lenin, Vladimir Ilyich Ulyanov. *Collected Works.* Trans. Clemens Dutt *et al.* Moscow: Foreign Languages Institute, l960 ff. (26 vols. by 1965).

———. *Materialism and Empirio-Critiásm.* New York: International Publishers, 1927.

———. *Philosophical Notebooks* (1914–16), in *Collected Works,* Vol. 38.

Lévy-Bruhl, Lucien. *L'Idée de responsabilité.* Paris: Alcan, 1885.

———. *La philosophie d'Auguste Comte.* Paris: Alcan, 1900.

———. *La morale et la science des moeurs.* Paris: Alcan, 1903. Trans. by Elizabeth Lee as *Ethics and Moral Science.* London: Constable, 1905.

Lopatin, L. M. "The Philosophy of Vladimir Solovyev," Trans. by A. Bakshy, in *Mind,* XXV (1916), 425–60.

Lubac, Henri de. *The Drama of Atheist Humanism.* Trans. Edith M. Riley. New York: Sheed & Ward, 1950.

Lukacs, Georg. *Geschichte und Klassenbewusstsein.* Berlin: Malik-Verlag, 1923.

———. *Existentialisme ou Marxisme?* Paris: Nagel, 1948.

McGovern, W. M. *From Luther to Hitler.* New York: Houghton, 1941.

Mankiewicz, H. *La conception nationalsocialiste du sens de la vie et du monde.* Lyon: Université de Lyon, l937.

Marx, Karl. *Zur Kritik der Hegelschen Rechtsphilosophie.* Berlin, 1843.

———. *Karl Marx: Early Writings,* ed. T. B. Bottomore. New York: McGraw-Hill, 1964.

Marx, Karl, and Engels, F. *Historisch-kritische Gesamtausgabe,* hrsg. D. Rjazanow und V. Adoratsky. Frankfurt-am-Main, 1927 ff.

———. *The Communist Manifesto.* London-Brussels, 1848.

———. *Das Kapital.* 3 vols. Berlin, 1867–94. Trans. as *Capital, The Communist Manifesto, and Other Writings,* ed. Max Eastman. New York: Random House, 1932.

Merleau-Ponty, Maurice. *Les aventures de la dialectique.* Paris: Gallimard, 1955.

Meyer, H. *Houston S. Chamberlain als völkischer Denker.* Berlin: Hoheneichen, i939.

Meyerhoff, Hans (ed.). *The Philosophy of History in Our Time, An Anthology.* Garden City, N.Y.: Doubleday Anchor, 1959.

Popper, K. R. *The Open Society and Its Enemies.* 2 vols. London: Routledge, Kegan Paul, 1945. Vol. II, chap. 8: "Marx's Ethics."

Rauh, Frédéric. *Essai sur le fondement métaphysique de la morale.* Paris, 1890; Paris: Alcan, 1903.

———. *L'Experience morale.* Paris: Alcan, 1903.

———. *Etudes de morale.* Paris: Alcan, 1911.

Romanelli, Patrick. *Croce versus Gentile.* New York: Macmillan, 1947.

Rosenberg, Alfred. *Der Mythus des 20 Jahrhunderts.* München: Hoheneichen, 1938.

Rubel, M. *Pages choisies pour une Ethique socialiste.* Paris: Rivière, 1948.

Rühle, Jürgen. "The Philosopher of Hope: Ernst Bloch," in *Revisionism: Essays on the History of Marxist Ideas,* ed. L. Labedz. London-New York: Praeger, 1962. Pp. 166–78.

Sade, Donatien de. *Les Infortunes de la vertu.* Paris, 1787.

———. *Histoire de Juliette.* Paris, 1790.

Saint-Simon, Claude Henri de. *Oeuvres.* 6 vols. Paris: Anthropos, 1966 ff.

———. *La Société européenne.* Paris, 1814.

———. *Le Système industriel.* Paris, 1821.

Sartre, Jean-Paul. *Critique de la raison dialectique.* Tome I. Paris: Gallimard, 1960.

Seillière, E. *Le Comte de Gobineau et l'Arianisme historique.* Paris: Nourrit, 1903.

———. *Houston Stewart Chamberlain.* Paris: Renaissance du Livre, 1917.

Selsam, Howard. *Socialism and Ethics.* New York: International Publishers, 1943.

Shestov, Leon. *L'Idée de bien chez Tolstoi et Nietzsche.* Paris: Schiffrin, 1925.

———. *Kierkegaard et la philosophie existentielle.* Trad, par T. Rageot et Boris De Schloezer. Paris: Schiffrin, 1936.

Smith, T. V. "The Ethics of Fascism," *Ethics,* XLVI (1936), 151–77.

Solovyev, Vladimir. *The Justification of the Good.* Trans. Natalie Duddington. London: Constable, 1918.

———. *The Meaning of Love.* Trans. Janet Marshall. New York: Scribner's, 1947.

———. *A Solovyov Anthology,* ed. S. L. Frank. New York: Scribner's, 1950.

Stalin, Joseph (Iosif V. Dzhugashvili). *Leninism.* New York: International Publishers, 1942.

———. *Dialectical and Historical Materialism, id.,* 1940.

———. *Marxism and Linguistics, id.,* 1951.

Tansill, C. C. "Racial Theories in Germany from Herder to Hitler," *Thought,* XV (1940), 453–68.

Titarenko, Boldyrev, *et. al. O Kommunisticheskoi Morali.* Moscow: Academy of Sciences, 1951.

Tucker, R. C. *Philosophy and Myth in Karl Marx.* New York: Cambridge University Press, 1961.

Vico, Giambattista. *Opere.* 8 vols. Bari: Laterza, 1914–41.

———. *De universi juris uno principio et fine uno.* Napoli, 1720.

———. *Scienza Nuova.* Napoli, 1725. ed. 2^{e}, 1744 (in *Opere,* Vols. III–IV). Trans. by T. C. Bergin and M. H. Fisch as *The New Science of Giambattista Vico.* Ithaca, N.Y.: Cornell University Press, 1948.

Voinea, Serban. *La Morale et le socialisme.* Gand: La Flamme, 1953.

Westermarck, Edward. *The Origin and Development of the Moral Ideas.* 2 vols. London: Macmillan, 1906.

Wetter, Gustav. *Dialectical Materialism: a Historical and Systematic Survey of Philosophy in the Soviet Union.* Trans. Peter Heath, New York: Praeger, 1958.

Zenkovsky, V. V. A *History of Russian Philosophy.* Trans. G. L. Kline. New York: Columbia University Press, 1953.

Zis, A. Y. "Moral burzhuaznaya i moral kommunisticheskaya," *Pod Znamenem Marksizma,* VI (1939), 72 ff.

Zitta, Victor. *Georg Lukacs' Marxism: Alienation, Dialectics, Revolution.* The Hague: Nijhoff, 1964.

Chapter XIV

Allers, Rudolf. *Das Werden der sittlichen Person.* Freiburg im Breisgau: Herder, 1929. Trans. by E. B. Strauss as *The Psychology of Character.* New York: Sheed & Ward, 1930.

———. "Ethics and Anthropology," *New Scholasticism,* XXIV (1950), 237–62.

———. "Reflections on Co-operation and Communication," *Proceedings of the American Catholic Philosophical Association,* XXXIV (1960), 13–27.

———. *The Philosophical Work of Rudolf Allers: A Selection,* ed. J. A. Mann. Washington, D.C.: Georgetown University Press, 1965.

Blau, J. L. *Men and Movements in American Philosophy.* New York: Prentice-Hall, 1952.

Borzaga, Reynold. *Contemporary Philosophy.* Milwaukee: Bruce, 1966.

Brentano, Franz C. *Psychologie vom empirischen Standpunkte.* 3 Bde. Leipzig: Meiner, 1874.

———. *Vom Ursprung sittliches Erkenntnis.* Leipzig: Meiner, 1884. Trans. by Cecil Hague as *The Origin of the Knowledge of Right and Wrong.* Westminster: Constable, 1902.

———. *Grundlegung und Aufbau der Ethik,* hrsg. Franziska Mayer-Hillebrand. Berne: Francke, 1952.

Breton, Stanislas. "Le problème de la liberté dans l'éthique de Nicolai Hartmann," *Revue Thomiste,* XLIX (1949), 310–35. Brightman, Edgar S. *Religious Values.* New York: Abingdon Press, 1925.

———. *Moral Laws.* New York: Abingdon Press, 1933.

———. *Person and Reality,* ed. P. A. Bertocci *et al.* New York: Ronald Press, 1958.

Brock, Werner. *An Introduction to Contemporary German Philosophy.* London-New York: Cambridge University Press, 1935.

Collins, James. "The Moral Philosophy of Max Scheler," *Encyclopedia of Morals* (1956). Pp. 517–24.

Dupuy, Maurice. *La philosophie de Max Scheler. Son Evolution et son unité. 2* vols. Paris: Presses Universitaires, 1959.

Eaton, H. O. *The Austrian Philosophy of Values.* Norman, Okla.: University of Oklahoma Press, 1930.

———. "The Content of Axiological Ethics," *Ethics,* XLII (1932), 132–47; XLIII (1933), 20–36, 253–68. Ehrenfels, Christian von. "The Ethical Theory of Value," *Ethics,* VI (1896), 371–84.

———. *System der Werttheorie.* 2 Bde. Leipzig, 1897–1918.

Eklund, H. *Evangelisches und Katholisches in Max Schelers Ethik.* Lund: Uppsala University, 1932.

Finance, Joseph de. *Existence et liberté.* Paris: Vitte, 1955.

———. *Ethica Generalis.* Roma: Universitas Gregoriana, 1959.

———. *Essai sur l'âgir humain.* Rome: Université Grégorienne, 1962.

Findlay, J. N. *Meinong's Theory of Objects.* London: Oxford University Press, 1933.

Frings, Manfred. *Max Scheler.* Pittsburgh: Duquesne University Press, 1965.

Gibson, W. R. Boyce. "The Ethics of Nicolai Hartmann," *Australasian Journal of Psychology and Philosophy,* XI (1933), 12–28; XII (1934), 33–61; XIII (1935), 1–23.

Groos, Reinhold. *Die Prinzipien der Ethik Nicolai Hartmanns.* München: Kaiser, 1932.

Gurvitch, Georges. *Morale théorique et science des moeurs,* Paris: Alcan, 1937.

———. *Les tendances actuelles de la philosophie allemande.* Paris: Vrin, 1949.

Hartmann, Nicolai. *Ethik.* 3 Bde. Berlin: De Gruyter, 1926. Trans. by Stanton Coit as *Ethics.* London: Allen & Unwin, 1932.

Hessen, Johannes. *Max Scheler: eine kritische Einführung in seine Philosophie.* Essen: Chamier, 1948.

———. *Ethik: Grundzüge einer personalistischen Wertethik.* Leiden: Brill, 1954.

———. *Religionsphilosophie.* 2 Bde. München-Basel: Reinhardt, 1955.

Hildebrand, Dietrich von. "Max Scheler als Ethiker," *Hochland,* XXI (1924), 626–37.

———. "Die Rolle des 'objektiven Gutes für die Person' innerhalb des Sittlichen," in *Philosophia Perennis,* ed. F. J. von Rintelen. Regensburg: Habbel, 1930. Pp. 975–95.

———. *Sittliche Grundhaltungen.* Mainz: M. Grünewald, 1933. Trans. as *Fundamental Moral Attitudes.* New York: Longmans, 1950.

———. *Christian Ethics.* New York: David McKay, 1952.

———. *True Morality and Its Counterfeits.* New York: David McKay, l955.

Johnson, O. A. *Ethics. Selections from Classical and Contemporary Writers.* New York: Holt, Rinehart, 1965.

Lauer, Quentin. "The Phenomenological Ethics of Max Scheler," *International Philosophical Quarterly,* I (1961), 273–300.

———. *The Triumph of Subjectivity.* New York; Fordham University Press, 1958.

Lepley, Ray (ed.). *The Language of Value.* New York: Columbia University Press, 1957.

Lewis, Clarence Irving. *An Analysis of Knowledge and Valuation.* La Salle, Ill.: Open Court, 1946.

———. *The Ground and Nature of the Right.* New York: Columbia University Press, 1955.

Margolius, Hans. *Die Ethik Franz Brentanos.* Berlin: Levy, 1929.

Mayer, P. E. *Der Objektivität der Werterkenntnis bei Nicolai Hartmann.* Meisenheim: Hain, 1952.

Meinong, Alexius. *Psychologisch-ethische Untersuchungen zur Wert-Theorie.* Graz: Leuschner u. Lubensky, 1894.

———. *Zur Grundlegung der allgemeinen Werttheorie.* Graz: Leuschner u. Lubensky, 1923.

Melden, A. I. (ed.). *Ethical Theories. A Book of Readings.* New York: Prentice-Hall, 1950.

Messer, A. *Deutsche Wertphilosophie der Gegenwart.* Leipzig: Reinicke, 1926.

Most, O. *Die Ethik Franz Brentanos und ihre geschichtlichen Grundlagen.* Berlin: Mittler, 1931.

Muirhead, J. H. (ed.). *Contemporary British Philosophy.* 2 vols. New York: Macmillan, 1931.

Parker, DeWitt H. *Human Values. An Interpretation of Ethics Based on a Study of Values.* New York: Harper, 1931. Reprinted, Ann Arbor, Mich.: Wahr, 1944.

Pepper, S. C. "A Brief History of General Theory of Value," *History of Philosophical Systems,* ed. V. Ferm. New York: Philosophical Library, 1950. Pp. 493–503.

Perry, Ralph Barton. *General Theory of Value.* Cambridge: Harvard University Press, 1926.

Polin, Raymond. *La création des valeurs.* Paris: Presses Universitaires, 1944.

———. *La compréhension des valeurs, id.,* 1945.

———. *Du laid, du mal, du faux, id.,* 1948.

———. "La Philosophic des valeurs en France," in *L'Activité Philosophique,* II (1950), 216–32.

Reck, Andrew. "The Value-Centric Philosophy of W. M. Urban," in *Recent American Philosophy.* New York: Pantheon, 1964. Pp. 154–80.

Rintelen, F. J. von. *Der Wertgedanke in der europäischen Geistesentwicklung.* Mainz: Matthias-Grünewald, 1939–40.

Scheler, Max. *Gesammelte Werke,* hrsg. Maria Scheler. Berne: Francke, 1954 ff.

———. *Beiträge zur Feststellung der Beziehungen zwischen den logischen und ethischen Prinzipien.* Jena: Universitäts Dissertation, 1899.

———. *Ueber Ressentiment und moralisches Werturteil.* Leipzig:

Engelmann, 1912. Trans. by W. W. Holdheim as *Ressentiment.* Glencoe, Ill.: Free Press, 1961.

———. *Der Formalismus in der Ethik und die materiale Wertethik,* in *Jahrbuch für Philosophie und phänomenologische Forschung.* Halle, 1913–16.

———. *Vom Ewigen im Menschen.* Berlin: Neue Geist Verlag, 1921. Trans. by B. Noble as *On the Eternal in Man.* New York: Harper, 1960.

———. *Wesen und Formen der Sympathie.* Berlin: Neue Geist Verlag, 1921; Frankfurt: Schulte-Bulmke, 1948. Trans. by Peter Heath as *The Nature of Sympathy.* New Haven: Yale University Press, 1954.

———. *Die Stellung des Menschen im Kosmos.* Berlin: Neue Geist Verlag, 1928. Trans. as *Man's Place in Nature.* Boston: Beacon Press, 1961.

Schlick, Moritz. *Fragen der Ethik.* Wien: Springer, 1930. Trans. by David Rynin as *Problems of Ethics.* New York: Prentice-Hall, 1939.

———. *Gesammelte Aufsaetze,* 1926–1936. Wien: Springer, 1938.

Schutz, Alfred. "Max Sender's Epistemology and Ethics," *Review of Metaphysics,* XI (1957–58).

Schwarz, B. V. (ed.). *The Human Person and the World of Values: a Tribute to Dietrich von Hildebrand.* New York: Fordham University Press, 1960.

Shaw, C. G. "The Theory of Value and Its Place in the History of Ethics," *Ethics,* XI (1901), 306–20.

Shein, Louis. *A Critique of Nicolai Hartmann's Ethics.* Toronto: University of Toronto Dissertation, 1946.

Sorley, W. S. *The Moral Life and Moral Worth.* Cambridge, Eng.: University Press, 1911.

———. *Moral Values and the Idea of God, id.,* 1918.

———. "Value and Reality," *Contemporary British Philosophy,* II (1925), 245–67.

Spaemann, Robert. "Courants philosophiques dans l'Allemagne d'aujourd'hui," *Archives de Philosophic,* XXI (1958), 274–97.

Stern, Alfred. *La Philosophie des valeurs en Allemagne.* Paris: Alcan, 1933.

Störring, Gustav. *Die moderne ethische Wertphilosophie.* Leipzig: Engelmann, 1935.

Urban, Wilbur M. *Valuation. Its Nature and Laws.* New York: Macmillan, 1909.

———. *The Intelligible World—Metaphysics and Value.* London: Allen & Unwin, 1929.

———. *Fundamentals of Ethics.* New York: Holt, 1930.

Walraff, Charles. *Max Scheler's Theory of Moral Obligation.* Berkeley, Calif.: University of California Press, 1939.

Ward, Leo R. *Philosophy of Value.* New York: Macmillan, 1930.

———. *Values and Reality.* New York: Sheed & Ward, 1935.

———. *Ethics and the Social Sciences.* Notre Dame, Ind.: University of Notre Dame Press, 1959.

———. *Ethics.* New York: Harper, 1965.

Werkmeister, William H. "Ethics and Value Theory," *Proceedings XI International Congress of Philosophy,* X (Brussels, 1953), 119–23.

———. *Theories of Ethics: A Study in Moral Obligation,* Lincoln, Neb.: Johnsen, 1961.

Wittmann, Michael. *Die moderne Wertethtk.* Dusseldorf: Schwann, 1940.

Chapter XV

Adams, G. P., and Montague, W. P. (eds.). *Contemporary American Philosophy.* 2 vols. New York: Macmillan, 1930.

Adler, Felix. *Life and Destiny.* New York: McClure, Phillips, 1905.

———. *An Ethical Philosophy of Life.* New York: Appleton, 1918.

Barrett, W., and Aiken, H. D. (eds.). *Philosophy in the Twentieth Century.* 2 vols. New York: Random House, 1962.

Beck, Lewis White. "A Neglected Aspect of Butler's Ethics," *Sophia,* V (1937), 11–15.

———. "The Formal Properties of Ethical Wholes," *Journal of Philosophy,* XXXVIII (1941), 160–68.

———. "Apodictic Imperatives," *Kant-Studien,* XLIX (1957), 7–24.

Blanshard, Brand. *The Impasse in Ethics.* Berkeley: University of California Press, 1945.

———. *Reason and Goodness.* New York: Macmillan, 1961.

Bosanquet, Bernard. *Psychology of the Moral Self.* London: Macmillan, 1897.

———. *The Principle of Individuality and Value.* London: Macmillan, 1912.

———. *The Value and Destiny of the Individual.* London: Macmillan, 1913.

———. *Some Suggestions in Ethics.* London: Macmillan, 1918.

Bradley, Francis Herbert. *Ethical Studies.* London: King, 1876. 2nd ed., Oxford: Clarendon Press, 1927. Reprinted, New York: Oxford University Press, 1962.

Braithwaite, R. B. *Theory of Games as a Tool for the Moral Philosopher.* Cambridge: University Press, 1955, 1963.

Brandt, R. B. *Ethical Theory.* Englewood Cliffs, N.J.: Prentice-Hall, 1959.

Brogan, A. P. "A Study in Statistical Ethics," *Ethics,* XXXIII (1923), 119–34.

———. "Ethics as Method," *Ethics,* XXXVI (1926), 263–70.

Buchanan, J. M., and Tullock, G. *The Calculus of Consent.* Ann Arbor, Mich.: University of Michigan Press, 1962.

Carritt, E. F. *The Theory of Morals: an Introduction to Ethical Philosophy.* London: Oxford University Press, 1928.

———. *Morals and Politics,* London: Oxford University Press, 1935.

———. *An Ambiguity of the Word Good.* London: Oxford University Press, 1937.

Chubb, Percival. *On the Religious Frontier: From an Outpost of Ethical Religion.* New York: Macmillan, 1931.

Clark, Henry. *The Ethical Mysticism of Albert Schweitzer.* Boston: Beacon Press, 1962. (Includes two essays by Schweitzer: "The Ethic of Self-Perfection," pp. 38–52; and "Reverence for Life," pp. 99–105.)

Cornett, R. A. "Individualism in the Ethics of Elijah Jordan," *Ethics,* LXVI (1956), 61–66.

Cotton, J. H. *Royce on the Human Self.* Cambridge: Harvard University Press, 1954.

Davidson, D., and Suppes, P. *Decision Making,* Stanford, Calif.: Stanford University Press, 1957.

Dewey, R. E., *el al.* (eds.). *Problems of Ethics.* New York: Macmillan, 1961.

Diggs, B. J. "Rules and Utilitarianism," *American Philosophical Quarterly,* I (1964), 32–44.

Ekman, Rosalind (ed.). *Readings in the Problems of Ethics.* New York: Scribner's, 1965.

Ewing, A. C. *The Definition of Good.* New York: Macmillan, 1946.

———. *Ethics,* London: English Universities Press, 1960.

Frankena, W. K. *Ethics.* Englewood Cliffs, N.J.: Prentice-Hall, 1963.

Fuss, Peter. *The Moral Philosophy of Josiah Royce.* Cambridge: Harvard University Press, 1965.

Green, Thomas Hill. *Works.* 3 vols. Oxford: Clarendon Press, 1885–88.

———. *Prolegomena to Ethics.* Oxford: Clarendon Press, 1883.

———. *Principles of Political Obligation.* Oxford: Clarendon Press, 1895.

Harrod, R. F. "Utilitarianism Revised," *Mind,* XLV (1936), 137–56.

Hocking, W. E. *Human Nature and Its Remaking.* New Haven: Yale University Press, 1918, 1932.

———. *Types of Philosophy.* New York: Scribner's, 1929, 1959.

Johnson, O. A. *Rightness and Goodness, A Study in Contemporary Ethical Theory.* The Hague: Nijhoff, 1959.

Jordan, Elijah. *The Good Life.* Chicago: University of Chicago Press, 1949.

Joseph, H. W. B. *Some Problems in Ethics.* Oxford: Clarendon Press, 1931.

Kant, Immanuel. *Kant: Critique of Practical Reason and Other Writings in Moral Philosophy,* ed. and trans. L. W. Beck. Chicago: University of Chicago Press, 1949.

Kiernan, Thomas (ed.). *A Treasury of Albert Schweitzer.* New York: Philosophical Library, 1965.

Lamont, W. D. *An Introduction to Green's Moral Philosophy.* London: Allen & Unwin, 1934.

Lyons, David. *Forms and Limits of Utilitarianism.* London: Oxford University Press, 1965.

Mack, R. D. "Individualism and Individuality in the Ethics of Elijah Jordan," *Ethics,* LXVH (1957), 139–42.

McCloskey, H. J. "An Examination of Restricted Utilitarianism," *Philosophical Review,* LXVI (1957), 466–85.

McGlynn, J. V., and Toner, J. J. *Modern Ethical Theories.* Milwaukee: Bruce, 1962.

Martineau, James. *Types of Ethical Theory.* 2 vols. Oxford: Clarendon Press, 1886–91.

Mises, Ludwig von. *Human Action.* New Haven: Yale University Press, 1949.

Muirhead, J. H. *Elements of Ethics.* London: John Murray, 1892, 1910.

———. *The Platonic Tradition in Anglo-Saxon Philosophy.* London: Macmillan, 1931.

Munitz, M. K. *The Moral Philosophy of Santayana.* New York: Humanities Press, 1957.

Neumann, J. von. "Zur Theorie der Gesellschaftspiele," *Mathematische Annalen,* C (1928), 295–320.

Neumann, J. von, and Morgenstern, Ó. *Theory of Games and Economic Behavior.* Princeton, N.J.: Princeton University Press, 1947.

Passmore, John. *A Hundred Years of Philosophy.* London: Duckworth, 1957.

Paton, H. J. *The Good Will, a Study in the Coherence Theory of Goodness.* London: Allen & Unwin, 1927.

———. *The Categorical Imperative: a Study in Kant's Moral Philosophy.* London: Hutchinson's Library, 1946.

———. *The Moral Law; or, Kant's Groundwork of the Metaphysic of Morals.* Trans. with analysis and notes. New York: Barnes & Noble, 1950.

Patterson, C. H. *Moral Standards.* New York: Ronald Press, 1957.

Prichard, H. A. *Duty and Interest.* Oxford: Clarendon Press, 1928.

———. *Moral Obligation.* Oxford: Clarendon Press, 1949.

———. "Does Moral Philosophy Rest on a Mistake?" *Mind,* XXI (1912), 487–99.

Rashdall, Hastings. "A Critique of Self-Realization," in *The Theory of Good and Evil.* Oxford: Clarendon Press, 1907. Reprinted in Dewey, R. E. *Problems of Ethics* (1961), pp. 257–60.

Rawls, John. "Two Concepts of Rules," *Philosophical Review,* LXIV (1955), 3–32.

Ross, W. D. *The Right and the Good.* Oxford: Clarendon Press, 1930.

———. *Foundations of Ethics.* Oxford: Clarendon Press, 1939.

Royce, Josiah. *The Religious Aspect of Philosophy.* Boston: Houghton Mifflin, 1885.

———. *The World and the Individual.* 2 vols. New York: Macmillan, 1900–01.

———. *Studies of Good and Evil.* New York: Appleton, 1902.

———. *The Philosophy of Loyalty.* New York: Macmillan, 1908, 1924.

———. *The Hope of the Great Community.* New York: Macmillan, 1916.

———. *Fugitive Essays.* Cambridge: Harvard University Press, 1920.

Santayana, George. *Works.* 15 vols. New York: Scribner's, 1936–40.

———. *The Life of Reason.* 5 vols. New York: Scribner's, 1905–06.

———. *Skepticism and Animal Faith,* New York: Scribner's, 1923.

———. *Realms of Being.* 4 vols. New York: Scribner's, 1940, 1942.

Schweitzer, Albert. *Kultur und Ethik.* Leipzig: Barth, 1922. Trans. by John Naish as *Civilization and Ethics.* New York: Macmillan, 1923. Reprinted 1962.

———. *Aus meinen Leben und Denken.* Leipzig: Barth, 1931. Trans. as *Out of My Life and Thought.* New York: Holt, 1933.

———. *The Philosophy of Civilization.* Trans. C. T. Campion. New York: Macmillan, 1949. Reprinted 1964.

———. *The Teaching of Reverence for Life.* London; Peter Owen, 1964.

Segerstedt, T. T. *Value and Reality in Bradley's Philosophy.* Lund: Gleerup, 1934.

Shubik, Martin (ed.). *Game Theory and Related Approaches to Social Behavior.* New York: Wiley, 1964.

Sidgwick, Henry. *Lectures on the Ethics of T. H. Green, Mr. Herbert Spencer and J. Martineau.* London: Macmillan, 1902. Singer, M. G. "Moral Rules and Principles," in A. I. Melden (ed.), *Essays in Moral Philosophy.* Seattle: University of Washington Press, 1958.

———. *Generalization in Ethics.* New York: Knopf, 1961.

Smart, J. J. C. "Extreme and Restricted Utilitarianism," *Philosophical Quarterly,* VI (1956), 344–54.

———. *An Outline of a System of Utilitarian Ethics.* Melbourne: Melbourne University Press, 1961.

Stace, Walter T. *The Concept of Morals.* New York: Macmillan, 1937. Reprinted 1962.

———. *Mysticism and Philosophy.* New York: Macmillan, 1961. Taylor, A. E. "Self-Realization—A Criticism," *Ethics,* VI (1896), 356–71.

———. *The Problem of Conduct.* London: Macmillan, 1901.

———. *The Faith of a Moralist.* London: Macmillan, 1930.

Thompson, George. "Game Theory and 'Social Value' Ethics," *Ethics,* LXXV (1965), 36–39.

Urmson, J. O. "The Interpretation of the Moral Philosophy of J. S. Mill," *Phüosophical Quarterly,* III (1953), 33–39.

Warnock, Mary. *Ethics Since 1900.* London: Oxford University Press, 1960.

Whitman, M. J. "Forms and Limits of Utilitarianism," *Ethics,* LXXVI (1966), 309–17.

———. *The Public Interest.* New York: Wiley, 1966.

Wolff, R. P. "Reflections on Game Theory and the Nature of Value," *Ethics,* LXXII (1962), 171–79.

Wright, H. W. *Self-Realization. An Outline of Ethics.* New York: Holt, 1913, 1924, 1940.

———. *The Moral Standards of Democracy.* New York: Appleton, 1925.

Chapter XVI

Adams, E. M. *Ethical Naturalism and the Modern World-View.* Chapel Hill, N.C.: University of North Carolina Press, 1960.

Aiken, H. D. *Reason and Conduct.* New York: Knopf, 1962.

Allers, Rudolf. "Ethics and Anthropology," *New Scholasticism,* XXIV (1950), 237–62. Reprinted in *Philosophical Work of Rudolf Allers* (1965), pp. 94–110.

Baruk, H. *Psychiatrie morale expérimentale, individuelle et sociale.* Paris: Presses Universitaires, 1950.

Bausola, Adriano. *L'Etica di John Dewey.* Milano: Vita e Pensiero, 1960.

Blewett, J. E. *The Origins and Early Mutations of John Dewey's Ethical Theory (1884–1904).* St. Louis, Mo.: St. Louis University Dissertation, 1959.

———. (ed.). *John Dewey: His Thought and Influence.* New York: Fordham University Press, 1960.

Brennan, B. P. *The Ethics of William James.* New York: Bookman Associates, 1961.

Cuénot, Claude. "La morale et l'homme selon Pierre Teilhard de Chardin," in *Morale chrétienne et morale marxiste.* Paris-Genève: La Palatine, 1960, pp. 117–47.

Cunningham, R. L. "The Direction of Contemporary Ethics," *New Scholasticism,* XXXIX (1965), 330–48.

Dennes, William R. *Some Dilemmas of Naturalism.* New York: Columbia University Press, 1960.

Dewey, John. *Collected Works* (20 vols. to be published). Carbondale, Ill.: Southern Illinois University Press, 1966ff.

———. *The Ethics of Democracy.* New York: Andrews, 1888.

———. *Outlines of a Critical Theory of Ethics.* Ann Arbor, Mich.: Register Publ., 1891.

———. *The Study of Ethics.* Ann Arbor, Mich.: Wahr, 1894.

———. *Logical Conditions of a Scientific Treatment of Morality.* Chicago: University of Chicago Press, 1903.

———. *Ethics.* New York: Columbia University Press, 1908.

———. *Moral Principles in Education.* Boston: Houghton Mifflin, 1909.

———. *Reconstruction in Philosophy.* New York: Holt, 1920.

———. *Human Nature and Conduct.* New York: Holt, 1922.

———. *The Quest for Certainty.* New York: Minton, Balch, 1929.

———. A *Common Faith.* New Haven: Yale University Press, 1934.

———. *Theory of Valuation. (International Encyclopedia of Unified Science,* II, 4.) Chicago: University of Chicago Press, 1939.

Dewey, John, and Tufts, J. H. *Ethics.* New York: Holt, 1908, 1932, 1960.

———. *Theory of the Moral Life* (Part II of this *Ethics),* ed. Arnold Isenberg. New York: Holt, Rinehart & Winston, 1960.

Dougherty, Jude. "Recent Developments in Naturalistic Ethics,"*Proceedings, American Catholic Philosophical Association,* XXXIII (1959), 97–108.

Dubois, J. *Spencer et le principe de lamorale.* Paris, 1899.

Edel, Abraham. S"ome Trends in American Naturalistic Ethics," *Philosophic Thought in France and the U.S.* (1950), pp. 589–611.

———. *Ethical Judgment: The Use of Science in Ethics.* Glencoe, Ill.: Free Press, 1955.

———. *Method in Ethical Theory.* New York: Bobbs-Merrill, 1963.

Edel, Abraham and May. *Anthropology and Ethics.* Springfield, Ill.: Thomas, 1959.

Edwards, Paul. *The Logic of Moral Discourse.* Glencoe, Ill.: Free Press, 1955.

Edwards, Paul, and Pap, Arthur (eds.). *A Modern Introduction to Philosophy.* Glencoe, Ill.: Free Press, 1965.

Feuer, L. S. *Psychoanalysis and Ethics.* Springfield, Ill.: Thomas, 1955.

Flugel, J. C. *Man, Morals and Society: A Psychoanalytical Study.* London: Duckworth, 1945.

Foot, Philippa R. "Moral Arguments," *Mind,* LXVII (1958), 502–13.

Frankena, W. K. "The Naturalistic Fallacy," *Mind,* XLVIII (1939), 464–77.

Freud, Sigmund. *Standard Edition of the Complete Psychological Works,* ed. James Strachey. 24 vols. New York: Norton, 1953.

———. *Vorlesungen zur Einführung in die Psychoanalyse.* Wien, 1916–17. Trans. by Joan Riviere as *Introductory Lectures on Psychoanalysis.* London: Hogarth, 1922.

———. *Civilization and Its Discontents.* Trans. J. Riviere. London: Hogarth, 1949; New York: Doubleday Anchor, 1958.

———. *Beyond the Pleasure Principle.* Trans. J. Strachey. New York: Liveright, 1922, 1950.

———. *Basic Writings of Sigmund Freud,* ed. A. A. Brill. New York: Random House, 1938.

Fromm, Erich. *Escape from Freedom.* New York: Rinehart, 1941.

———. *Psychoanalysis and Religion.* New Haven: Yale University Press, 1950.

———. *Man for Himself. An Inquiry into the Psychology of Ethics.* New York: Rinehart, 1947.

———. *Socialist Humanism: An International Symposium.* New York: Doubleday, 1965.

Fuchs, Joseph. *Lex Naturae: Zur Theologie des Naturrechts.* Düsseldorf: Schwann, 1955. Trans. as *The Natural Law. A Theological Investigation.* New York: Sheed & Ward, 1964.

Giddings, F. H. "The Heart of Mr. Spencer's Ethics," *Ethics,* XIV (1904), 496–99.

Glass, Bentley. *Science and Ethical Values.* Chapel Hill, N.C.: University of North Carolina Press, 1965.

Hamburg, C. H. "Fromm's 'Scientific' Ethics of Human Nature," in *Studies in Ethics.* (Tulane Studies, VI.) New Orleans, La.: Tulane University Press, 1957.

Handy, Rollo. "The Naturalistic Reduction of Ethics to Science," *Journal of Philosophy,* LIII (1956), 829–35.

Harding, A. L. (ed.). *Origins of the Natural Law Tradition.* Dallas, Tex.: Southern Methodist University Press, 1954.

Hartmann, Heinz. *Psychoanalysis and Moral Values.* New York: International Universities Press, 1960.

Hartshome, Charles. *The Divine Relativity.* New Haven: Yale University Press, 1948.

Hawkins, D. J. B. *Nature as the Ethical Norm.* London: Aquinas Society, 1951.

Holmes, Samuel J. *The Trend of the Race.* New York: Harcourt, Brace, 1921.

———. *Life and Morals.* New York: Macmillan, 1948.

Holt, E. B. *The Freudian Wish and Its Place in Ethics.* New York: Holt, 1915.

Hook, Sidney. "The Ethical Theory of John Dewey," in *Quest for Being.* New York: St. Martin's Press, 1934. Pp. 49–70.

———. "The Desirable and Emotive in Dewey's Ethics," in *John Dewey: Philosopher of Science and Freedom.* New York: Dial Press, 1950.

Huxley, Julian. *Evolutionary Ethics.* (Romanes Lecture, 1943.) London: Oxford University Press, 1943. Reprinted in *Touchstone for Ethics.* New York: Harper, 1947.

———. *Evolution in Action.* New York: Harper, 1953.

Huxley, Thomas H. *Man's Place in Nature.* London, 1863.

———. *Evolution and Ethics.* (Romanes Lecture, 1893.) London, 1893. Reprinted in *Touchstone for Ethics* (see Julian Huxley, above).

James, William. "The Moral Philosopher and the Moral Life," *Ethics,* I (1891), 330–54. Reprinted in *Essays on Faith and Morals,* ed. R. B. Perry. New York: Meridian, 1962.

———. *The Will to Believe, and Other Essays.* New York: Longmans, 1897.

———. *Talks to Teachers on Psychology: and to Students on Some of Life's Ideals.* New York: Longmans, 1899, 1939.

Klemke, E. D. "Vivas on 'Naturalism' and 'Axiological Realism,'" *Review of Metaphysics,* XII (1958), 310–21.

Krikorian, Y. H. (ed.). *Naturalism and the Human Spirit.* New York: Columbia University Press, 1944.

Kurtz, P. W. "Naturalistic Ethics and the Open Question," *Journal of Philosophy,* LII (1955), 113–28.

———. "Decision Making and Ethical Naturalism," *Journal of Philosophy,* LVIII (1961), 693–94.

Lamont, Corliss. *The Illusion of Immortality.* New York: Philosophical Library, 1935.

———. *Humanism as a Philosophy.* New York: Philosophical Library, 1040.

Leclerq, Jacques. *Du droit naturel à la sociologie.* 2 vols. Paris: Spes, 1960.

———. "Natural Law the Unknown," *Natural Law Forum,* VII (1962), 1–15.

Macbeath, Alexander. *The Relationship of Primitive Morality and Religion.* London: Macmillan, 1949.

———. *Experiments in Living.* London: Macmillan, 1952.

Margolis, Joseph. *Psychotherapy and Morality.* New York: Random House, 1966.

———. (ed.). *Contemporary Ethical Theory.* New York: Random House, 1966.

Maritain, Jacques. *Science et sagesse: suivi d'échircissements sur la. philosophie morale.* Paris: Labergerie, 1935. Trans. by Bernard Wall as *Science and Wisdom.* New York: Scribner's, 1940.

———. *Les droits de l'homme et la loi naturelle.* New York: Maison Française, 1942. Trans. by Doris C. Anson as *The Rights of Man and the Natural Law.* New York: Scribner's, 1942.

———. *Neuf Leçons sur les notions premières de la philosophie morale.* Paris: Téqui, 1951.

———. *La philosophie morale.* Paris: Gallimard, 1960. Trans. by Joseph Evans *et al.* as *Moral Philosophy.* New York: Scribner's, 1964.

Mead, Margaret. "Some Anthropological Considerations concerning Natural Law," *Natural Law Forum,* VI (1961), 51–64.

Messner, Johannes. *Das Naturrecht: Handbuch der Gesellschaftsethik.* Innsbruck: Tyrolia Verlag, 1950. Trans. by J. J. Doherty as *Social Ethics, Natural Law in the Modern World.* St. Louis: Herder, 1949, 1965.

———. *Kulturethik, mit Grundlegung durch Prinzipienethik und Personalichkeitsethik.* Innsbruck: Tyrolia Verlag, 1954.

———. *Ethics and Facts.* St. Louis: Herder, 1952.

———. "The Postwar Natural Law Revival and Its Outcome," *Natural Law Forum,* IV (1959), 101–05.

Minkiel, S. J. *The General Ethics of John Dewey in the Light of Thomism.* Rome: Angelicum, 1959.

Monist, The (Summer, 1903). Special issue on "Ethics and Anthropology." (Articles by M. and A. Edel, A. C. Gamett, Paul Taylor, John Ladd, and David Bidney.)

Nielsen, Kai. "Examination of the Thomistic Theory of the Natural Law," *Natural Law Forum,* IV (1959), 44–71.

Odier, Charles. *Les deux sources consciente et inconsciente de la vie morale.* 2me éd. Neuchâtel: La Baconnière, 1947.

Otto, Max. *Science and the Moral Life.* New York: Mentor, 1949.

———. "Humanism," in *American Philosophy,* ed. R. B. Winn. New York: Philosophical Library, 1955. Pp. 172–82.

Pepper, Stephen C. *The Sources of Value.* Berkeley, Calif.: University of California Press, 1958.

———. *Ethics.* New York: Appleton-Century-Crofts, 1960.

Perry, Ralph Barton. *The Moral Economy,* New York: Scribner's, 1909.

———. "The Question of Moral Obligation," *Ethics,* XXI (1911), 282–98.

———. *General Theory of Value.* Cambridge: Harvard University Press, 1926.

Prall, D. W. *Naturalism and Norms.* Berkeley, Calif.: University of California Press, 1925.

Quillian, W. F. "Evolution and Moral Theory in America," in *Evolutionary Thought in America,* ed. S. Persons. New Haven: Yale University Press, 1950. Pp. 398–419.

Ramirez, J. M. "De philosophia morali Christiana. Responsio quaedam responsionibus 'completis et adaequatis' Domini Jacobi Maritain," *Divus Thomas (Fribourg),* XIV (1936), 87–122.

Rice, Philip Blair. "Objectivity in Value Judgments," *Journal of Philosophy.* XL (1943), 132–41.

———. "Public and Private Factors in Valuation," *Ethics,* LIV (1944), 41–52.

———. *On the Knowledge of Good and Evil.* New York: Random House, 1955.

Rieff, Philip. *Freud: The Mind of the Moralist.* Garden City, N.Y.: Doubleday Anchor, 1961.

———. "Freudian Ethics and the Idea of Reason," *Ethics,* LXVII (1957), 169–83.

Romanell, Patrick. *Toward a Critical Naturalism.* New York: Macmillan, 1958.

Roth, R. J. *John Dewey and Self-Realization.* Englewood Cliffs, N.J.: Prentice-Hall, 1963.

Sartre, Jean-Paul. *L'Existentialisme est un humanisme.* Paris: Nagel, 1947. Trans. by B. Frechtman as *Existentialism.* New York: Philosophical Library, 1947. Also Trans. by P. Mairet. London: Methuen, 1962.

Shelton, H. S. "Spencer as an Ethical Teacher," *Ethics,* XX (1910), 424–37.

Simon, Yves. *The Tradition of Natural Law,* ed. V. Kuic. New York: Fordham University Press, 1965.

Spencer, Herbert. *On Moral and Physical Education.* London, 1861.

———. *The Principles of Ethics.* 2 vols. London-New York: Appleton, 1879–92.

———. *Data of Ethics* (first part of the foregoing). New York: Hurst, 1923.

Stuart, H. W. "Dewey's Ethical Theory," in *The Philosophy of John Dewey,* ed. P. A. Schilpp. Chicago: Northwestern University Press, 1939.

Teilhard de Chardin, Pierre. *Oeuvres.* Paris: Editions du Seuil, 1956 ff.

———. *Le phénomène humain,* in *Oeuvres.* Tome I, 1956. Trans. by Bernard Wall as *The Phenomenon of Man.* New York: Harper, 1959.

———. *Le Milieu divin,* in *Oeuvres.* Tome IV, 1957. Trans. by B. Wall *et al.* as *Le Milieu Divin.* London: Collins, 1960. Reprinted New York: Harper, 1960, 1965.

Tresmontant, Claude. *Pierre Teilhard de Chardin: His Thought.* Baltimore: Helicon Press, 1959.

Vivas, Eliseo. "Julian Huxley's Evolutionary Ethics," *Ethics,* LVIII (1948), 275–84.

———. *The Moral Life and the Ethical Life.* Chicago: University of Chicago Press, 1950.

———. "Animadversions on Naturalisitc Ethics," *Ethics,* LVI (1946), 157–79.

Whitehead, Alfred North. *Science and the Modern World.* New York: Macmillan, 1925.

———. *Process and Reality.* New York: Macmillan, 1929.

———. *Adventures of Ideas.* New York: Macmillan, 1933.

———. *Modes of Thought.* New York: Macmillan, 1938.

Wild, John. "Natural Law and Modern Ethical Theories," *Ethics,* LXIII (1953), 1–13.

———. *Introduction to Realistic Philosophy.* New York: Harper, 1948.

Williams, Gardner. *Humanistic Ethics.* New York: Philosophical Library, 1951.

Chapter XVII

Abelson, Raziel (ed.). *Ethics and Metaethics.* New York: St. Martin's Press, 1963.

Aiken, Lillian W. *Bertrand Russell's Philosophy of Morals.* New York. Humanities Press, 1963.

Ayer, Alfred J. *Language, Truth and Logic.* London: Gollancz, 1936. Reprinted New York: Dover, 1946.

———. "On the Analysis of Moral Judgments," *Horizon* (London), 1949. Reprinted in *Philosophical Essays.* New York: St. Martin's Press, 1954.

———. *Logical Positivism.* New York: Free Press, 1959.

———. *The Concept of a Person and Other Essays.* London: Macmillan, 1963.

Baier, Kurt. "Doing My Duty," *Philosophy,* XXVII (1952), 253–60.

———. "Good Reasons," *Philosophical Studies,* IV (1953), 1–15.

———. "Proving a Moral Judgment," *Philosophical Studies,* IV (1953), 33–44.

———. *The Meaning of Life.* Canberra: University College, 1957.

———. *The Moral Point of View.* Ithaca, N.Y.: Cornell University Press, 1958.

Binkley, L. J. *Contemporary Ethical Theories.* New York: Philosophical Library, 1961.

Black, Max. "Some Questions about Emotive Meaning," *Philosophical Review,* LVII (1948), 111–26.

Brandt, R. B. "The Emotive Theory of Ethics," *Philosophical Review,* LIX (1960), 305–18.

———. (ed.). *Value and Obligation. Systematic Reading in Ethics.* New York: Harcourt, Brace & World, 1961.

Broad, C. D. "Is Goodness a Name of a Simple Non-natural Quality?" Proc, *Aristotelian Society,* XXXIV (1933–34), 249–68.

———. "Certain Features of Moore's Ethical Doctrines," in P. A. Schilpp, *The Philosophy of G. E. Moore.* Evanston, Ill.: Northwestern University Press, 1942.

———. "G. E. Moore's Latest Published Views on Ethics," *Mind,* LXX (1961).

Camap, Rudolf. *Philosophy and Logical Syntax.* London: Routledge, Kegan Paul, 1936.

———. "Empiricism, Semantics and Ontology," in *Semantics and the Philosophy of Language,* ed. L. Linsky. Urbana, Ill.: University of Illinois Press, 1952. Pp. 209–12.

Castañeda, H. N., and Nakhnikian, George (eds.). *Morality and the Language of Conduct.* Detroit: Wayne State University Press, 1963.

Charlesworth, M. J. *Philosophy and Linguistic Analysis.* Pittsburgh: Duquesne University Press, 1959.

Copleston, F. *Contemporary Philosophy.* Westminster, Md.: Newman Press., 1956.

Ellis, Frank. "Analytic-Positivist Thought," in Mann-Kreyche, *Approaches to Morality* (1966). Pp. 434–557.

Ewing, A. C. "Recent Developments in British Ethical Thought," in *British Philosophy in the Mid-Century,* ed. C. A. Mace. London: Macmillan, 1957. Pp. 65–95.

———. *Second Thoughts in Moral Philosophy.* New York: Macmillan, 1959.

Falk, W. D. "Goading and Guiding," *Mind,* LXII (1953), 145–71–

Frankena, W. K. "Moral Philosophy at Mid-Century," *Philosophical Review,* LX (1951), 44–55.

Hägerström, Axel. *Inquiries into the Nature of Laws and Morals,* ed. K. Olivecrona. Trans. C. D. Broad. Stockholm: Almqvist & Wiksell, 1938.

———. *Philosophy and Religion,* ed. R. T. Sandin. New York: Humanities Press, 1964.

Hall, E. W. "Stevenson on Disagreement in Attitude," *Ethics,* LVIII (1948), 51–56.

———. "Practical Reason(s) and Ethics," *Mind,* LXIV (1955), 319–32.

Hampshire, Stuart. "Fallacies in Moral Philosophy," *Mind,* LVIII (1949), 466–82.

———. *Thought and Action.* London: Chatto & Windus, 1959.

———. (ed.). *The Age of Reason.* New York: Mentor, 1956.

Hampshire, Stuart, and Hart, H. L. A. "Decision, Intention, and Certainty," *Mind,* LXVII (1958), 1–12.

Hancock, Roger. "The Refutation of Naturalism in Moore and Hare," *Journal of Philosophy,* LVII (1960), 326–34.

Hare, Richard M. *The Language of Morals.* Oxford: Clarendon Press, 1952.

———. "Universalizability," *Proceedings, Aristotelian Society,* LV (1954–55), 295–312.

———. *Freedom and Reason.* Oxford: Clarendon Press, 1963.

Hare, Richard M., and Gardiner, P. M. "Pain and Evil," *Proceedings, Aristotelian Society,* Suppl. XXXVIII (1964), 91–124.

Hospers, John. *An Introduction to Philosophical Analysis.* New York: Prentice-Hall, 1953.

Joad, C. E. M. *A Critique of Logical Positivism.* Chicago: University of Chicago Press, 1950.

Kerner, G. C. *The Revolution in Ethical Theory.* New York: Oxford University Press, 1966.

Laird, John. *Recent Philosophy.* London: Butterworth, 1936.

Lawler, Ronald. "The Nature of Analytic Ethics," *Proceedings, American Catholic Philosophical Association,* XXXIV (1960), 151–57.

Lewis, H. D. (ed.). *Contemporary British Philosophy.* London: Allen & Unwin, 1957.

"Logical Positivism and Ethics," symposium in *Proceedings, Aristotelian Society,* Suppl. XXII (London, 1948).

McCloskey, H. J. "Nowell-Smith's Ethics," *Australasian Journal of Psychology and Philosophy,* XXXIX (1961).

Mehta, Ved. *Fly and the Fly Bottle. Encounters with British Intellectuals.* Boston: Little, Brown, 1963.

Milne, A. J. M. *The Social Philosophy of English Idealism.* London: Allen & Unwin, 1962.

Moore, Asher. "Elmotivism: Theory and Practice," *Journal of Philosophy,* LV (1958).

Moore, G. E. *Principia Ethi*ca. Cambridge, Eng.: University Press, 1903. Reprinted New York: Cambridge University Press, 1959.

———. *Ethics.* London: Home University Library, 1912. Reprinted New York: Cambridge University Press, 1949.

———. "The Nature of Moral Philosophy," in *Philosophical Studies.* London: Kegan Paul, 1922. Pp. 310–29.

———. *Philosophical Papers.* New York: Macmillan, 1959.

Munitz, M. K. (ed.). *A Modern Introduction to Ethics.* New York: Free Press, 1958.

Newsom, G. E. *The New Morality.* New York: Scribner's, 1933.

Nowell-Smith, Patrick H. "Free Will and Moral Responsibility," *Mind,* LVII (1948), 45–61.

———. *Ethics.* London-Baltimore: Penguin, 1954. Reprinted New York: Philosophical Library, 1958.

———. "Determinists and Libertarians," *Mind,* LXII (1954), 317–37.

———. "Psycho-analysis and Moral Language," *The Rationalist Annual* (1954). Reprinted in Edwards-Pap, *Modern Introduction to Philosophy (1965).* Pp. 86–93.

———. "Choosing, Deciding and Doing," *Analysis,* XVIII (1958), 63–69.

———. "Contextual Implication and Ethical Theory," *Proceedings, Aristotelian Society,* Suppl. XXXVI (1962), 1–18.

Ofstad, Harald. "Objectivity of Norms and Value-Judgments according to Recent Scandinavian Philosophy," *Philosophy and Phenomenological Research,* XII (1951–52), 42–68.

Oldenquist, Andrew (ed.). *Readings in Moral Philosophy.* Boston: Houghton Mifflin, 1964.

Rawls, John. "Outline of a Decision Procedure for Ethics," *Philosophical Review,* LX (1951), 177–97.

———. "Two Concepts of Rules," *Philosophical Review,* LXIV (1955), 3–32.

———. "Justice as Fairness," *Philosophical Review,* LXVII (1958), 164–94.

———. "The Sense of Justice," *Philosophical Review,* LXXII (1963), 281–305.

Rhees, Rush. "Some Developments in Wittgenstein's Views of Ethics," *Philosophical Review,* LXXIV (1965), 17–26.

Ross, Alf. *On Law and Justice.* Berkeley-Los Angeles: University of California Press, 1959.

Russell, Bertrand. "A Free Man's Worship," in *Mysticism and Logic.* New York: Norton, 1929. Pp. 46–57. Reprinted New York: Doubleday, 1957.

———. *Marriage and Morals.* New York: Norton, 1929.

———. *Religion and Science.* London: Oxford University Press, 1935.

———. "The Elements of Ethics," in Sellars and Hospers, *Readings in Ethical Theory* (1952). Pp. 1–17.

———. *Human Society in Ethics and Politics.* London: Allen & Unwin, 1955.

Stapledon, Olaf. "Mr. Bertrand Russell's Ethical Beliefs," *Ethics,* XXXVII (1927), 390–402.

Stevenson, Charles L. "The Emotive Meaning of Ethical Terms," *Mind,* XLVI (1937), 10–31.

———. "Ethical Judgments and Avoidability," *Mind,* XLVII (1938), 45–67.

———. "Persuasive Definitions," *Mind,* XLVII (1938), 331–50.

———. *Ethics and Language.* New Haven: Yale University Press, 1944.

———. "The Emotive Conception of Ethics and Its Cognitive Implications," *Philosophical Review,* LIX (1950). Reprinted in *Facts and Values: Studies in Ethical Analysis.* New Haven: Yale University Press, 1963. Pp. 55–70.

Strawson, Peter F. "Ethical Intuitionism," *Philosophy,* XXIV (1949), 347–57.

———. *Individuals.* Oxford: Clarendon Press, 1959.

———. "Social Morality and Individual Ideals," *Philosophy,* XXXVI (1961), 1–17.

Stroll, Avrum. *The Emotive Theory of Ethics.* Berkeley, Calif.: University of California Press, 1954.

Taylor, P. W. *Normative Discourse.* Englewood Cliffs, N.J.: Prentice-Hall, 1961.

———. (ed.). *The Moral Judgment: Readings in Contemporary Meta-Ethics.* New York: Free Press, 1966.

Toulmin, Stephen E. "Knowledge of Right and Wrong," *Proceedings, Aristotelian Society,* LI (1950–51).

———. *An Examination of the Place of Reason in Ethics.* London: Cambridge University Press, 1950.

———. "Principles of Morality," *Philosophy,* XXXI (1956), 142–53.

———. "The Emotive Theory of Ethics," a symposium in *Proceedings, Aristotelian Society,* Suppl. XXII (1948), 76–140.

Urmson, James O. "On Grading," *Mind,* LIX (1950), 145–69.

———. *Philosophical Analysis: Its Development between the Two Wars.* Oxford: Clarendon Press, 1956.

Veatch, H. B. "Non-Cognitivism in Ethics," *Ethics,* LXXVI (1966), 102–16.

Waismann, F. *The Principles of Linguistic Philosophy.* London: Macmillan, 1965.

Weitz, Morris (ed.). *20th-Century Philosophy: The Analytic Tradition.* New York: Free Press, 1966.

White, A. R. G. E. Moore; *A Critical Exposition.* Oxford: Clarendon Press, 1958.

White, Morton (ed.). *Age of Analysis.* New York: Mentor, 1955.

———. *Toward Reunion in Philosophy.* Cambridge: Harvard University Press, 1956.

Williams, Bernard, and Montefiore, Alan (eds.). *British Analytical Philosophy.* New York: Humanities Press, 1966.

Wittgenstein, Ludwig. "Logisch-philosophische Abhandlung" *Annalen der Naturphilosophie* (Leipzig, 1921). Reprinted as *Tractatus Logico-Philosophicus* (German and English). London: Routledge, Kegan Paul, 1922. New Trans. by D. F. Pearson and B. F. McGuiness. New York: Humanities Press, 1958.

———. *Philosophical Investigations.* Trans. G. E. M. Anscombe. Oxford: Blackwell, 1953.

———. *The Blue and Brown Books.* Foreword by Rush Rhees. Oxford: Blackwell, 1958.

———. *Wittgenstein Notebooks,* 1914–1916, ed. and trans. G. E. M. Anscombe. New York: Harper, 1961.

———. *Philosophische Bemerkungen,* ed. Rush Rhees. New York: Barnes & Noble, 1965.

———. "Lecture on Ethics," plus "Notes on Talks with Wittgenstein," edited by Friedrich Waismann, *Philosophical Review,* LXXIV (1965), 3–12, 12–16.

Wolter, Allan. "The Unspeakable Philosophy of the Late Wittgenstein," *Proceedings, American Catholic Philosophical Association,* XXX (1960), 168–93.

Chapter XVIII

Alcala, Manuel. *La etica de la situación y Thomas Steinbüchel.* Madrid: Consejo Superior de Investigaciones Cientificas, 1963.

Alluntis, Felix. "Social and Political Ideas of José Ortega y Gasset," New *Scholasticism,* XXXIX (1965), 467–90.

Aranguren, J. L. L. *La etica de Ortega.* Madrid: Taurus Ediciones, 1958.

Barrett, William. *Irrational Man. A Study in Existential Philosophy.* Garden City, N.Y.: Doubleday, 1958, 1962.

Barth, Karl. *The Word of God and the Word of Man.* Boston: Pilgrim Press, 1928.

———. *The Doctrine of the Word of God.* Trans. G. T. Thomson. New York: Scribner's, 1936.

———. *Protestant Thought from Rousseau to Ritschl.* New York: Harper, 1959.

Beauvoir, Simone de. Pour *une morale de l'ambiguité.* Paris: Gallimard, 1946. Trans. by Bernard Frechtman as *The*

Ethics of Ambiguity. New York: Philosophical Library, 1948.

Beis, R. H. "Atheistic Existentialist Ethics: a Critique," *The Modern Schoolman,* XLII (1965), 153–77.

Benn, A. W. "The Morals of an Immoralist—Friedrich Nietzsche," *Ethics,* (1909), 1–13, 192–203.

Bonhoeffer, Dietrich. *Letters and Papers from Prison,* ed. E. Bethge. Trans. Reginald Fuller. New York: Macmillan, 1962.

———. *Ethics,* ed. E. Bethge. Trans. Neville Smith. New York: Macmillan, 1965.

Borzaga, R. *Contemporary Philosophy. Phenomenological and Existential Currents.* Milwaukee: Bruce, 1966.

Brisebois, Edmond. "Le Sartrisme et le problème moral," *Nouvelle Revue Théologique,* LXXIV (1952), 30–48, 124–45.

Brunner, Emil. *Justice and the Social Order.* Trans. M. Hottinger. New York: Harper, 1945.

———. *The Divine Imperative.* Trans. Olive Wyon. Philadelphia: Westminster Press, 1947.

Buber, Martin. *Ich und Du.* Berlin, 1923. Trans. by R. G. Smith as *I and Thou,* New York: Scribner's, 1958, 1960.

———. *Good and Evil. Two Interpretations.* New York: Scribner's, 1953.

———. *The Writings of Martin Buber,* ed. Will Herberg. Cleveland: World, 1956.

Camus, Albert. *Le mythe de Sisyphe.* Paris: Gallimard, 1942. Trans. by Justin O'Brien as *The Myth of Sisyphus and Other Essays.* New York: Knopf, 1955.

———. *L'Homme révolté.* Paris: Gallimard, 1951. Trans. by Anthony Bower as *The Rebel: an Essay on Man in Revolt.* New York: Knopf, 1954, 1961.

Cassem, N. H. "The Way to Wisdom: A Biodoctrinal Study of Friedrich Nietzsche," *The Modern Schoolman,* XXXIX (1962), 335–58.

Collins, James. "Three Kierkegaardian Problems: II, The Ethical View and Its Limits," *New Scholasticism,* XXIII (1949), 3–37.

———. "Freedom as Atheistic Heroism," *Giornale di Metafisica,* IV (1949), 573–80.

———. *The ExistentL.lists:* A *Critical Study.* Chicago: Regnery, 1959.

Copleston, F. C. *Friedrich Nietzsche: Philosopher of Culture.* London: Burns, Oates, 1942.

Diamond, M. L. *Martin Buber: Jewish Existentialist.* New York: Oxford University Press, 1960.

Dondeyne, Albert. *Contemporary European Thought and Christian Faith.* Pittsburgh: Duquesne University Press, 1958.

Dostoyevsky, Feodor M. *Works.* 13 vols. Trans. Constance Garnett. London: Macmillan, 1949–50.

———. *Notes from Underground* (1864). Trans. C. Garnett. New York: Macmillan, 1949. Excerpted in Walter Kaufmann. *Existentialism.* Pp. 52–82.

Ferrater Mora, José. *Ortega y Gasset.* New Haven: Yale University Press, 1957.

———. *Unamuno: A Philosophy of Tragedy.* Trans. Philip Silver. Berkeley, Calif.: University of California Press, 1962.

———. *Philosophy Today: Conflicting Tendencies in Contemporary Thought.* Berkeley: University of California Press, 1962.

Fletcher, Joseph. *Situation Ethics.* Philadelphia: Westminster Press, 1966.

Friedman, Maurice. *Martin Buber: The Life of Dialogue.* Chicago: University of Chicago Press, 1955. Chap. 21: "Ethics." Fuchs, Joseph. "Situation Ethics and Theology," *Theology Digest,* II (1954), 25–30.

———. *Situation und Entscheidung, Grandfragen christlicher Situationsethik.* Frankfurt: Carolusdruckerei, 1952.

Fullat, Octavio. *La moral atea de Albert Camus.* Barcelona: Pubul, 1963.

Garnett, A. C. "Phenomenological Ethics and Self-Realization," *Ethics,* LIII (1943), 159–72.

Greene, N. N. *Jean-Paul Sartre: The Existentialist Ethic.* Ann Arbor, Mich.: University of Michigan Press, 1960.

Grisebach, Eberhard. *Gegenwart: eine kritische Ethik.* Halle: Niemeyer, 1928.

Gusdorf, Georges. *Traité de l'existence morale.* Paris: Colin, 1949.

Hartmann, Klaus, *Sartres Sozialphilosophie.* Berlin: De Gruyter, 1966.

Henry, C. F. H. *Christian Personal Ethics.* Grand Rapids, Mich.: Eerdmans, 1957.

Hildebrand, Dietrich von. *True Morality and Its Counterfeits.* New York: McKay, 1955.

Hochberg, Herbert. "Albert Camus and the Ethics of Absurdity," *Ethics,* LXXV (1965), 87–102.

Holmer, P. L. "Kierkegaard and Ethical Theory," *Ethics,* LXIII (1953), 157–70.

Huertas-Jourda, José. *The Existenthlism of Miguel de Unamuno.* Gainesville, Fla.: University of Florida Press, 1963.

Husserl, Edmund. *Ideen zu einer reinen Phänomenologie und phänomenologischen Philosophic,* in *Jahrbuch für Philosophie* (Halle: Niemeyer), Vol. I, 1913. Ed. W. Biemel.

Ten Haag: Nijhoff, 1950. Trans. by W. R. Boyce Gibson as *Ideas: General Introduction to Pure Phenomenology.* London: Macmillan, 1931.

Jeanson, Francis. *Le Problème moral et la pensée de Sartre.* Paris: Editions du Myrte, 1947.

Jolivet, Régis. "La morale de l'ambiguité," *Revue Thomiste,* XLIX (1949), 278–85.

Kaufmann, Walter (ed.). *Existentialism from Dostoevsky to Sartre.* New York: Meridian, 1957.

Kierkegaard, Søren. *Samlede Vaerker,* ed. A. B. Brachmann. 20 vols. J. L. Heiberg & H. O. Lange. Copenhagen: Gyldendalske Boghandel, 1903–06.

———. *Either/Or: a Fragment of Life,* 2 vols. (1843). Trans. by D. F. and Lillian Swenson of Vol. I, *The Aesthetic Life.* Trans. by Walter Lowrie of Vol. II, *The Ethical Life.* Princeton, N.J.: Princeton University Press, 1944.

———. *Fear and Trembling* (1843). Trans. W. Lowrie. Princeton, 1941; with *Sickness unto Death,* New York: Doubleday Anchor, 1954.

———. *Philosophical Fragments* (1844). Trans. D. F. Swenson. Princeton, 1936; New York: Harper, 1938.

———. *The Concept of Dread* (1844). Trans. W. Lowrie, Princeton, 1944.

———. *Stages of Life's Way.* Trans. W. Lowrie. Princeton, 1940.

———. *Concluding Unscientific Postscript* (1846). Trans. D. F. Swenson and W. Lowrie. Princeton, 1941.

———. *Christian Discourses* (1848). Trans. W. Lowrie. New York: Oxford University Press, 1939.

———. *The Sickness unto Death* (1849). Trans. W. Lowrie. Princeton, 1954.

———. *Purity of Heart Is to Will One Thing.* Trans. D. V. Steere. New York: Harper, 1938, 1956.

———. *A Kierkegaard Anthology,* ed. R. A. Bretall. Princeton, N.J.: Princeton University Press, 1946.

Laing, R. D., and Cooper, D. G. *Reason and Violence. A Decade of Sartre's Philosophy.* New York: Humanities Press, 1964.

Lauer, Quentin. *The Triumph of Subjectivity.* New York: Fordham University Press, 1958.

Lawrence, Nathaniel, and O'Connor, D. D. (eds.). *Readings in Existential Phenomenology.* Englewood Cliffs, N.J.: Prentice-Hall, 1967.

Lehman, Paul. *Ethics in a Christian Context.* New York: Harper & Row, 1963.

Lindbeck, G. A. "Natural Law in the Thought of Paul Tillich," *Natural Law Forum,* VII (1962), 84–96.

McInerny, Ralph. "Ethics and Persuasion: Kierkegaard's Existential Dialectic," *The Modern Schoolman,* XXXIV (1956), 219–39.

Mandelbaum, Maurice. *The Phenomenology of Moral Experience.* Glencoe, Ill.: Free Press, 1955.

———. "On the Use of Moral Principles," *Journal of Philosophy,* LIII (1956), 662–70.

———. "Determinism and Moral Responsibility," *Ethics,* LXX (1960), 204–16.

Marcel, Gabriel. *Etre et avoir.* Paris: Aubier, 1935. Trans. by Katharine Farrer as *Being and Having.* Boston: Beacon, 1951.

———. *Homo viator.* Paris: Aubier, 1944. Trans. by Emma Craufurd as *Homo Viator.* Chicago: Regnery, 1951.

———. *The Mystery of Being* (Gifford Lectures, 1949–50.) 2 vols. London: Harvill Press, 1951; Chicago: Regnery, 1951.

———. *L'Homme problématique.* Paris: Aubier, 1955.

———. *The Philosophy of Existence.* Trans. Manya Harari. London: Harvill Press, 1948.

Marty, Martin E. (ed.). *The Place of Bonhoeffer.* New York: Association Press, 1962.

Mehl, Roger, *et al. Le problème de la morale chrétienne.* Paris: Presses Universitaires, 1948.

Minnema, T. *The Social Ethics of Reinhold Niebuhr.* Grand Rapids, Mich.: Eerdmans, 1959.

Morgan, G. A. *What Nietzsche Means.* Cambridge: Harvard University Press, 1941.

Mortimer, R. C. *Christian Ethics.* London: Hutchinson, 1950.

Nabert, Jean. *Eléments pour une éthique.* Paris: Presses Universitaires, 1943.

———. *Essai sur le mal.* Paris: Presses Universitaires, 1955.

Niebuhr, H. Richard. *Kingdom of God in America.* New York: Harper, 1937.

Niebuhr, Reinhold. *An Independent Christian Ethics.* New York: Harper, 1935.

———. *Moral Man and Immoral Society.* New York: Scribner's, 1949.

———. *The Nature and Destiny of Man.* (Gifiord Lectures, 1941–43.) 2 vols. New York: Scribner's, 1941–43.

Nietzsche, Friedrich W. *Nktzsches Werke und Briefe: Historischekritische Gesamtausgabe,* hrsg. von C. A. Emge. München: Beck, 1933 ff.

———. *The Complete Works,* ed. Oscar Levy. 18 vols. London: Allen & Unwin, 1923–24.

———. *Die Geburt der Tragödie* (1872). Trans. by Francis Golffing as *The Birth of Tragedy.* New York: Doubleday, 1956.

———. *Jenseits von Gut und Böse* (1886). Trans. by Helen Zimmern as *Beyond Good and Evil.* In *The Philosophy of Nietzsche.* New York: Random House, 1954.

———. *Zur Genealogie der Moral* (1887). Trans. by H. B. Samuel as *Toward a Genealogy of Morals.* In *The Philosophy of Nietzsche.* New York: Random House, 1954.

———. *The Philosophy of Nietzsche,* ed. W. H. Wright. New York: Scribner's, 1937.

———. *The Portable Nietzsche,* ed. W. Kaufmann. New York: Viking, 1954.

Ortega y Gasset, José. *Obras completas.* Madrid: Editorial Aguilar, 1947 ff.

———. *La rebelión de la masas.* Madrid: Aguilar, 1930. In *Obras,* IV, 113–313. Trans. as *The Revolt of the Masses.* New York: Norton, 1956.

———. *El hombre y la gente.* Madrid: Aguilar, 1958. In *Obras,* VI, 13–167. Trans. by W. R. Trask as *Man and People.* New York: Norton, 1957.

Pigou, A. C. "The Ethics of Nietzsche," *Ethics,* XVIII (1908), 343–55.

Poppi, Antonino. "The Background of Situation Ethics," *Philosophy Today,* I (1957), 266–77.

Rahner, Karl. "On the Question of a Formal Existential Ethics," in *Theological Investigations.* Trans. K. H. Kruger. Baltimore: Helicon, 1963. Pp. 421–31.

Ramsey, Paul. *Basic Christian Ethics.* New York: Scribner's, 1952.

———. *Nine Modern Moralists.* Englewood Cliffs, N.J.: Prentice-Hall, 1962.

Rau, Catherine. "The Ethical Theory of J. P. Sartre," *Journal of Philosophy,* XLVI (1949), 536–45.

Rauche, G. A. *The Philosophy of Actuality.* Fort Hare, Republic of South Africa: Fort Hare University Press, 1964. (A complete English analysis of the ethics of Eberhard Grisebach.)

Robinson, John A. *Honest to God.* Philadelphia: Westminster Press, 1963.

———. *Christian Morals Today.* Philadelphia: Westminster Press, 1964.

Roth, Alois. *Edmund Husserls ethische Untersuchungen.* (Phaenomenologica, 7.) Ten Haag: Nijhoff, 1960.

Sartre, Jean-Paul. *Esquisse d'une théorie des émotions.* Paris: Hermann, 1939. Trans. by Bernard Frechtman as *Outline of a Theory of the Emotions.* New York: Philosophical Library, 1948. Trans. by P. Mairet as *Sketch for a Theory of the Emotions.* London: Methuen, 1962.

———. *L'Etre et le néant: essai d'ontologie phénoménologique.* Paris: Gallimard, 1943. Trans. by Hazel Barnes as *Being and Nothingness.* New York: Philosophical Library, 1956.

———. *L'Existentialisme est un humanisme.* Paris: Nagel, 1946. Trans. by P. Mairet as *Existentialism and Humanism.* London: Methuen, 1948.

———. *Saint Genet: comédien et martyr.* Paris: Gallimard, 1952. Trans. by B. Frechtman as *Saint Genet, Actor and Martyr.* London: Allen & Unwin, 1964.

———. *Critique de la raison dialectique.* Vol. I. Paris: Gallimard, 1960.

Sittler, Joseph. *The Structure of Christian Ethics.* Baton Rouge: Louisiana State University Press, 1958.

Smith, Colin. *Contemporary French Philosophy.* London: Methuen, 1964.

Spiegelberg, Herbert. *The Phenomenological Movement.* 2 vols. The Hague: Nijhoff, 1960.

Stavrides, Ria. "French Existentialism and Moral Philosophy," in *Encyclopedia of Morals,* ed. V. Ferm. New York: Philosophical Library, 1956. Pp. 163–71.

Stern, A. "Nietzsche et le doute méthodologique en morale," *Revue Philosophique de la France et de l'Etranger,* CXXXIX (1949), 48–59.

Thibon, G. "Friedrich Nietzsche, analyste de la causalité matérielle en psychologie et en morale," *Revue Thomiste,* XL (1935), 3–36.

Thomas, G. F. *Christian Ethics and Moral Philosophy.* New York: Scribner's, 1955.

Tillich, Paul. *Systematic Theology.* 3 vols. Chicago: University of Chicago Press, 1951–63.

———. *The Courage to Be.* New Haven: Yale University Press, 1952, 1959.

———. *Love, Power, and Justice.* New York: Oxford University Press, 1960.

———. *Morality and Beyond.* New York: Harper & Row, 1963.

Unamuno y Jugo, Miguel de. *Obras completas.* Madrid: Editorial Aguilar, 1951 ff.

———. *Del sentimiento tragico de la vida.* 2 vols. Madrid: Aguilar, 1914, 1945. Trans. by J. E. C. Fitch as *The Tragic Sense of Life.* New York: Dover, 1954.

Villaseñor, J. S. *Onega y Gasset, Existentialist.* Trans. J. Small. Chicago: Regnery, 1949.

Virasoro, Rafael. *Existendalismo y moral.* Santa Fe, Argentina: Libreria Castellvi, 1957.

Wahl, Jean. *Existence humaine et transcendence.* Neuchâtel: La Baconnière, 1944.

———. *A Short History of Existentialism.* Trans. F. Williams and S. Maron. New York: Philosophical Library, 1949, 1962. Wild, John. *The Challenge of Existentialism.* Bloomington, Ind.: Indiana University Press, 1955.

———. *Human Freedom and Social Order: An Essay in Christian Philosophy.* Durham, N.C.: Duke University Press, 1959.

———. *Existence and the World of Freedom.* Englewood Cliffs, N.J.: Prentice-Hall, 1963.

Williams, Martha. "Gabriel Marcel's Notion of Value," *The Modern Schoolman,* XXXVII (1959), 29–38.

Wolff, Edgar. *L'Individualisme radical fondé sur la caractérologie. Pour un renouveau des idées de Nietzsche.* Paris: Bordas, 1955. Wolff, P. (ed.). *Christliche Philosophie in Deutschland 1920 bis 1945.* Regensburg: Habbel, 1949.

Index

A

Abelard. *See* Peter Abelard
Abubacer (Ibn-Tufail) **I:** 148
Abulfaragius **I:** 134
Achillini, Alexander **I:** 224
"act" and "rule" utilitarianism **II:** 168
Adams, E. M. **II:** 205
Addresses to the German Nation **II:** 34
Adler, Felix **II:** 158
Advancement of Learning **I:** 248, 249
Against Celsus **I:** 89
Ages of the World, The **II:** 48
Ailly, Pierre d' **I:** 258
Aklaq-i Jalali (Jalal's Ethics) **I:** 158
al-Ameri **I:** 139
Albanenses **I:** 114
Albert the Great **I:** 53, 162, 178
Albigensians **I:** 114
Albo, Joseph **I:** 132, 133
Albrecht von Eyb **I:** 200
Alciphron **I:** 270, 275
al-Dimishqi, abu-Uthman **I:** 140
Alexander of Hales **I:** 175–176
Alexandria, Egypt **I:** 72, 74, 88, 136

al-Farabi **I:** 127, 136–138, 141, 151
Algazel (al-Ghazzali) **I:** 144
alienation **II:** 65, 103, 106, 256
Allers, Rudolph **II:** 145, 146
al-Razi, Mohammed ibn-Zakariya **I:** 135
Ambiguities (Patrologia Graeca) **I:** 92
Ambrose, Bishop of Milan **I:** 84, 95, 97, 169
Analogy of Religion **I:** 277
Analysis Aristotelica ex Euclide restituta **I:** 238
Analysis of Knowledge and Valuation **II:** 144
Analysis of the Phenomena of the Human Mind **II:** 21
analytic ethics **II:** 205, 209, 224, 236
Anaxagoras **I:** 15, 17
Andreas Capellanus **I:** 164
Andreas de Novo Castro **I:** 258
Andronicus **I:** 52, 113
Annals of the Parish **II:** 4
Année Sociologique, L' **II:** 110
Anniceris **I:** 25
Anselm of Canterbury, St. **I:** 95, 108–110, 116, 186, 191
Anthony of Parma **I:** 53
Anti-Dühring **II:** 104
Antipater **I:** 62
anti-Semitism (racism). *See* Jews (Judaism)
Antisthenes **I:** 24
Antoninus of Florence **I:** 200
apathy (*apatheia*) **I:** 24, 115
Apology (Plato) **I:** 21, 26
Appeal from the New to the Old Whigs **II:** 16
Appearance and Reality **II:** 153
Aquinas. *See* Thomas Aquinas
Arabs. *See* Moslems
Archytas of Tarentum **I:** 15
Areopagiticum **I:** 90
Aretino **I:** 223
Aretus **I:** 62
Aristippus of Cyrene **I:** 25
Aristo **I:** 62
Aristophanes **I:** 20
Aristotle (Aristotelianism) **I:** 14, 17–20, 22, 25–26, 37–53, 58, 62, 67, 74–75, 84, 98, 104, 106, 109, 111,

127, 136–137, 139–141, 143, 147–148, 150–151, 156, 158–159, 161–163, 166–168, 176, 178, 185–187, 200, 209–211, 214, 222–224, 227, 230, 235, 237, 239, 249, 258, 282, 290, 292, 312; **II:** 23–24, 133–134, 167, 230–231
Arriaga, Rodrigo de **I:** 289
Aspasius **I:** 53
astrologers, Maimonides on **I:** 131
ataraxia **I:** 16, 66, 70
athambiē **I:** 16
Athens **I:** 17, 20, 24–27, 38, 56, 62
atoms **I:** 69; **II:** 7
Augustine, St. **I:** 24, 63, 78, 84, 91, 95, 97–104, 109, 116, 169, 172–173, 176, 189–190, 211, 244, 260; **II:** 24, 60, 65, 86, 130, 146, 241
Austin, John **II:** 22, 23, 28, 221
Austria, axiology in **II:** 126–130, 139
Austrian Philosophy of Values, The **II:** 139
Autobiography of Benjamin Franklin **I:** 275
Avempace **I:** 147
Averroës **I:** 137, 149, 150–152, 159
Averroism, Latin **I:** 186
Avicebrón **I:** 79, 123, 159
Avicenna **I:** 78, 127, 137, 141–144, 148, 151–152, 159, 163, 173
  and mystical love **I:** 163
axiological ethics **II:** 125–148
axiology **II:** 56, 126, 133, 139, 148
Ayer, Alfred J. **II:** 220, 224, 225, 226

B

Baader, Franz von **I:** 240; **II:** 49
Bacon, Francis **I:** 172, 231, 248, 249
Bacon, Roger **I:** 172, 173, 174, 178
Bad Conscience **II:** 79
Bahya ibn Pakuda **I:** 125
Baier, Kurt **II:** 232–233
Bain, Alexander **II:** 30, 151
Baldwin, William **I:** 222
Balguy, John **I:** 283–284
Bardaisan of Edessa **I:** 86

Bar-Hebraeus **I:** 134, 146
Barrett, William **II:** 167
Bartholomew of Messina **I:** 163
Baruk, H. **II:** 197
Basis of Natural Right **II:** 34
Baumgarten, Alexander G. **I:** 318, 320
Beattie, James **II:** 16
Beauvoir, Simone de **II:** 258, 259
Beck, Lewis W. **II:** 168
Being and Having **II:** 251
Being and Nothingness **II:** 255
Bellarmine, Robert **I:** 182, 227–228
Beneke, Friedrich E. **II:** 47–48
Bentham, Jeremy **I:** 273; **II:** 4, 18–23, 28–29, 151, 171
Berdyaev, Nikolai **II:** 109–110
Bergson, Henri **II:** 75–81, 83–84, 130, 183, 191, 195
Berkeley, George **I:** 275
Bernard of Clairvaux **I:** 112
Bessarion, Cardinal **I:** 210
Beyond Good and Evil **II:** 242
Beyond Realism and Idealism **II:** 139, 140
Bible **I:** 84, 115, 118, 125, 173, 201. *See also* specific Books
  and Jewish ethics B: 117ff
Birth of Tragedy **II:** 242
Blackstone, Sir William **II:** 18–19
Blanquerna **I:** 190, 191
Blanshard, Brand **I:** 164; **II:** 166–167
Bloch, Ernst **II:** 106
Blondel, Maurice **II:** 24
Boethius (Anicius Manlius Severinus Boethius) **I:** 84, 95, 104–106; **II:** 14
Boethius of Dacia **I:** 187
Böhme (Behmen), Jakob **I:** 238–239
Boke Named the Governour, The **I:** 221
Bolingbroke, Henry St. John **I:** 268, 274
Bonaventure, St. **I:** 175–178
Bondage of the Will, The **I:** 236
Bonhoeffer, Dietrich **II:** 249–250
Book of Dispositions **I:** 146

Book of Doctrines and Beliefs **I:** 121
Book on Felicity **I:** 187
Book on Pleasure **I:** 213
Book of the Dove **I:** 134
Book of the Laws of Countries **I:** 86
Bosanquet, Bernard **II:** 155
Bourget, Paul **II:** 72
Boutroux, Émile **II:** 74, 75
Bowring, John **II:** 18
Bradley, Francis H. **II:** 151, 153–155, 207
Braithwaite, R. B. **II:** 169–171
Bramhall, John **I:** 256, 259, 260
Brentano, Franz C. **II:** 127–129, 139, 141, 148, 180, 238
Brief Disquisition of the Law of Nature, A **I:** 256
Brightman, Edgar S. **II:** 144
Brisbane, Albert **II:** 97
British. *See* Great Britain and the English
Broad, C. D. **II:** 227
Brook Farm, Massachusetts **II:** 97
Brothers Karamazov, The **II:** 244
Brown, Thomas **II:** 15
Browne, Sir Thomas **I:** 256
Brownson, Orestes **II:** 60, 97
Bruni, Leonardo **I:** 163, 223
Brunner, Emil **I:** 84
Bruno, Giordano **I:** 210, 215–216, 218, 243
Brunschbicg, Leon **II:** 77–78
Buber, Martin **II:** 245–247
Bucer (or Butzer), Martin **I:** 236
Buffier, Claude **II:** 14
Burgersdijck, Francis **I:** 234, 235, 238
Burgundio of Pisa **I:** 92
Burke, Edmund **II:** 16, 21
Burleigh, Walter **I:** 162, 170
Butler, Joseph **I:** 277, 278, 279; **II:** 12

C

Cabal of the Horse Pegasus **I:** 215
Cajetan (Cardinal Tommaso de Vio) **I:** 224
Callicles **I:** 19, 20, 258
Calvin, John **I:** 237, 238, 239
Cambridge University **I:** 237; **II:** 169, 210

analytic ethics **II:** 210–214
Platonism **I:** 257
Campanella, Tommaso **I:** 210, 217–218
Campbell, Archibald **I:** 279
Camus, Albert **I:** 242; **II:** 108, 244, 259–260
Capital (Marx) **II:** 101
Carnap, Rudolf **II:** 219, 224
Cartesian Ethics **I:** 298
Cartesianism **I:** 298; **II:** 14, 92
Catechism of Positive Religion **II:** 97
Catharism **I:** 114
catharsis **I:** 77
Catholics and Catholicism **I:** 182, 186, 201, 219, 225, 228, 234, 239, 289, 295, 297, 306, 314, 317; **II:** 23–24, 49, 63, 68, 79–80, 82, 86, 100, 127, 145–147, 187, 193–196, 215, 250
Cato Uticensis **I:** 64
cave, Plato's allegory of the **I:** 32
Chamberlain, Houston S. **II:** 120
Chapman, George **I:** 245
Characteristics (Shaftesbury) **I:** 266
Charmides **I:** 27
Charron, Pierre **I:** 242
Christian Discussions **II:** 61
Christian Ethics (Hildebrand) **II:** 147
Christian Morals (Browne) **I:** 256
Christian Morals Today **II:** 250
"Christian philosophy" movement **II:** 78
"Christian Socratism" **I:** 113
Christianity **I:** 56, 67, 79, 87–89, 92, 96, 104, 115, 121, 124, 189, 201, 225, 241, 257, 273–274; **II:** 39, 45, 96, 107, 115, 162, 243, 249. *See also* specific denominations
Chrysippus of Soli **I:** 57, 62
Chubb, Percival **II:** 159
Church Council of Florence **I:** 209
Cicero **I:** 52, 62–64, 97–98, 113, 185, 209, 269
City of God **I:** 63, 98, 103, 312

City of the Sun **I:** 217
Civilization and Ethics **II:** 165
Civilization and Its Discontents **II:** 181
Clarke, John **I:** 269
Clarke, Samuel **I:** 268, 269; **II:** 12, 31
Claudius Galen. *See* Galen
Cleanthes **I:** 57, 58, 61
Clement IV, Pope (Guido Fulcodi) **I:** 172
Clement of Alexandria **I:** 88
Clouds, The **I:** 20
Clough, Arthur Hugh **II:** 32
Code of the Law of Peoples **I:** 308
Cohen, Hermann **II:** 56
Coit, Stanton **II:** 159
Coleridge, Samuel Taylor **II:** 22
Collingwood, R. G. **II:** 116, 117
Commentaria in libros Sententiarum **I:** 179
Commentaries on the Laws of England **II:** 18
Commentary on the Second Part of the Summa Theologiae **I:** 225
Common Faith **II:** 200
Communia Naturalium **I:** 173
Communism **II:** 100, 102–103, 105, 259. *See also* Marx and Marxism
Communist Manifesto **II:** 101
Comte, Auguste **I:** 173; **II:** 25, 72–73, 85, 97–100, 150
Concept of Dread **II:** 239
Concept of Morals **II:** 166
Concerning the Fundamental Principle of Virtue or Morality **I:** 268
Concerning the Infinite **I:** 243
Concluding Unscientific Postscript **II:** 240
Concorenses **I:** 114
Condemnation of 219 Propositions **I:** 187
Condillac, Étienne Bonnot de **I:** 274; **II:** 64–65, 95
Condorcet, Antoine Nicholas de **II:** 25, 94–95, 98
Conduct in Regard to Others **II:** 82

Confessions (Augustine) **I:** 98, 99
Consciousness of Self **II:** 82
Considérant, Victor **II:** 97
Consolation of Philosophy **I:** 104, 106
Contemporary British Philosophy **II:** 137
contemporary ethics **I:** 48; **II:** 148, 174, 180, 188, 196–197, 220, 226, 234, 248, 262
Contra Faustum **I:** 101
Corpus Dionysiacum **I:** 90
courage **I:** 22, 27–28, 35, 46, 52, 77, 140, 157, 184, 217; **II:** 118, 135, 243, 256
Courage to Be, The **II:** 246
Course in Philosophy **II:** 69
Course of Positive Philosophy **II:** 97
Cousin, Victor **II:** 16, 60, 66–67, 70, 74
Crates **I:** 6 2
Crates of Thebes **I:** 24
Creative Evolution **II:** 75
Creative Liberty **II:** 83
Crime and Punishment **II:** 244
Critique de la raison dialectique **II:** 255, 257
Critique of Practical Reason **I:** 320, 322, 325–327; **II:** 155
Critique of Pure Reason **I:** 320–322
Crito **I:** 21, 26
Croce, Benedetto **II:** 91, 113
Crusius, Christian A. **I:** 319
Cudworth, Ralph **I:** 244, 257–260, 266; **II:** 8, 12, 151
Culverwel, Nathanael **I:** 257
Cumberland, Richard **I:** 261, 269; **II:** 5, 6
Cursus Conimbricensis **I:** 227
Cynics **I:** 24
Cyrenaics **I:** 25, 68

D

Dana, Charles A. **II:** 97
Dante Alighieri **I:** 192
Darwin, Charles **II:** 151, 177–178
Daub, Karl **II:** 45
Dawson, Miles **I:** 21
De amore **I:** 164, 223
De amore divino **I:** 223
De Anima (Aristotle) **I:** 39, 41, 49, 137, 142, 151

De Anima (Avicenna) **I:** 142
De Anima (Suárez) **I:** 228, 233
De bona fortuna **I:** 52, 163
Decalogue (Ten Commandments) **I:** 85, 90, 118, 185, 212; **II:** 31
Decartes, René **II:** 83 86 92 95 150 239
  existentialism and **II:** 239
  spiritual ethics and **II:** 60, 64, 74
Decisive Treatise **I:** 150–152
De cive **I:** 250
De corpore (On Body) **I:** 250
De divisione naturae **I:** 107
De fide orthodoxa (On the True Faith) **I:** 92
De finibus **I:** 52, 63
Definition of Good, The **II:** 219
De Hebdomadibus **I:** 105
De homine (On Man) **I:** 250
De imperio **I:** 288, 290
De Isaac et anima **I:** 97
Deism (Deists) **I:** 268, 271–275
De l'Homme **II:** 19
Deliverance from Error **I:** 144
Democritus of Abdera **I:** 16
Dennes, William R. **II:** 201
Deontology **I:** 44, 326; **II:** 4, 168
Deschamps, Dom Léger-Marie **II:** 93
Destiny of Man **II:** 109, 248
Deuteronomy, Book of **I:** 118, 121
De veritate **I:** 245
De Virtutibus et vitiis **I:** 140
De vita beata **I:** 296
De voluptate **I:** 213
Dewey, John, II **II:** 126, 144, 184–187, 200–201, 203, 223–224, 235
Dialogue between a Conservative and a Reformer **II:** 96
Dialogue on Truth **I:** 109
Dialogues on Metaphysics **II:** 61
Diderot, Denis **II:** 93
Diogenes of Seleucia **I:** 62

Diogenes of Sinope **I:** 24
Dionysius the Areopagite **I:** 78
Dionysius the Pseudo-Areopagite **I:** 90
Disciple, The **II:** 72
Discourse on the Arts and Sciences **I:** 315
Discourse on the General View of Positivism **II:** 97
Discourse of Liberty and Necessity **I:** 259
Discourse on Method **I:** 293
Discourse on Natural Religion **I:** 268
Discourses (Diatribai) **I:** 65
Disputations on the Highest Good **I:** 297
Dissertation upon the Nature of Virtue **I:** 277
Divine Comedy **I:** 192
Divine Institutes **I:** 96
Divine Milieu **II:** 190
Doctrine of Right **II:** 45
dogs (dogness) **I:** 40
Dominicans **I:** 161, 178
Dostoyevsky, Feodor **II:** 108, 243, 244
Duns Scotus, John **I:** 175, 193–194, 197–198, 209, 229
Durkheim, Émile **II:** 110, 111
Duties of the Heart **I:** 125
Duty (Le Senne) **II:** 80
Du Vair, Guillaume **I:** 244–245

E

Early Theological Writings **II:** 38
Eastern Church **II:** 107
Eaton, Howard O. **II:** 139
Eckhart, Meister Johannes. *See* Johannes Eckhart, Meister
Edel, Abraham **II:** 202–203
Edwards, Paul **II:** 204–205, 235
egoism, ethical **I:** 247ff
Ehrenfels, Christian von **II:** 129, 139
Either/Or **II:** 239, 240
Elean-Eretrian group **I:** 24
Elementa philosophiae moralis **I:** 237
Eléments pour une éthique **II:** 253
Elements of First Practical Philosophy **I:** 318
Elements of Law **I:** 250
Elements of Theology **I:** 79

Elizabeth of Bohemia, Princess **I:** 293, 295
Elyot, Sir Thomas **I:** 215, 221–222
Emmanuel College, Cambridge **I:** 257
Emotional Presentation **II:** 129
emotivism **II:** 202, 204, 221, 233
empiricism **I:** 248
Enarrationes in Psalmos **I:** 101
Enchiridion (Augustine) **I:** 98
Enchiridion (Epictetus) **I:** 65, 244
Enchiridion Ethicum **I:** 260
Engels, Friedrich **II:** 104–105
England. *See* Great Britain and the English
Enneads (the "Nines") **I:** 74, 79, 98, 213
Enquiry concerning Human Understanding **II:** 7
Enquiry into Goodness **II:** 235
Enquiry into the Origin of the Human Appetites and Affections **I:** 284
Enquiry into the Original of Moral Virtue **I:** 279
Enquiry (as title). *See also Inquiry . . .*
Enumeration of the Sciences **I:** 136
Epictetus **I:** 57, 64–66, 244, 249, 256
Epicurus and Epicureanism **I:** 25, 55, 67–71, 89, 98
  in the Renaissance **I:** 239–240
Epistola **I:** 102
equity (*epieikeia*) **I:** 47
Er, Tale of **I:**87
Erasmus, Desiderius **I:** 236
Erigena, John Scottus **I:** 78, 95, 107, 108
Erkenne dich selbst **I:** 239
Error of Narcissus **II:** 82
Escape from Freedom **II:** 198
Essai sur le Mérite et la Vertu **I:** 266
Essais de Théodicée **I:** 311
Essay concerning Human Understanding **I:** 263
Essay on Man **I:** 273
Essay on the Nature and Conduct of the Passions **I:** 280

Essays (F. Bacon) **I:** 248
Essays (Montaigne) **I:** 241
Essays, Moral and Political **II:** 7
Essays on the Law of Nature **I:** 262
Essays on the Principle of Morality and Natural Religion **I:** 279
Essays in Sociology and Social Philosophy **II:** 117
Eternal Gospel **I:** 115
Ethica (Geulinex) **I:** 298–299
Ethica nova (New Ethics) **I:** 162
Ethica vetus (Old Ethics) **I:** 162
Ethical Characters **I:** 52
ethical culture movement **II:** 158–159
Ethical Disputations **I:** 297, 298
ethical intuitionism **I:** 45, 123, 266, 278; **II:** 158
Ethical Judgment **II:** 203
Ethical Reason and Moral Intelligence **II:** 86
Ethical Relativity **II:** 112
Ethical Studies **II:** 153
Ethics (Bonhoeffer) **II:** 249
Ethics (Dewey and Tufts) **II:** 184
Ethics (Fries) **II:** 45
Ethics (Garnett) **II:** 168
Ethics (Geulincx) **I:** 297
Ethics (Hartmann) **II:** 49, 133–135
Ethics (Hessen) **II:** 146
Ethics (Moore) **II:** 157, 175–176, 191, 204, 207, 210–213, 215, 217, 220, 226, 238
Ethics (Nowell-Smith) **II:** 228–230
Ethics (Pepper) **II:** 192, 193
Ethics (Peter Abelard) **I:** 95, 110–112, 116, 191; **II:** 66
Ethics (Spinoza) **I:** 213, 216, 271, 299–306, 309, 311; **II:** 150
Ethics (Vasconcelos) **II:** 84–85
Ethics (Ward) **II:** 147
Ethics (Wundt) **II:** 56
Ethics and Language **II:** 223
Ethics and Moral Science **II:** 111
Ethics and Morality **II:** 86
Ethics and the Materialist Conception of History **II:** 105

Ethics of Ambiguity **II:** 258
Ethikon **I:** 134, 146
Etika **II:** 179
Eucken, Rudolf **II:** 56, 130
Euclid of Megara **I:** 23
Eudaimonism
  definitions, translations **I:** 43
  early Greek **I:** 13–36
  teleological (Aristotelian) **I:** 37–54
  Thomism **I:** 186
eudemian ethics **I:** 26, 38–39, 46, 51, 53, 163
Eudemus **I:** 38–39
Europe
  contemporary ethics **II:** 125, 132, 141, 146, 190
  rationalistic ethics (17th and 18th centuries) **I:** 287–327

Eustratios, Bishop of Nicaea **I:** 53
Euthydemus **I:** 27
Euthyphro **I:** 27
evolutionary ethics **II:** 138, 179–180
Ewing, Alfred Cyril **II:** 219–221
Examination of Sir William Hamilton's Philosophy **II:** 22
Examination of the Place of Reason in Ethics **II:** 234
existential ethics **II:** 80, 205, 241, 247, 258
Exodus, Book of **I:** 118
Experiments in Living **II:** 191
Expulsion of the Triumphant Beast **I:** 215

F

Fable of the Bees **I:** 269, 270
Facts and Values **II:** 223
Fada'il al-Nafs **I:** 140
Faith of a Moralist **II:** 156
fathers of the Church **I:** 209, 309
Fear and Trembling **II:** 239
Feigl, Herbert **II:** 224
Ferguson, Adam **II:** 15
Ferrier, James **II:** 22
Feuerbach, Ludwig **II:** 45, 102
Fichte, Johann Gottlieb **II:** 34–37, 39, 48, 53, 55, 71
Ficino, Marsilio **I:** 210, 213–214, 223
FitzGerald, Edward **I:** 146
Flavius Arrianus **I:** 64
Flowers of St. Francis **I:** 164
Fons Vitae **I:** 123–124

Foot, Philippa R. **II:** 204
Formalism and Ethics **II:** 130
Förster-Nietzsche, Elisabeth **II:** 241
Fortescue, Sir John **I:** 199, 200
Foundation of Moral Goodness **I:** 283
Foundation of Morality **I:** 269
Foundations of Ethics **II:** 157
Foundations of Psychology **II:** 63
Foundations of the Metaphysic of Morals **I:** 320, 322
Foundations of the Nineteenth Century **II:** 120
Fountain of Life **I:** 123–124
Four Saints **II:** 82
Foure Hymnes **I:** 222
Fourier, François Marie Charles **II:** 96–97, 99
Fourteenth-century ethics **I:** 193ff
Fox, George **I:** 150
Fragment on Government **II:** 18
France
  17th and 18th century rationalism **I:** 314; **II:** 81
  axiology in **II:** 148
  Deism **I:** 271, 274–275
  existential ethics **II:** 80, 258
  societal ethics **II:** 93, 97, 99, 108
  spiritistic ethics **II:** 59, 66–67, 69, 71, 74, 79–80
Francis of Assisi **I:** 164
Franciscans **I:** 115, 161, 164, 171, 176, 178, 188
Franco-Latin Spiritistic Ethics **II:** 59–87
Frank, Philipp **II:** 224
Franklin, Benjamin **I:** 275
Freedom and Reason **II:** 234
Freedom of the Will **II:** 52
Freud (Sigmund) and Freudianism **II:** 50, 127, 180–182, 186, 198
Friars Minor, Order of **I:** 164, 175
friendship **I:** 70–71
Fries, Jakob Friedrich **II:** 45–46

Fromm, Erich **II:** 197–200
Fundamental Moral Attitudes **II:** 147
Fundamental Principles of the Torah **I:** 128

G

Gabriel Biel **I:** 199
Galen **I:** 52
Galt, John **II:** 4
games theory **II:** 168
Garnett, A. C. **II:** 168
Gassendi, Pierre **I:** 243–244, 258
Gauthier of Chatillon **I:** 113
Gay, John **I:** 268
Gegenwart: eine kritische Ethik **II:** 249
Gemistus Pletho **I:** 210
Genealogy of Morals **II:** 242–243
General Theory of Value **II:** 189
General View of Positivism **II:** 99
"general will" **I:** 316, 317
Generalization in Ethics **II:** 173
Genesis and Structure of Society **II:** 116
Genesis, Book of **I:** 165; **II:** 116
Gentile, Giovanni **II:** 113, 115–116
Georgios Scholarios **I:** 210
Gerardus de Borgo San Domino **I:** 115
Gerardus Odonis **I:** 162
Gerdil, Sigismond Cardinal **I:** 317
German Writings **II:** 119
Germany
  axiology **II:** 139
  idealism **II:** 50, 66, 133, 181, 241
  Marxism **II:** 106, 197, 198
  situation ethics **II:** 249
  societal ethics **II:** 100, 101, 102, 106, 108, 118, 119, 120, 121, 126, 133
Gersonides (Levi ben Gerson) **I:** 132
Gesetz und Sittengesetz . . . **II:** 245
Geulincx, Arnold **I:** 297, 298
Gianfrancesco **I:** 215
Giles of Rome **I:** 53, 162, 188
Gilson, Étienne **II:** 78
Ginsberg, Morris **II:** 117, 118

Gioberti, Vincenzo **II:** 60, 68, 69, 70, 71
Giornale di Metafisica **II:** 86
Gobineau, Count Arthur de **II:** 118, 120
God
  and Peter Abelard **I:** 110–111
  in analytic ethics **II:** 208, 218–220
  in Augustine **I:** 91, 97–104, 109, 116, 169, 172–173; **II:** 60, 65
  in Boethius **I:** 104–106
  in British ethics **I:** 247–286
  in Christian ethics **I:** 56, 63, 104, 114, 116, 243; **II:** 108, 146, 188, 194, 246–250
  in Erigena **I:** 107–108
  in Jewish ethics **I:** 117–133
  in the Middle Ages **I:** 83–116
  in modern theories **II:** 17–18, 23, 32, 37, 40, 44, 49, 55, 61–79, 82, 85
  in spiritistic ethics **II:** 59–87
  in Stoicism **I:** 57–61, 67
  Renaissance and **I:** 207–221, 231–246
  right reason and **I:** 161–201
Gödel, Kurt **II:** 224
Godwin, William **II:** 21
Good and Evil **II:** 155–156, 159, 202, 242, 246
Good Life, The **II:** 164
good reasons ethics **II:** 223–234
Gorgias **I:** 28, 35
Gorgias the Sophist **I:** 24
Gouhier, Henri **II:** 63
Governance of the Solitary **I:** 147
Grammar of Assent **II:** 23
Great Britain and the English **I:** 247ff
  Aristotelianism **I:** 192
  analytic ethics **II:** 207–236
  egoism **I:** 247ff
  naturalism **II:** 248, 302, 306
  Platonism **I:** 215, 217–223
  societal ethics **II:** 115–118
  stoicism **I:** 98–99
  utilitarian and subjectivist ethics **II:** 3–32, 149–174
  value ethics **II:** 188

Greek (Hellenistic) ethics **I:** 16, 75, 116, 118, 283
Greek Christian writers **I:** 87–95
Green, Thomas Hill **II:** 151, 152, 153, 207
Gregorius Abu al-Faraj **I:** 133
Gregory I (the Great), Pope **I:** 107
Gregory of Nyssa, St. **I:** 90
Gregory of Rimini **I:** 232
Gregory of Valencia **I:** 289
Grisebach, Eberhard **II:** 249
Grote, John **II:** 22
Grotius, Hugo **I:** 287, 288, 289, 290, 291, 292, 313
Guide for the Perplexed **I:** 121, 126
Guido Fulcodi (later Pope Clement IV) **I:** 172
Gumplowicz, Ludwig **II:** 119–120
Gusdorf, Georges **II:** 252
Guyau, Marie Jean **II:** 72–75
Gyges **I:** 33

H

Hägerström, Axel **II:** 226, 227
Halevi, Judah **I:** 124, 125
Hamilton, Sir William **II:** 22, 25
Hampshire, Stuart **II:** 231–234
Hare, R. M. **II:** 169, 233–234
Hartley, David **I:** 284
Hartmann, Eduard von **II:** 49
Hartmann, Nicolai **II:** 133, 201, 238, 261
Hartshorne, Charles **II:** 188
Hasdai ben Abraham Crescas **I:** 132
Hawthorne, Nathaniel **II:** 97
Hayy ibn Yaqzan **I:** 148
Hecker, Thomas **II:** 97
hedonism **I:** 25, 50, 68, 123, 46
Heereboord, Andriaan **I:** 235, 238
Hegel, G. W. F. **II:** 34, 38–45, 51, 54, 68, 71, 75, 100-103, 113, 115, 133, 159
  existentialism and **II:** 238, 239, 240, 241, 251, 256
hēgemonikon **I:** 63
Hegesias **I:** 25

Helvétius, Claude Adrian **I:** 225; **II:** 19
Henning, Leopold von **II:** 45
Henry de Bracton **I:** 199
Henry of Ghent **I:** 189, 195, 229
Henry VIII **I:** 219
Heraclitus **I:** 15
Herbart, Johann Friedrich, II: **II:** 46–47
Herbert of Cherbury **I:** 219, 245, 263, 271
Hermannus Alemannus **I:** 162
Hermes Tresmegistos **I:** 74
Heroic Frenzies **I:** 215
Hexaëmeron **I:** 165
Hildebert of Tours **I:** 113
Hildebrand, Dietrich von **II:** 146, 147
Hillel ben Samuel **I:** 132
Hippias Minor **I:** 28
Hippias of Elis **I:** 20
Hippolytus **I:** 87, 88
Histoire de Juliette **II:** 94
Historical Sketch of the Progress of the Human Mind **II:** 25
History of Ethics (Sidgwick) **II:** 30
Hitler, Adolf **II:** 37, 118, 120, 249
Hobbes, Thomas **I:** 219, 221, 234, 244, 248–259, 261, 263–264, 267–269, 271, 273, 277, 292, 302, 305, 309, 315; **II:** 12, 31, 151
  ethical egoism of **I:** 219, 244
Hocking, William Ernest **II:** 164
Holbach, Baron d' **I:** 225
Holland **I:** 234, 289, 300
Holmes, Samuel Jackson **II:** 189
Homenajae a Xavier Zubiri **II:** 86
Homer **I:** 245; **II:** 92
Homme problématique, L' **II:** 251
Homo Viator **II:** 251
Honest to God **II:** 250
Hooker, Richard **I:** 202–203, 218, 253, 257
Hope of the Great Community **II:** 159, 162
How to Do Things with Words **II:** 221
Human Nature and Conduct **II:** 185
Human Nature and Its Remaking **II:** 164

Human Person and the World of Values, The **II:** 147
humanism **I:** 18; **II:** 198–200
Renaissance **I:** 207ff
Humanism as a Philosophy **II:** 200
Humanisme et Terreur **II:** 259
Humanity and Duty **II:** 141
Human Values **II:** 144
Hume, David **II:** 6–16, 25, 208–209
Husserl, Edmund **II:** 85, 129–130, 238, 245
Hutcheson, Francis **I:** 279–284; **II:** 151
Huxley, Julian **II:** 189–191
Huxley, Thomas Henry **II:** 178

I

I and Thou **II:** 246
Iamblichus **I:** 13, 79
Ibn-Bajjah (Avempace) **I:** 147
Ibn-Gabirol (Avicebrón). *See* Avicebrón (ibn-Gabirol)
Ibn-Haylan, Yuhanna **I:** 136
Ibn-Hazm **I:** 146
Ibn-Ishaq, Hunaïn **I:** 133, 140
Ibn-Tufail **I:** 148, 150
Idea philosophiae moralis **I:** 235
ideal forms **I:** 22, 31, 32, 40, 74, 166; **II:** 134
idealism **II:** 60, 159
Germany (modern) **II:** 33–57
Ideas: General Introduction to Pure Phenomenology **II:** 245
Idiot, The **II:** 244
Ignatius of Loyola **I:** 227
Ihya al-Ulum **I:** 134, 144
immortality
in Aristotle **I:** 41, 151, 224
in Averroes **I:** 151
in Epicurus **I:** 71
in Gregory of Nyssa **I:** 90
in Plato **I:** 26, 41, 87
Immortality of the Soul **I:** 224
Independent Christian Ethics **II:** 248
Individual and His Unique Quality **II:** 54
Inequality of Human Races **II:** 118

Inquiries into the Nature of Law and Morals **II:** 227
Inquiry **I:** 266, 280. *See also* Enquiry
Inquiry concerning Political Justice **II:** 21
Inquiry concerning the Principles of Morals **II:** 6
Inquiry concerning Virtue **I:** 266
Inquiry into the Distinctness of the Principles of Natural Theology and Morals **I:** 319
Inquiry into the Human Mind on the Principles of Common Sense **II:** 14
Inquiry into the Original of Our Ideas of Beauty and Virtue **I:** 280
Intelligible World, The **II:** 139, 140
International Journal of Ethics **II:** 155
Introduction to Moral Instruction **I:** 223
Introduction to Stoic Philosophy **I:** 244
Introduction to the Jurisprudence of Holland **I:** 288
Introduction to the Principles of Morals and Legislation **II:** 18
Irrational Man **II:** 167
Islam. *See* Moslems
Italy and the Italians **I:** 114
  Aristotelianism **I:** 223
  Epicureanism **I:** 243–244
  Platonism **I:** 209ff
  Renaisance **I:** 213–246
  societal ethics **II:** 112–114
  spiritistic ethics **II:** 59, 60, 68–70
intuitionism, ethical **II:** 3–32, 176, 158, 219, 221, 228

J

Jalal al-Din Muhammad ibn-Asad Dawani **I:** 158
James, William **II:** 159, 182, 183, 184
Jankélévitch, Vladimir **II:** 79, 80
Jansenism **I:** 298
Jean Buridan **I:** 162
Jerome, St. **I:** 169
Jesuits **I:** 227, 229
Jews (Judaism) / anti-Semitism **II:** 119

contemporary ethics **II:** 180, 197
medieval ethics **I:** 84, 117–160
Joachim of Flora **I:** 115
Joad, C. E. M. **II:** 225
Johannes Eckhart, Meister **I:** 191
John Baconthorpe **I:** 162
John Damascene, St. **I:** 84, 92, 93, 94
John Duns Scotus.. *See* Duns Scotus, John
John of La Rochelle **I:** 175, 176
Jordan, Elijah **II:** 164
Jouffroy, Théodore **II:** 67
Judah Halevi **I:** 124, 125
justice **I:** 19–22, 27–35, 38, 44, 46–48, 52, 77, 100, 102, 106, 110, 113, 118, 132, 135, 140–141, 157, 184–185, 197, 216, 222, 244–245, 258–259, 288, 305, 308–310, 315, 317
in Aristotle **I:** 38, 44–48, 185
Justification of the Good **II:** 108

K

Kalam, The **I:** 135, 136
Kames, Henry Home, Lord **I:** 279
Kant, Immanuel **I:** 110, 116, 145, 186, 191, 245, 259, 270, 287, 308, 313, 316–327; **II:** 13, 30, 33, 37–39, 51, 56, 111, 115, 131, 149–157, 161, 168, 173–174, 246, 258
Coleridge and **II:** 22
existential ethics and **II:** 246, 257–258
Fries and **II:** 45–46
Price and **II:** 13
Scheler and **II:** 56
Schopenhauer and **II:** 53
self-realization ethics **II:** 152–155, 168
spiritistic ethics and **II:** 64, 78, 83, 86

Kautsky, Karl **II:** 105
Keckermann, Bartholomaeus **I:** 238
Kierkegaard, Søren **I:** 23; **II:** 45, 108, 239, 239–241, 240, 241, 242, 253
Kindi, al- **I:** 135, 137

King and the Education of the King, The **I:** 227
King, William, Archbishop of Dublin **I:** 268
Kingdom of God in America **II:** 249
Kleine Schriften **II:** 55
Knutzen, Martin **I:** 318
Kolakowski, Leszek **II:** 107
Koran **I:** 134, 135, 144, 145, 156
Korn, Alejandro **II:** 83, 84
Kropotkin, P. A. **II:** 179

L

Lactantius **I:** 96, 97
Laches **I:** 27
Lagarde, Paul Anton de **II:** 119
Lamont, Corliss **II:** 200
Lange, Joachim **I:** 318
language analysis **II:** 207, 208, 216, 221, 231, 235, 262
Language of Morals **II:** 233, 234
Language, Truth, and Logic **II:** 224
Latest Decalogue **II:** 31
Lavelle, Louis **II:** 82, 83, 148
law **I:** 16, 133, 168ff, 181 (*See also* natural law)
Aristotle on **I:** 43
Augustine on **I:** 95
Judaism and **I:** 120–128
rationalistic ethics and (17th and 18th centries) **I:** 287ff
Stoicism and **I:** 58
Law of Nature and of Nations **I:** 291
Law, Edmund **I:** 268
Laws (Plato) **I:** 29, 35, 136
Laws of Nature (Cumberland) **I:** 261; **II:** 5
Le Senne, René **II:** 80, 80–82, 81, 82, 148
Leclercq, Jacques **II:** 196, 197
Lectura in libros Ethicorum Aristotelis **I:** 179
Lectures on Ethics (Kant) **I:** 319
Lectures on the Ethics (Albert the Great) **I:** 180
Lectures on the Summa of Theology **I:** 228
Leibniz, Gottfried Wilhelm von **I:** 216, 237, 238, 271, 290, 297, 306, 306–313, 307, 308, 309, 310, 311, 312, 313, 318, 319; **II:** 46, 55, 71
Lenin, V. I. **II:** 105, 106

Leonardo Bruni d'Arezzo **I:** 163
Leonardo da Vinci **I:** 208
Letter on Apostasy **I:** 130
Letter on Astrology **I:** 126
Letters (Pseudo-Dionysius) **I:** 91
Letters and Moral Essays **I:** 64
Letters on the Study of History **I:** 274
lex talionis **I:** 120
Leviathan **I:** 250, 256, 258
Leviathan Drawn Out with a Hook **I:** 256
Leviticus, Book of **I:** 121
Lévy-Bruhl, Lucien **II:** 111
Lewis, C. I. **II:** 143, 144, 168
Libellus de beata vita **I:** 239
Liber de Bona Fortuna **I:** 52
Liber Sextus Naturalium **I:** 142
Life of Jesus **II:** 38
Life of Reason **II:** 163
Life of the Spirit **II:** 56
Light of Nature Pursued **I:** 284
"limiting" and "non-limiting" opposites **I:** 15
Lipsius, Justus (Lips, Joest) **I:** 244
Locke, John **I:** 261, 262, 263, 264, 265, 266, 267, 271, 274, 284, 293, 310, 317, 318; **II:** 12, 14
Logic of Moral Discourse **II:** 204
Logic of the Moral Sciences **II:** 25
Lollard movement **I:** 201
Lombard, Peter. *See* Peter Lombard
Loquentes **I:** 135
Lotze, Rudolf Hermann **II:** 55, 159
love
  in England **I:** 177
  in medieval thought **I:** 162–164, 212
  in modern theories **II:** 39
  in Renaissance **I:** 198
Love, Power, and Justice **II:** 246
Lucretius **I:** 70, 71, 243
Lukacs, Georg **II:** 106, 107
Lull, Ramón. *See* Ramón Lull
Luther, Martin **I:** 200, 235, 236, 239; **II:** 45

M

Macbeath, Alexander **II:** 191, 192

Mach, Ernst **II:** 106
Machiavelli, Niccolò **I:** 219, 240; **II:** 115
Macrobius **I:** 77, 113
Magna Moralia **I:** 39, 53, 163
Maimon, Salomon **I:** 126, 327
Maimonides (Moses ben Maimon) **I:** 121
Maine de Biran **II:** 63, 64, 65, 68, 77, 83
Malebranche, Father Nicolas **I:** 317; **II:** 60, 61, 62, 63, 64, 69, 150
Man for Himself **II:** 198
Mandelbaum, Maurice **II:** 260, 261, 262
Mandeville, Bernard **I:** 269, 270, 271, 275
Manichaeanism **I:** 114
Marcel, Gabriel **II:** 80, 195, 250, 251, 252, 254
Marcus Aurelius **I:** 57, 66, 67
Marheineke, P. K. **II:** 45
Mariana, Juan de **I:** 227
Maritain, Jacques **II:** 78, 194, 195, 196, 209
Marius Victorinus **I:** 78
Martin of Dumio, Bishop of Braga **I:** 107
Martineau, Harriet **II:** 97
Martineau, James **II:** 24, 25, 97, 150, 151, 152
Marx and Marxism **II:** 45, 100, 101, 102, 103, 104, 105, 106, 107, 197, 255, 257
materialism **I:** 225; **II:** 60, 85, 102, 103, 105, 106, 138, 257
mathematics and ethics **I:** 14, 33, 265; **II:** 98, 104
Matthew of Aquasparta **I:** 176
Matthew, Gospel of **I:** 85
Maurus, Sylvester **I:** 227
Maximus of Scythopolis **I:** 92
Maximus the Confessor **I:** 78
McCosh, James **II:** 16
McLuhan, Marshall **II:** 216
Medici, Cosimo de' **I:** 210, 256
Medieval and patristic theories **I:** 15
Meditations (Descartes) **I:** 293
Meditations (Marcus Aurelius) **I:** 66
Megarics **I:** 23

Meinong, Alexius **II:** 128, 129, 139
Meister Eckhart. *See* Johannes Eckhart, Meister
Melanchthon, Philip **I:** 237
Memorabilia (Xenophon) **I:** 21
Mendemus of Eretria **I:** 24
Mental and Moral Science **II:** 30
Merleau-Ponty, Maurice **II:** 259
Messner, Johannes **II:** 196
Metaphysical Disputations **I:** 229
Metaphysical Principles of Christian Morality **I:** 317
Metaphysics (Aristotle) **I:** 39, 49
Metaphysics (Lotze) **II:** 55
Metaphysics of Morals **I:** 320
metempsychosis **I:** 14
Method in Ethical Theory **II:** 203
Methods of Ethics **II:** 30
Mexico **II:** 84
Michael Ephesius **I:** 53
Microcosmus **II:** 55
"middle Stoicism" **I:** 62, 63
Milhamot Adonai I: 132
Mill, James **II:** 20–21
Mill, John Stuart **I:** 235; **II:** 18, 21–31 *passim*, 263
Mind (Stevenson) **II:** 213, 222, 223
Miscellanies (Stromata) **I:** 88
Mishneh Torah (the Code) **I:** 126, 128
Miskawaihi, Ahmed ibn-Muhammad-ibn Yaqub **I:** 133, 139, 140, 141, 156, 157, 159
Modern Theory of Ethics **II:** 180
Mohammed, Prophet **I:** 130, 133, 134, 135, 138
monads **I:** 307; **II:** 71
Montaigne, Michel de **I:** 241, 242
Montesquieu, Charles Louis de Secondat, baron de **I:** 314, 315
Moore, G. E. **II:** 30, 157, 175–176, 191, 204, 207
Moral Experience **II:** 112, 260
Moral Life and Moral Worth **II:** 138
Moral Life and the Ethical Life **II:** 201

Moral Man and Immoral Society **II:** 248
Moral Obligation **II:** 158
Moral Philosopher (Morgan) **I:** 273
Moral Philosophy (Maritain) **II:** 195
Moral Philosophy (Wolff) ***I:*** *313*
Moral Philosophy in the Eighteenth Century **II:** 66
Moral Philosophy of Antonio Rosmini **II:** 86
Moral Philosophy of the Good-in-itself and the Useful Good **I:** 113
Moral Philosophy of the Stoics **I:** 244
Moral Point of View **II:** 233
Moral Science **II:** 30, 71, 111
Moral Values and the Idea of God **II:** 138
Moralists (Shaftesbury) **I:** 266
Morality of Self-Interest **II:** 200
More, Henry **I:** 257, 260
More, Thomas **I:** 215, 219, 221
Morgan, Thomas **I:** 273
Morgenstern, O. **II:** 168
Moses **I:** 85, 101, 126, 134, 185
Moslems **I:** 78, 136, 159. *See also* Islam; Mohammedans
Muirhead, J. H. **II:** 155
Munk, Solomon **I:** 124
Musonius, Rufus **I:** 65
Mussolini, Benito **II:** 113
Mutual Aid **II:** 179
Mystery of Being **II:** 251
Mystical Theology **I:** 91, 92
Myth of Sisyphus **II:** 259
Myth of the Twentieth Century **II:** 121

N

Nabert, Jean **II:** 253, 254
Najat (*Salvation*) **I:** 141
Nasir ad-Din Tusi **I:** 152, 159
Nasirean Ethics, The **I:** 152
natural law **I:** 49, 58, 86, 132, 180, 183, 199, 229, 231, 232, 233, 238, 253, 255, 262, 288, 289, 290, 291, 292, 309, 313, 314, 317; **II:** 16, 18, 91, 156, 177, 196, 197, 200, 202, 248

naturalism **II:** 138, 141, 176, 177, 181, 190, 193, 197, 199, 200, 201, 202, 203, 204, 205, 220, 261, 262
Natural System of Practical Philosophy **II:** 47
Nature and Destiny of Man **II:** 248
Nature of Sympathy, The **II:** 130
Nature, History and God **II:** 85
Naville, Pierre **II:** 257
Nazism **II:** 119, 121, 242, 249
Nelson, Leonard **II:** 46
Nemesius, Bishop **I:** 93
neoclassicism **I:** 209, 248
Neoplatonism **I:** 55, 79, 80, 124, 179, 215
Neumann, J. von **II:** 168
New Atlantis **I:** 248
New Essays in Anthropology **II:** 63
New Science **II:** 90, 91, 92
New World of Industry and Society **II:** 96
Newman, John Henry **II:** 23
Nicholas of Cusa **I:** 78, 210, 213, 215, 238, 239, 242
Nicomachean Ethics **I:** 38, 39, 42, 43, 44, 46, 47, 49, 51, 53, 84, 98, 104, 111, 133, 147, 150, 157, 161, 162, 163, 170, 179, 182, 188, 200, 223, 227, 237
Nicomachus **I:** 37, 39
Niebuhr, H. Richard **II:** 248, 249
Niebuhr, Reinhold **II:** 248, 249
Nietzsche, Friedrich **II:** 54, 74, 83, 130, 136, 241, 242, 243, 244, 253
Nifo, Agostino **I:** 224
Nine Lectures . . . (Maritain) **II:** 194
noemata **I:** 260, 261
Non-Religion of the Future **II:** 72
Notebooks (Leonardo) **I:** 208
Notes from the Underground **II:** 244
Notion of Responsibility **II:** 111
Notulae **I:** 53, 170
Nouveaux essais sur l'entendement humain **I:** 310
Nouveaux mélanges philosophiques **II:** 67

Nowell-Smith, P. H **II:** 228, 229, 230

O

Observations on Man **I:** 284
Obstacle and Value **II:** 80
Ockham (Ockhamism). *See* William of Ockham
Ogden, C. **II:** 222
Olivi, Peter John **I:** 188
Olson, Robert G. **II:** 200
Omar Khayyam **I:** 146
On Authority in Matters of Religion **I:** 274
On Cheerfulness **I:** 16
On Divine Love **I:** 213
On Duty **I:** 57
On Ecclesiastical Power **I:** 188
On Eudaimonia **I:** 52
On First Principles **I:** 89
On Free Choice **I:** 213
On Human Freedom **II:** 49
On Human Nature **I:** 57
On Intelligence **II:** 72
On Justice **I:** 38
On Law and Justice **II:** 227
On Laws **I:** 229
On Learned Ignorance **I:** 211
On Living in Accord with Nature **I:** 57
On Logical and Ethical Principles **II:** 130
On Love **I:** 164
On Moral Customs **I:** 52
On Nature **I:** 68
On Order **I:** 101
On Seeking and Causing Happiness **I:** 139
On the Basis of Morality **II:** 53
On the Celestial Hierarchy **I:** 91
On the Divine Names **I:** 91
On the Ecclesiastical Hierarchy **I:** 91
On the Functions of the Clergy **I:** 97
On the Good (Gioberti) **II:** 69
On the Good (Plato) **I:** 26
On the Infinite, Universe and Worlds **I:** 216
On the Knowledge of Good and Evil **II:** 201
On the Knowledge of Self **II:** 78
On the Law of War **I:** 225
On the Laws and Customs of England **I:** 199

On the Life and Moral Teachings of Epicurus **I:** 243
On the Merits of the Laws of England **I:** 199
On the Nature of Man **I:** 93
On the Nature of Things **I:** 70, 71, 243
On the Necessity of Loving God **I:** 112
On the Origin of Ethical Knowledge **II:** 127
On the Origin of Evil **I:** 268
On the Passions **I:** 52
On the Peace of Faith **I:** 212
On the Rights of War and Peace **I:** 288
On the Soul (John of La Rochelle) **I:** 175
On the Soul (Tertullian) **I:** 96, 147, 228
On the Spirit and the Letter **I:** 102
On the Trinity **I:** 98, 99
On the Union between the Intellect and Man **I:** 148
On the Vision of God **I:** 211
On Truth **I:** 245
On University Studies **II:** 48, 49
On Virtues and Vices **I:** 39
On Wisdom (Charron) **I:** 242
On Wisdom (Leibniz) **I:** 308
Opera Omnia **I:** 227, 229
opposites, theory of **I:** 15
Opus Majus (Greater Work) **I:** 173, 174
Opus Postumum **I:** 320
Or Adonai **I:** 132
Oration on the Dignity of Man **I:** 208, 214
Ordinatio (Duns Scotus) **I:** 193
Ordinatio (William of Ockham) **I:** 196
Origen **I:** 89
Origin and Development of the Moral Ideas **II:** 112
Origin of Species **II:** 177
Ortega y Gasset, José **II:** 253
Outline of a System of Utilitarian Ethics **II:** 171
Outline of a Theory of the Emotions **II:** 255
Outlines of a Critique of the Doctrine of Morals up to the Present **II:** 37

Outlines of the Philosophy of Epicurus **I:** 243
Oxford Collection of Moral Writings **I:** 113
Oxford University **II:** 221

P

Paley, William **II:** 17, 23, 151
Panaetius of Rhodes **I:** 62
Parerga and Paralipomena **II:** 54
Paris, University of **I:** 162, 175, 182, 186, 189, 227
Parker, DeWitt H. **II:** 144, 145, 147
Passions of the Soul **I:** 293, 295, 298
Passive Obedience **I:** 276
Paton, H. J. **II:** 168
patristic and medieval theories **I:** 81
Paulsen, Friedrich **II:** 56
Pecock, Reginald. *See* Reginald Pecock
Pepper, Stephen C. **II:** 192, 193
Peripatetic school **I:** 52
Perry, Ralph Barton **II:** 125, 126, 141, 144, 147, 188, 189, 192, 223
Persaeus **I:** 62
Peter Abelard **I:** 95, 110, 111, 112, 116, 191; **II:** 66
Peter Lombard **I:** 177, 179, 193, 196
Pfänder, Alexander **II:** 245
Phaedo **I:** 21, 26, 27, 35, 76
Phaedrus **I:** 29, 30, 35, 76
Phänomenologie des Wollens **II:** 245
Phenomenological ethics **I:** 190; **II:** 56, 126, 237, 245, 253, 256, 259, 260
Phenomenology of Mind **II:** 38, 40
Phenomenology of Moral Experience **II:** 260
Phenomenon of Man **II:** 190
Philebus **I:** 29
Philo Judaeus **I:** 72, 118
Philosophia rationalis **I:** 235
Philosophical Analysis **II:** 221
Philosophical Commentaries **I:** 276
Philosophical Dictionary **I:** 274
Philosophical Ethics **I:** 318
Philosophical Fragments **II:** 251

Philosophical Inquiry into the Origin of Our Ideas **II:** 16
Philosophical Investigations on the Essence of Human Freedom **II:** 48
Philosophical Lectures **II:** 22
Philosophical Papers **II:** 221
Philosophical Proof of the Truth of the Christian Religion **I:** 318
Philosophical Rudiments **I:** 255
Philosophical Thoughts on the Sciences **I:** 274
Philosophie de la volonté **II:** 259
philosophie de l'esprit **II:** 59, 147
Philosophie des deutschen Idealisms, Die **II:** 133
Philosophumena **I:** 87
Philosophy and Logical Syntax **II:** 219
Philosophy of Freedom **II:** 68
Philosophy of G. E. Moore **II:** 212
Philosophy of History **II:** 39, 44, 113
Philosophy of Loyalty **II:** 159, 161
Philosophy of Right **II:** 38, 42, 44
Philosophy of the Active and Moral Powers of Man **II:** 15
Philosophy of the Person **II:** 84
Philosophy of the Practical **II:** 114
Philosophy of Value **II:** 147
Physico-Theology **I:** 273
Pico della Mirandola, Giovanni **I:** 208, 210, 213, 214, 215, 221
Pindar **I:** 20
Plato (Platonic ethics; Platonism) **I:** 17–36 *passim*, 40, 45, 62, 67, 88, 94, 98, 106, 136, 179, 210, 215, 217; **II:** 182, 241
  Aristotle and **I:** 40–41
  Cambridge **I:** 218, 257ff
  in England **I:** 217ff
  Freud and **II:** 182
  and ideal forms **I:** 166; **II:** 134
  in Italy **I:** 209ff
  Maimonides and **I:** 127
  Moslems and **I:** 136, 139–140, 156

Platonic Theology **I:** 213
Plotinus **I:** 72, 73, 74, 75, 76, 78, 79, 89, 98, 191, 209, 211, 213, 214; **II:** 70
Plutarch **I:** 16, 72, 73
Plutarch of Chaeronea **I:** 72, 73
Polin, Raymond **II:** 148
Political Treatise **I:** 305, 306
Politics (Aristotle) **I:** 39, 158, 223
Polus **I:** 258
Pomponazzi, Pietro **I:** 224, 225
Pope, Alexander **I:** 268
Porphyry **I:** 13, 74, 79, 98, 133
Portugal **I:** 225
Poseidonius **I:** 62, 93
Practical Philosophy **II:** 46, 47
Price, Richard **I:** 283; **II:** 12, 13, 151
Prichard, H. A. **II:** 157, 158, 260
Primary Science (*Protologia*) **II:** 69
Prince, The **I:** 219, 240
Principes de la nature et de la Grâce **I:** 311
Principia Ethica **II:** 211, 212, 213, 214
Principia Mathematica **II:** 188, 208
Principien der Ethik im historischer Entwicklung **II:** 45
Principle of Individuality and Value **II:** 155
Principle of Morality **II:** 68
Principles of Ethics **II:** 178
Principles of Human Knowledge **I:** 275
Principles of Moral and Political Philosophy **II:** 17
Principles of Morals **II:** 6, 10, 18, 20, 21
Principles of Philosophy **I:** 293, 294, 299
Prize Essays **II:** 50
Problem of Conduct **II:** 156
Problems concerning Providence **I:** 79
Problems of Ethics **II:** 50, 141
Proclus **I:** 55, 79, 80, 91
Prolegomena to Ethics **II:** 152
Protagoras **I:** 18, 19, 25, 28, 258

Protestants and Protestanism **I**: 218, 228, 292, 297, 306, 314; **II**: 188, 198, 239, 247, 249, 254
reform ethics **I**: 235ff Protrepticus **I**: 38
Proverbs, Book of **I**: 120
Providence and Fate **I**: 79
Province of Jurisprudence Determined **II**: 22
Przywara, Erich **II**: 24
Pseudo-Alexander of Aphrodiasis **I**: 53
Pseudo-Dionysius **I**: 92
Pseudo-Heliodorus **I**: 53
Psychology from the Empirical Standpoint **II**: 127
Psychology of Character **II**: 146
Pufendorf **I**: 238, 289, 291, 292, 293, 314
Purity of Heart Is to Will One Thing **II**: 239
Pythagoras (of Samos) and the Pythagoreans **I**: 13-16, 33, 45, 211, 216
Pyrrho **I**: 242

Q

Quest for Certainty **II**: 186

R

Ramirez, J. M. **II**: 194
Ramón Lull **I**: 189, 190
Rashdall, Hasting **II**: 155, 156
Rational Man **II**: 167
rationalism (rationality, reason) **I**: 15, 23, 29, 30, 34, 35, 40, 49, 57, 58, 61, 63, 65, 72, 88, 90, 94, 126, 153, 154, 159, 176, 313, 314, 318
  British ethics and **I**: 257ff
  existential ethcs and **II**: 103
  Judaic **I**: 121–132 *passim*
  Middle Ages **I**: 167–203
  Moslem **I**: 135
  right reason theories **I**: 161ff
  17th and 18th century European **I**: 287ff
  spiritistic ethics and **II**: 59ff
Rauh, Frédéric **II**: 112
Rawls, John **II**: 235
Razi, Mohammed ibn-Zakariya al- **I**: 135
Reason and Goodness **II**: 167
Reason and Religion **II**: 78

reason. *See* rationalism (rationality, reason)
Rebel: an Essay on Man in Revolt, The **II:** 259
Reconstruction in Philosophy **II:** 185
Reflections on the Common Concept of Justice **I:** 309
Reflections on the Revolution in France **II:** 21
Reformation (Protestant) ethics **I:** 235ff
Reginald Pecock **I:** 200
Reid, Thomas **II:** 14, 15, 22, 67
Relations between the Physical and the Moral in Man **II:** 63
Religio Medici **I:** 256
Religion and Science **II:** 214
Religion of Nature Delineated **I:** 272
Religion of the Gentiles **I:** 245
Religious Aspect of Philosophy, The **II:** 159
Renaissance ethics **I:** 207, 210, 242
  Aristotelianism **I:** 186–188
  neoclassicism **I:** 206, 248
  Platonism **I:** 209ff
Renan, Ernest **II:** 71, 72
Renouvier, Charles **II:** 71
Reportatio **I:** 196
Republic **I:** 19, 26, 27, 29, 30, 31, 32, 33, 34, 35, 36, 87, 136, 140, 156, 166, 216, 217, 219, 221; **II:** 95
Review of the Principal Questions in Morals **II:** 12
Rewards of the Soul **I:** 132
Rhetoric **I:** 39, 188
Rice, Philip Blair **II:** 202
Richards, I. A. **II:** 223
Rickert, Heinrich **II:** 139
Ricoeur, Paul **II:** 259
Right and the Good, The **II:** 156
right reason theories **I:** 161ff, 196, 200, 272; **II:** 4
Rintelen, Fritz von **II:** 146
Risalat **I:** 144
Robert Grosseteste **I:** 53, 162, 170
Robinson, John A. **II:** 250
Roger Bacon **I:** 172, 173, 174, 178
Roman Catholicism. *See* Catholics and Catholicism

Romanell, Patrick **II:** 203, 204
Romans, Epistle to the **I:** 85
Romans, ethical theories of **I:** 62, 63
Romero, Francisco **II:** 84
Rosenberg, Alfred **II:** 121
Rosmini, Antonio **II:** 68, 69, 70, 86, 87
Ross, Alexander **I:** 256
Ross, Alf **II:** 227, 228
Ross, W. D. **I:** 53; **II:** 156, 228, 260
Rousseau, Jean Jacques **I:** 315, 316, 317, 324; **II:** 36, 56, 93, 94, 167
Royce, Josiah **II:** 159
Rubáiyát **I:** 146
Rüdiger, Johann Andreas **I:** 318
Rules for the Direction of the Mind **I:** 293
Rules of a Christian Lyfe **I:** 215
Russell, Bertrand **II:** 188, 200, 213, 214
Russia. *See* U.S.S.R.

S

Saadia ben Joseph al-Fayyumi **I:** 121, 122, 123, 126
Sade, Marquis de **II:** 93, 94
Saint Genet **II:** 255
Saint-Simon, Count Claude Henri de **II:** 95, 96
Salter, W. M. **II:** 159
Sanchez, Franciscus **I:** 242
Sane Society **II:** 199
Santayana, George **II:** 162, 163, 164, 183, 214
Sartre, Jean-Paul **II:** 251, 252, 255, 256, 257, 258, 259
Scheler, Max **II:** 56, 130, 131, 132, 133, 134, 136, 137, 139, 145, 146, 147, 238, 245, 260, 261
Schelling, Freidrich W. J. von **II:** 34 39 48–49 159
Schleiermacher, Friedrich **II:** 37, 38
Schlick, Moritz **II:** 141, 142, 143, 215, 218, 219, 224
Scholasticism **I:** 106, 142, 199, 225, 232, 235, 238, 248, 262, 273
Schopenhauer, Arthur **I:** 234; **II:** 34, 50, 51, 52, 53, 54, 159
Schweitzer, Albert **II:** 165, 166

Sciacca, M. F. **II:** 69, 86
Science and Wisdom **II:** 194
Scienza Nuova **II:** 113
Scotland **I:** 282; **II:** 14, 16
Scotus Erigena **I:** 78
Search for Truth **II:** 61
Second Thoughts in Moral Philosophy **II:** 220
Sécrétan, Charles **II:** 67, 68
Sefer ha-ikkarim **I:** 132
Sefer ha-Kuzari **I:** 124
Self-Realization **II:** 149, 166
self-realization ethics **I:** 113, 183, 186; **II:** 37, 71, 126, 137, 141, 149, 152, 154, 155, 156, 158, 159, 160, 164, 166, 168, 185
Seneca **I:** 16, 57, 64, 107, 113, 173, 209, 244, 249, 256, 296, 311
Sens et non-sens **II:** 259
Sentences (Peter Lombard) **I:** 177, 179, 182, 193, 196
Sermon on the Mount **I:** 85
Sermons (Joseph Butler) **I:** 277
Sextus Empiricus **I:** 19
Shaftesbury, Anthony Ashley Cooper, Lord **I:** 266, 267, 268, 270, 273, 274, 275, 277; **II:** 151
Shestov (or Chestov), Léon **II:** 108, 109
Shifa (*Book of Healing*) **I:** 141
Short Treatise **I:** 299
Sickness unto Death, The **II:** 239
Sidgwick, Henry **II:** 4, 6, 30, 31, 165, 191, 213
Siger de Brabant **I:** 53
Simmel, Georg **II:** 253
Singer, Marcus G. **II:** 173–174
"situation ethics" **II:** 249, 250
skepticism **I:** 17, 18, 24, 239, 240, 242; **II:** 143, 163, 215
Sketch of a Historical Table on the Progress of the Human Mind **II:** 94
Sketch of Morality . . . **II:** 72, 73
Smart, J. J. C. **II:** 171
Smith, Adam **II:** 13, 14
Sobre la esencia **II:** 86

Social Contract **I:** 316
societal ethics in Europe **II:** 118
Society of Jesus **I:** 227
sociology **II:** 26, 73, 97, 98, 99, 110, 119, 196, 203, 225
Socrates **I:** 13, 18, 20, 21, 22, 23, 24, 25, 26, 27, 28, 33, 41, 43, 211, 297; **II:** 195, 240
Soloviev, Vladimir **II:** 108
Some Dilemmas of Naturalism **II:** 201
Somnium Scipionis, In **I:** 77
Sophists **I:** 17, 18, 19, 20
Sorley, William R. **II:** 137, 138
soul **I:** 14, 16, 17, 21, 26, 29, 30, 31, 34, 35, 36, 38, 40, 41, 44, 63, 66, 72, 73, 74, 75, 76, 77, 78, 79, 80, 87, 88, 89, 90, 91, 93, 94, 96, 97, 98, 99, 100, 107, 108, 109, 112, 115, 121, 126, 127, 128, 135, 137, 138, 139, 140, 141, 142, 143, 146, 152, 153, 154, 157, 175, 176, 177, 189, 191, 195, 197, 214, 217, 223, 224, 260, 283, 295, 296, 303, 307, 316, 326; **II:** 46, 64, 65, 68, 72, 76, 78, 90, 107, 121, 182
Source of Knowledge **I:** 92
Sources of Value **II:** 192
Spain **I:** 126, 132, 146, 159, 225, 228, 289; **II:** 59, 85
Sparshott, F. E. **II:** 235
Spencer, Herbert **II:** 151, 178, 179
Spenser, Edmund **I:** 222, 223
Sphaerus **I:** 62
Spiegelberg, Herbert **II:** 245
Spinoza, Benedict de **I:** 213, 216, 271, 299, 300, 301, 302, 303, 304, 305, 306, 309, 311; **II:** 150
Spirit of Christianity, The **II:** 39
Spirit of the Laws **I:** 314
spiritistic ethics **II:** 59–87
Stace, Walter T. **II:** 166
Stalin, Joseph **II:** 106
Stapleden, Olaf **II:** 180
Statesman **I:** 29

Stevenson, Charles L. **II:** 212, 222, 223, 224, 225, 226, 235
Stewart, Dugald **II:** 14, 15
Stilpo **I:** 24
Stirner, Max **II:** 54
Stoicism **I:** 55, 56, 57, 62, 63, 64, 65, 98, 106, 168, 215, 239, 244, 245, 296, 311. *See also* specific individuals
Strauss, David F. **II:** 45
Strawson, Peter F. **II:** 233
Studies of Good and Evil **II:** 159
Suárez, Francis **I:** 174, 228, 229, 230, 231, 232, 233, 234, 235; **II:** 86
subjectivist (intuitionist) ethics **I:** 17, 111, 112; **II:** 5, 6, 37, 164, 166, 220, 222, 225, 226
Subsistence of Evil **I:** 79
Subyektivizm i individualizm **II:** 109
Summa de creaturis **I:** 179
Summa Fratris Alexandri **I:** 175
Summa Theologiae **I:** 179, 182, 225, 229, 290
Switzerland **I:** 315; **II:** 67
Symposium **I:** 28, 35, 76, 166
synderesis, defined **I:** 169, 177, 181, 195, 216
Syrian ethical scholars **I:** 134
System of Ethics (Fichte) **II:** 34
System of Ethics (Hegel) **II:** 39
System of Ethics (Keckermann) **I:** 238
System of Logic **II:** 25
System of Moral Philosophy, A **I:** 280, 282
System of Value Theory **II:** 129
Systematic Theology **II:** 246

T

Tahafut al-Falasifa **I:** 144
Tahdhib al-Akhlaq (*Correction of the Dispositions*) **I:** 133, 156
Taine, Hippolyte **II:** 72
Tale of Er **I:** 36
Taylor, A. E. **II:** 156
Teachings of the Moral Philosophers **I:** 113
Teilhard de Chardin, Pierre **II:** 190, 191
teleological eudaimonism **I:** 37–53

Tempier, Etienne, Bishop of Paris **I:** 149, 164, 187
Ten Commandments **I:** 118
Teodoro Gaza **I:** 210
Tertullian **I:** 95, 96
That Nothing Is Known **I:** 242
Theaetetus **I:** 76, 166
Theodorus the Atheist **I:** 25
Theological-Political Treatise (Spinoza) **I:** 300, 305
Theophrastus **I:** 52
Theories of Ethics **II:** 145
Theory of Games as a Tool for the Moral Philosopher **II:** 169
Theory of Good and Evil, The **II:** 155, 156
Theory of Moral Sentiments **II:** 13
Theory of Objects **II:** 128
Theory of the Moral Life **II:** 184
Theory of Valuation **II:** 126, 187
Thomas Aquinas (and Thomism) **I:** 53, 94, 95, 162, 168, 175, 176, 177, 179, 180, 182, 183, 184, 185, 186, 191, 192, 193, 195, 197, 200, 201, 202, 209, 218, 224, 225, 228, 229, 234, 253, 289, 314; **II:** 16, 60, 80, 86, 109, 145, 194, 195
Thomasius, Christian **I:** 292, 314
Thought and Action **II:** 232
Thrasymachus of Chalcedon **I:** 19
Three Truths, The **I:** 242
Thus Spake Zarathustra **II:** 242
Tillich, Paul **II:** 246, 247
Tobit, Book of **I:** 120
Toulmin, Stephen E. **II:** 234, 235
Toward a Critical Naturalism **II:** 203
Toward a Genealogy of Morals **II:** 242
Tractatus Logico-Philosophicus **II:** 215
Tractus de natura boni **I:** 99
Tragic Sense of Life **II:** 253
Traité de l'existence morale **II:** 252
Traité des premières vérités **II:** 14

Traité des sensations **I:** 274
Treatise concerning Eternal and Immutable Morality **I:** 258
Treatise of the Laws of Nature **II:** 5
Treatise on Free Choice **I:** 213
Treatise on General Morality **II:** 80
Treatise on Human Nature **II:** 6
Treatise on Morality **II:** 61
Treatise on the Love of God **II:** 61
Treatise on the Virtues **II:** 79
True Intellectual System of the Universe, The **I:** 258
True Morality and Its Counterfeits **II:** 147
True System, The **II:** 93
True, the Beautiful, and the Good, The **II:** 66
Tucker, Abraham **I:** 284
Tufts, J. H. **II:** 184
Twain, Mark **II:** 263
Two Basic Problems of Ethics, The **II:** 50
Two Books of Constancy **I:** 244
Two Sources of Morality and Religion **II:** 75, 191
Two Treatises of Civil Government **I:** 263
Types of Ethical Theory **II:** 24, 150
Tyrrell, Sir James **I:** 256

U

U.S.S.R. **II:** 106
Unamuno, Miguel de **II:** 253
United States **I:** 228, 275; **II:** 15, 16, 46, 56, 60, 97, 139, 143, 145, 147, 158, 159, 164, 168, 182, 186, 201, 222, 232, 235, 250, 260
Universal Practical Philosophy **I:** 312
Urban, Wilbur M. **II:** 125
Urmson, James O. **II:** 221, 222
utilitarianism **I:** 68, 186, 217, 241, 249, 250, 261, 279, 281; **II:** 4, 5, 6, 11, 21, 22, 27, 30, 31, 72, 90, 95, 149, 150, 155, 163, 168, 171, 172, 173, 179, 203, 212, 222
Utilitarianism (Mill) **II:** 25, 28, 29, 31

Utopia (More) **I:** 219

V

Valla, Laurentius **I:** 210, 213, 243
Value and Destiny of the Individual **II:** 155
Value and Meaning of Life **II:** 56
values (value ethics), axiology as study of, **II:** 125ff
Vanini, Lucilio **I:** 225
Varro, M. Terentius **I:** 63
Vasconcelos, José **II:** 84, 85
Vásquez, Gabriel **I:** 232
Veatch, Henry B. **I:** 53; **II:** 167
Vico, Giambattista **II:** 91, 92, 95, 113
Virgil **I:** 249
Vitoria, Francisco de **I:** 225, 226
Vivas, Eliseo **II:** 201, 203, 204
Vocation of Man **II:** 34
Voice of Reason, The **II:** 93
Voltaire (François Marie Arouet) **I:** 274
von Eyb, Albrecht **I:** 200

W

Wagner, Eva **II:** 120
Waismann, Friedrich **II:** 218
Ward, Leo R. **II:** 147
Warnock, Mary **II:** 226
Wealth of Nations, The **II:** 13
Weigel, Erhard **I:** 238, 239
Weigel, Valentine **I:** 239
Werkmeister, William H. **II:** 145
Westermarck, Edward **II:** 112, 117
Whately, Richard **II:** 23
Whitehead, Alfred North **II:** 188, 208
Wieman, Henry Nelson **II:** 188
Will to Power **II:** 241
William of Conches **I:** 113
William of Moerbeke **I:** 79
William of Ockham **I:** 175, 211, 229, 232, 291; **II:** 63
Windelband, Wilhelm **II:** 139
Wisdom, John **II:** 216
Witherspoon, John **II:** 16
Wittgenstein, Ludwig **II:** 215, 216, 217, 218, 219, 220

Wolff, Christian von **I:** 312, 313, 314
Wollaston, William **I:** 272, 273, 277, 281
World and the Individual **II:** 159
World as Will and Idea, The **II:** 50
Wright, Henry W. **II:** 166
Wundt, Wilhelm **II:** 56

X

Xenophon **I:** 20

Y

Yahweh **I:** 118, 119, 120
Yahya ibn-Adi **I:** 133

Z

Zabarella, Giacomo **I:** 224
Zaraguëta, Juan **II:** 85
Zeno the Stoic **I:** 24, 249
Zeus **I:** 58, 59, 60, 66, 69
Zimara, Marcantonio **I:** 224
Zubiri, Xavier **II:** 85, 86